"A refreshingly new view of learning and learning problems; it is seldom that we find something so really original and groundbreaking written about education. Knowledge from the neurosciences, information about how bodily movement, emotional expression, nutrition, and the social and physical environment influence learning, are all brought together in a remarkable synthesis. I have never seen a better guide to creating more effective learning situations in home and school."

— *Dr. Willis Harman, President, Institute of Noetic Sciences*

"A powerful revelation of the full potential of the human mind and body. Carla Hannaford shows why and how the body plays an essential role in all learning. Her book will surprise, inspire, and delightfully instruct every reader."

— *Jack Canfield, author of **Chicken Soup for the Soul***

"Carla Hannaford brings together key information and ideas that brilliantly illuminate the learning process. This book should be required reading for teachers and parents. For me, her ideas have the ring of truth and common sense. The heart of the book is a clear call for a more caring, compassionate schooling of our children."

— *Dr. Betty Edwards, Director, the Brain/Ed Center, CSULB and author of **Drawing from the Right Side of the Brain***

"Carla Hannaford reveals the amazing mystery of how we move, grow, and learn. A perceptive teacher and committed learner, she makes a forceful argument that children must move in order to think, create and learn."

— *Dr. Paul E. Dennison, Educational Kinesiologist and author of **Brain Gym***

Smart Moves

Why Learning Is Not All In Your Head

By Carla Hannaford, Ph.D.

Second Edition
Revised and Enlarged

Introduction by Candace B. Pert, Ph.D.

Great River Books
Salt Lake City, Utah

Permission for use of the following is gratefully acknowledged:

Brain Gym® is a Registered Trademark of the Educational Kinesiology Foundation.
Frances Park Stryk kindly loaned me the name of her exercise and physical training company,
Smart Moves. Illustration on page 74 is from Anthony Trowbridge's model. Illustration on
page 75, "Caution: Children Not at Play" is copyright American Heart Association. The
Domi-Know figure on page 199 and the other Dominance Profiles in Chapter 13 are from
The Dominance Factor by Carla Hannaford, copyright Great River Books.

Book and cover design by M. M. Esterman
Cover painting by Paige Billin-Frye

For information contact:

GREAT RIVER BOOKS
161 M STREET
SALT LAKE CITY, UTAH 84103

www. greatriverbooks.com

Library of Congress Cataloging in Publication Data
Hannaford, Carla
    Smart Moves : why learning is not all in your head / Carla Hannaford — 2nd ed.
    p. cm.
    Includes bibliographical references and index.
    ISBN 0-915556-37-5 (alk. paper)
    1. Learning — Physiological aspects . 2. Mind and body. I. Title
QP408.H36   2005   95-32775
612.8—dc20   CIP

Printed in the United States of America   10 9   8 7 6 5 4 3 2

*To my mother, Minnie, for life, tenacity,
and her model of excellence and flexibility*

*To my father, Jim, for giving me the courage to risk
and make life an adventure*

*To my daughter, Breeze, for her deep love, wisdom, insights,
and being my teacher, co-teacher and traveling partner.*

*To my husband, Ahti, for his love, support, gentle stability, patience
and heartfelt music*

Acknowledgements

My greatest thanks goes to the following individuals:

Mark and Margaret Esterman for believing in me, teaching me to write, encouraging me to update the first edition, and supporting me during every step of the process.

Candace Pert for her model of perseverance, passion, creativity, and her willingness to write the Introduction to this edition.

Chris Brewer, Cherokee Shaner, Johanna Bangeman, Yahuda Plaut and all my other wondrous friends throughout the U.S. who have shared their wisdom as teachers and assisted me in pulling together the current research presented here.

Sumi and Hadi from Singapore, and the Forest Kindgergarten for providing me with excellent models and research showing the importance of movement for learning.

Maryna Allan, Kolten Yamaguchi, Aaron Estoy, Shellsea Naihe-Lindsey, Kawela Benson, Breeze Hannaford, Aspen Moon, and my husband Ahti for being photo models, Jaz for his computer graphics, Amy Choi and John Wu for their dominance research in Hong Kong, and Penelope Mathes, first grade teacher, for sharing the figure in Chapter seven showing the writing improvement of one of her students.

My extended family world-wide in the thirty plus countries I have been fortunate enough to visit and learn much more than I came to teach.

Occupational and Physical therapists, Montessori and Waldorf teachers, development experts, and brain and movement researchers who have given me a deeper practical understanding of how learning optimally occurs.

Paul and Gail Dennison, and the whole Educational Kinesiology family world wide for their elegant work with Brain Gym.

All the children who have touched my life, in my work with them and their work with me.

Contents

∽

Illustrations

Introduction

Candace B. Pert, Ph.D.

❧

I first met Carla Hannaford in 1998 at a conference where we were each presenting our research to an international group of educators. I was excited to find in Carla a dynamic, warm woman whose modesty belied her achievements. We shared a few laughs about the challenges we'd faced working in the male-dominated scientific world. We shared another great interest as well — how to bring the joy and pleasure of learning back into the educational process for our children.

My work on the interconnectedness of mind and emotions and Carla's investigations into the role of play, movement and music for learning, greatly complement one another. I see in her a tremendous passion and dedication to transforming our schools into nurturing, inspiring environments in which all children can learn with dignity and pleasure. I admire her pioneering spirit as she travels around the globe propounding the enormity of human potential that science now shows we possess; and also teaching educators very practical ways to improve the quality of learning in their classrooms.

Carla Hannaford is a leader in bringing to the forefront the new insights from research showing the new paradigm of body/mind unity. She has successfully integrated the important scientific discoveries about how the body grows the brain through movement, enriched sensory environments and human connection, into the real world of life-long learning, education and parenting.

Those of you new to **Smart Moves** are about to embark on a fascinating journey into the process of human growth, development and empowerment. Carla Hannaford presents a vivid picture of the nervous system's development from the embryo to adulthood. You'll learn of the flexible nature of the human brain, its ability to reorganize and adapt itself and how its growth and capacities are influenced by the sensory-motor systems of the body. You'll learn how to create a rich, sensory learning environment, and, sadly, you'll see how some of the teaching methods we now employ hamper the creativity, imagination and joy of learning for our children.

I am delighted to see the new edition of this book, which for years has been a best selling, groundbreaking work important to children, adults and the world at large. I am thrilled that her ubiquitous inclusion of my research, ideas and concerns will now reach a wider general public of parents, teachers, health professionals and policy makers through her remarkable book. In this extensively updated new edition she has also highlighted new research and insights which go beyond my 1999 book *Molecules of Emotion*.

For example, it is now clear to me that anticipation of pleasure is the key to all learning. Only the neuropeptides and other information molecules that promote pleasure in our lives can stimulate and enhance the learning process. All other molecules of emotion diminish learning in deference to survival. Play is the important work of childhood and the base from which all learning grows. Environments that include pleasure, movement and creativity are truly the most successful for learning. Learning is naturally a pleasurable experience and Carla Hannaford shows us how to return to that state as she explores the research, and ways and means of achieving the optimal learning environment.

Georgetown University
School of Medicine
Washington, DC
(CandacePert.com)

Preface to the Second Edition

Carla Hannaford, Ph.D.

⤳

Through the advances of science we are realizing the importance of whole body/mind integration and the effect of coherent functioning not only on learning and memory, but also on all the people we come in contact with, and on the world at large. As a connected community of human beings, our lives and futures will be determined by how we love and empower our children. Learning is a highly natural process, invigorated by our interactions with other people through our sensory-motor experiences and sense of connectedness and appreciation. Until we understand this, learning will be preoccupied with survival, difficult and stifled.

Since the publication of the first edition of *Smart Moves*, research on the importance of sensory-motor experiences for brain growth and development has blossomed astonishingly. We can no longer limit the learning environment to "sitting still, being quiet, and memorizing stuff." It is time to return to the "good old days" when children played, sang, verbally interacted with other children and adults on a regular basis, and were encouraged in their curiosity, imagination, physical prowess and concern for their fellow human beings.

As the research continues to unfold, I have felt compelled to expand my own view of the body/mind connection. When I wrote the first edition, as exciting as our knowledge of the brain was, we were aware that we knew very little. The pieces of information and personal experiences showing the power of movement to assist learning were just touching the horizon of understanding. Today, it seems, we are finally coming to grasp that movement and sensory experiences are the fertile soil for continual brain development and growth for a lifetime — and that these experiences actually cause the brain to constantly transform itself in unimaginably plastic ways. It would seem that as we become more present, more connected and safe in our human experience, and more coherently active and aware, that we can accomplish almost anything in our lifetime.

It has been a wonderful experience to bring forward so much new research, which strongly supports our need as human beings to connect, love, laugh, play and share music with each other to make each moment the best learning experience possible. I invite and challenge you to partake of the new findings of science, and to explore simple ways to optimize our experience and that of our children, to live more complete, passionate, creative, satisfying lives.

1

~

Learning Is Not All In Your Head

The mind, the unfathomable generator of reality, culture, history and all human potentiality, continues to intrigue and baffle us in our quest to understand ourselves. We have attempted to explain the mind from the glimpses and pieces we are able to put together as we focus our attention and research on the brain. But we have missed a most fundamental and mysterious aspect of the mind: learning, thought, creativity and intelligence are not processes of the brain alone, but of the whole body. Sensations, movements, emotions and brain integrative functions are grounded in the body. The human qualities we associate with the mind can never exist separate from the body.

Of course we know that our brains are encased in our skulls and are in ceaseless communication with the rest of our bodies. But in practice — when we think about thinking, when we try to encourage it, to mold conditions favorable to learning and creative thought — we tend to regard it as a kind of disembodied process, as if the body's only role in that process were to carry the brain from place to place so it can do the important work of thinking.

The notion that intellectual activity can somehow exist apart from our bodies is deeply rooted in our culture. It is related to the attitude that the things we do with our bodies, and the bodily functions, emotions and sensations that sustain life, are lower, less distinctly human. This idea is also the basis of a lot of educational theory and practice that make learning harder and less successful than it could be.

Thinking and learning are not all in our head. On the contrary, the body plays an integral part in all our intellectual processes from our earliest moments in utero right through to old age. It is our body's senses that feed the brain environmental information with which to form an understanding of the world and from which to draw when creating new possibilities. And it is our movements that not only express knowledge and facilitate greater cognitive function, they actually grow the brain as they increase in complexity. Our entire brain structure is intimately connected to and grown by the movement mechanisms within our body.

How we take in and assimilate learning is first determined by our safety, and the quality of our relationships with parents, caregivers and siblings. If the mother is stressed, the unborn embryo and fetus will react with basic reflexive movements for survival and the learning of survival is initiated. When the mother is peaceful, joyful, enthusiastic, and learning, the embryo, fetus or newborn experiences safety and feels free to explore its body and environment through movement and sensory challenges. In a bonded and safe environment, the ever more complex movements involved in exploration become the fertile ground for the growing and developing brain. This is the conclusion which neuroscientific research supports in ever-richer detail. Although there is a tremendous amount that we don't know about the body/mind connection, there is a great deal we have learned in recent years. And I believe that knowledge will have a powerful effect on the way we raise and teach children, and the ways we see ourselves and learn throughout our lives.

We need to become more aware of the body's role in learning as it is being dramatically clarified by scientific research. This book attempts to incorporate these new insights into a more valid and dynamic view of learning. In particular it seeks to illuminate the many ways that movement and emotions initiate and support mental processes.

WHAT YOU WILL FIND IN THIS BOOK

Part One, *Ways of Knowing*, focuses on brain and physical development — the growth of the body/mind capacities with which we learn. Intelligence, which is too often considered to be merely a matter of analytical ability — measured and valued in I.Q. points — depends more on the body than we generally realize. Physical movement and emotional safety, from earliest infancy and throughout our lives, plays an important role in the creation of nerve cell networks, which are the fundamental ground of learning.

We will explore three distinct but interconnected kinds of body/mind processing: sensation, emotion, and thought. Sensations received through our eyes, ears, nose, tongue, skin, proprioceptors, and other sensory receptors we are just beginning to understand, are the foundation of knowledge. The body is the medium of this learning as it gathers all the sensations that inform us about the world and about ourselves.

Next we will examine the deep ties that bind body, emotion and thought together. Our view of the role of emotional processing is being transformed by recent brain and heart research. What is emerging is a new picture of emotions — as a body/mind system that optimizes brain growth, and provides important information to reasoning processes, and a healthy immune system.

Then we will turn our attention to thinking, and the need for movement to anchor thought and build the skills with which we express our knowledge as lifelong learners. No matter how abstract our thinking may appear to be, it can only be manifested through the use of the muscles in our bodies — speaking, writing, making music, computing, and so on. Our bodies do the talking, focus our eyes on the page, hold the pencil, play the music.

In Part Two, *Smart Moves*, we will zero in on the importance of movement and play, and explore why and how integrative movements like Brain Gym®, Tai Chi, yoga, singing, dancing, playing a musical instrument, and even rough-and-tumble play enhance learning for everyone.

Finally in Part Three, *Nurturing and Protecting Our Learning Systems*, we will consider the need to manage stress, as well as nutrition and other physical requirements of learning. As we shall see, stress, in addition to its already well-publicized effects on health, is extremely damaging to learning potential. Stress is a root cause of many of the learning problems that we see in people labeled hyperactive, ADD, ADHD, dyslexic and emotionally handicapped. You will learn valuable suggestions to reduce the effects of stress in your life including: more human interconnectedness, integrative movement and play.

WHERE THIS STORY BEGAN

My fascination with the role of movement and play in the learning process came out of the miracles I witnessed with children labeled "learning disabled." When working with these children I found that they were more easily able to learn when we began their learning sessions with simple, whole body integrative movements in a safe, playful, exploratory atmosphere. My fascination continued as I myself experienced measurably greater ease in thinking, communicating, and learning anything I undertook — from writing a book to downhill skiing — as I did the movements with them.

It had never been easy for me to learn. Indeed, if I were a child in school today I would be labeled "learning disabled" or "Attention Deficit Hyperactive Disorder" due to my inability to learn to read before the age of ten and my need to move to learn. My daughter had some of the same difficulties when she went to school. These realities gave me a personal stake in understanding why movement assisted learning so dramatically.

The changes brought about in "learning disabled" children by such simple integrative physical activities, in a playful context, intrigued me so much that I had to know why they worked. So the search for understanding began, and has led me to the recognition that movement activates the neural wiring throughout the body, making the whole body the instrument of learning. What a step away from the idea that learning occurs only in the brain.

Though modern science is helping us to appreciate the role of the body and the need for movement and play in learning, modern life may be making it harder than ever before to benefit from this insight. Children tend to spend large amounts of time with the TV, computers or video games, and — like their elders — develop lifestyles that preempt regular exercise, spontaneous, imaginative physical play, and intimate human connection. When we do move, it tends to be competitive or compulsive, risking early injuries. Our daily existence is highly stressful, and as a society we are plagued with a fear of personal violence, which is amplified by the media. We may feel a sense of isolation and even depression as personal, interactive communication decreases. Too often, the available and recommended alternatives to all this stress, hyperactivity and depression are drugs of one sort or another. All these factors and many more markedly decrease the ability to learn, and with it our ability to be creative and reach our full potential as human beings.

The first step in countering these harmful trends is, I believe, to understand the body/mind system's enormous innate capacity to learn, and the role of movement and play in activating that capacity. For me, this unfolding scientific story is endlessly fascinating — and immensely significant for our future as individuals and as a global civilization. Movement and play profoundly improve— not only learning — but creativity, stress management and health. The inclusion of these two elements can have, and has had, an immediate impact on business people who need to deal with stress and yet remain productive; on the elderly in their quest to maintain clear thought, memory and vitality; on educators, teachers and parents concerned with the success of all our children; and on the children and adults whom we have offhandedly labeled as "learning disabled," "Attention Deficit Hyperactive Disorder," or "emotionally handicapped," as if these were true pathologies. These people will find effective, non-drug options for taking charge of their own lives, enhancing their abilities to learn and create, and to lead enriched, joyful lives.

So to begin this journey of understanding, I'd like to start with a miracle — the amazing neural plasticity of the human body/mind system I observed in the transformation of a little girl named Amy.

AMY'S TRANSFORMATION

Amy was a beautiful ten-year old with long golden curls and a brilliant smile. She was the right height for a fifth grader, but she walked with a noticeably bad limp as she dragged one leg behind her. And she spoke with an erratic, monosyllabic speech pattern that made very little sense. Amy had suffered brain damage from physical abuse at six weeks of age. With a very supportive mother and stepfather, she had grown to be a loving, enthusiastic child.

Since Amy could neither read, write nor communicate, the school placed her in a self-contained classroom with five "emotionally handicapped" children. Working as an elementary school counselor, I offered to take three of the children from this group during recess each day just to give the teachers a break. Amy was one of the children. The other two children were eight-year old boys. One boy was labeled mentally retarded (both parents were also considered to be mentally retarded). The other boy was labeled emotionally handicapped due to his violent outbursts.

It was a cozy group in my office, the size of a large closet, and for me it was a highly memorable experience. During the first week I repatterned each child using Dennison Laterality Repatterning. Each day thereafter, we playfully did five minutes of Brain Gym® activities. These are simple, physical movements (described later in Chapter 7) that activate whole brain functioning, especially areas of the frontal lobes. We also drank lots of water.

After these activities, we would go outside and kick a soccer ball around for ten minutes. The boys loved this and Amy would run after the ball, squealing and giggling with laughter. On rainy days, we spent the time talking, doing art and singing. There was always much laughter. Sometimes I read the children stories. Other times we made up stories together with all sorts of funny voices and dialects, often including drawing and play-acting.

If a fight occurred, I had a two-minute rule that everyone get into a Brain Gym® sitting position called Hook-ups. After quieting and integrating themselves in this way, the children were able to responsibly express their frustration or needs. This process encouraged more temperate emotional expression and released their tensions. Sitting in Hook-ups became a valuable interpersonal tool that cultivated honesty without fear or violence.

The children and I became buddies, and our daily activities became routine. Two months after I began working with Amy, her mother called with extremely gratifying news. The family's pediatrician was amazed at Amy's sudden ability to speak in sentences. Because I was so close to Amy, I simply hadn't noticed the shift.

As the months proceeded, Amy was able to connect with the ball and actually kick it, so that the boys now enjoyed her in the game. With her limp much diminished, Amy could now kick the soccer ball "straight as an arrow." Amy loved horses, but the horse she had drawn for me our first day together resembled a horse only in color. The horse she drew for me at the end of the school year was an identifiable *horse*.

After five months Amy was reading at second grade level and loved to write. At seven months she had told a convincing lie demonstrating her ability to access creative, higher level reasoning. By the end of the school year, she was reading at close to grade level, wrote highly imaginative stories and could communicate effectively.

Amy had been in school for five years and had made only small progress under excellent resource teachers. Her sudden leap in ability coincided with the addition of movement to her daily experience — movement in the form of Brain Gym®, soccer, art, music and playing with other children. The two boys also showed remarkable progress in their academic work during that year, due perhaps to the caring and playful connection we had with each other. Their ability to remain calm and collected in emotionally challenging situations also improved.

This experience greatly reinforced my conviction that movement, play and interpersonal connection was somehow essential to learning. My growing realization that the body was just as important as the brain when it came to learning led to the questioning and study that resulted in this book. I had witnessed significant academic accomplishments in children and adults after Brain Gym® movements, but Amy's experience demonstrated increased ability in everything she did.

It was fascinating and baffling all at the same time. We have spent years and resources struggling to teach people to learn, and yet the standardized achievement test scores go down and illiteracy rises. Could it be that one of the key elements we've been missing is simply movement? My curiosity led me to a closer examination of the labyrinth of neurophysiology that I had been teaching at the university for years. My quest expanded to the exponentially growing information base about body/mind function and the essential link of movement, the senses and emotion to effective learning. It's time to take a serious look at our own misconceptions about our bodies. In so doing we can free the body/mind system to reclaim its infinite potential for learning, thought and creativity.

2

Neural Networks – Superhighways To Development

The growth of the human mind is still high adventure, in many ways the highest adventure on earth.

— Norman Cousins

Amy's dramatic progress was miraculous to all of us involved in her life. She provided us, first of all, with a vision of undaunted spirit. At the same time, her transformation gave me a profound and hopeful insight into the enormous plasticity and healability of the human body/mind system.

Human nature itself is highly adaptive and flexible. As a species we have adapted to and succeeded in a wide variety of environments from equatorial rainforest to arctic tundra. It is the plasticity of our body/mind system that enables us to adapt, to build tree houses and igloos.

Neural plasticity is an intrinsic, beneficial characteristic of the nervous system that gives us both the ability to learn, and the ability to adapt in response to damage — to relearn. From shortly after conception and throughout a lifetime, the nervous system is a dynamically changing, self-organizing system. It follows no single master plan and is never static. We develop our neural wiring in direct response to our life experiences. Ability and increased potential grow hand in hand. As we grow, as we move, as we learn, the cells of our nervous systems connect in highly complex patterns of neural pathways. These patterns are organized and reorganized throughout life, allowing us greater ability to receive outside stimuli and perform the myriad jobs of a human life.[1, 2]

This plasticity gives the nervous system enormous potential for change and growth. In the case of damage to neurons, as with Amy, other neurons can "kick in" and take over the lost function. We also see this dramatically with stroke patients who are able to reorganize their neural apparatus to reestablish lost functions, like speech.

Not only do neurons restructure themselves to accommodate for damage, new nerve cells actually arise from neural "stem cells" in the brain's ventricles (part of what we call the limbic system) until the day we die. From these stem cells, as many as 6,000 new nerve cells per day have been formed, mainly in two areas of the brain; the hippocampus, a structure crucial for learning and memory, and the olfactory bulbs, which receive input from odor-sensing cells in the nose, and are also associated with memory. [3, 4, 5, 6, 7]

Researchers studying rodents and birds discovered that new nerve cells grow in response to enriched, secure, complex environments with space to move and explore, fresh air, good food and water, playmates, and toys. These conditions offer expanded learning opportunities, increased social interaction, and spaces to explore and live. In attempting to understand what specific facet of an enriched environment stimulated the most nerve cell growth, researchers found that the integrated cross-lateral movements of rodents voluntarily running in running wheels *doubled* the number of surviving newborn nerve cells. Voluntary integrated movements appeared to be the key. This was not true when the animals were forced to perform on the running wheel, in fact these rodents lost nerve cells. In monkey experiments, researchers found that mere repetition of a behavior doesn't determine whether you learn it. Neural connections can be altered and grown only if there is full attention, focused interest on what we do. In three weeks we can get ten times more proficient at anything if we are emotionally engaged with focused interest.[8] Self-initiated movement, exploration, interaction and physical experience for the joy and challenge of it, facilitates neurogenesis (nerve growth) for a lifetime.[9, 10, 11]

Elderly people who dance regularly, decrease their risk of dementia/Alzeheimers Disease by 76% and those that play a musical instrument decrease the risk by 69%. Both of these activities are very physical, use integrated, cross-lateral movements, are playful and stimulating to the memory system.[12, 13] Rough-and-tumble play therapy was found to reduce hyperactivity in children labeled ADHD. [14] These findings underscore the importance of movement and play in growing and elaborating our learning mechanism.

HOW WE LEARN

In essence, the story of neural healing is also the story of learning. Typically, a newborn's brain is only slightly organized, responding to sounds and to gravity, and ready to take in and react to the material world. Though we vary genetically, we all have basically the same immense potential. Given the proper amounts of nutrients, oxygen, stimulation and freedom to move, we all design and redesign complex nervous systems — and think nothing of it. The inherent plasticity and capacity of our minds is awesome — and many people believe that as human beings we haven't even begun to tap into the full mental potential available to us.

Learning proceeds as we interact with the world. As we receive sensory stimuli and initiate movements, our neurons form extensions called dendrites to other neurons. Dendritic extensions bring the nerve cell into communication with other nerve cells. Neuronal groups form patterns of communication that become pathways and, with use, superhighways, through which we easily access and act upon our world.

The process of nerve cells connecting and networking is, in reality, learning and thought. As associations are made and information is synthesized, pathways become complex networks. These networks can be altered as the system continues to self-organize in ever more complex ways.

NEURONS

To proceed any further in the story of learning, we need to take a closer look at some important characters — our neurons. Neurons (nerve cells) are specialized cells, adapted specifically for transmission of electrical messages throughout the body. The human nervous system is thought to consist of 10^{11} neurons, about the same number as stars in the Milky Way galaxy. No two neurons are identical, yet their functional forms fall into a few broad categories.[15]

There are three main types of neurons: sensory, intermediate, and motor. The sensory neurons bring sensory information to the Central Nervous System (the brain and spinal cord) from all over the body: from the skin, the eyes, the ears, the tongue, the nose, and the proprioceptors. Proprioceptors are sense organs that relay information about muscle position or tension or activity of joints and equilibrium. The proprioceptors are located throughout muscles, tendons, joints and mechanisms of the inner ear.

Intermediate neurons have a networking function. In the spinal cord and brain, intermediate (association) neurons relay information via their dendrites to networks of other intermediate neurons all over the brain.[16] The great intermediate net of association neurons accounts for 99.98% of the neurons in the Central Nervous System (CNS). They bring all the information together, process it and then animate the body, the muscles and glands, to respond by way of motor neurons.[17] The great intermediate net can be considered *command central*, having instantaneous access to the brain's complete information network.

Once the information is processed, the great intermediate net initiates action by sending messages on to appropriate motor neurons that originate in the brain. Motor neurons carry the messages away from the CNS to muscles and glands to activate their function. Every action requires motor neuron activation. For gross motor movements, as in swinging your right arm back and forth, a single motor neuron may stimulate or cause the simultaneous contraction of 150 to 2,000 muscle fibers. For more precise movements, fewer than ten muscle fibers are stimulated by one neuron. This more focused distribution enables more exact control for the muscular actions of high level skills like those of concert pianists or brain surgeons.[18]

Bundles of neurons form nerves, like the sciatic nerve that is a conduit of millions of both sensory and motor neurons, supplying innervation to and from the leg and foot.

All of the structures in a neuron are involved in guiding and programming an organism's behavior.[19] The cell bodies contain the nucleus and other important organelles of the cell. The cell bodies are usually housed in the bony protection of the spinal column and skull because they contain the genetic and regenerative hardware for the whole cell.

Dendrites are the highly branched, thick extensions of the cell body that gather information and conduct impulses toward the cell body. The axon is usually a long, thin fiber that conducts nerve impulses away from the cell body to another neuron, a muscle or a gland. As neurons are used, over and over, they lay down over the axon a multilayered, white, phospholipid (fatty), segmented covering called myelin. Myelin increases the speed of nerve impulse transmission, and insulates, protects and assists axon regeneration if the nerve is damaged.

When we first learn something, it is slow going, like beating a path through untraveled terrain. But as the neurons are activated repeatedly, more myelin is laid down. The more myelin built up, the faster the transmission. In highly myelinated neurons, impulses travel at 100 meters per second. Therefore, the more practice, the more myelin, and the faster the processing — until it becomes easy and familiar, like driving fast on a superhighway. Researchers have discovered that thicker myelin coats translate into brains that are larger and better able to coordinate rapid perceptual decisions. Thicker myelin coating is associated with greater intelligence.[20] Myelin is responsible for the color of the white matter in the brain, spinal cord and nerves throughout the body. Unmyelinated nerve fibers look grey and, along with cell bodies, constitute the gray matter in the brain and spinal cord.

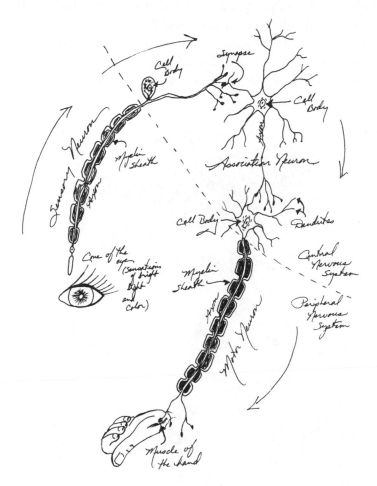

Figure 2.1: Types of Neurons

Multiple sclerosis and Tay-Sachs disease are related to destruction of myelin sheaths.[21] The movie Lorenzo's Oil, based on a true story, dealt with a rare disease that destroyed myelin on the neurons. Two dedicated parents, determined not to believe in the terminal diagnosis of this disease, studied myelin's composition and were able to arrest the disease. Then, with the use of specific fatty acids (oils), were able to assist the reformation of the lost myelin. This again, is an example of the remarkable healability of the nervous system.

At the ends of the axons are telodendria (telephone trees) with end feet. In these end feet are synaptic vesicles containing specific chemicals, called neurotransmitters. Upon activation, neurotransmitters cross the gap (synapse) between the neuron and the receptor sites on the cell membrane of the target neuron, muscle or gland to stimulate or inhibit activation of that membrane. Information is transferred from one cell to another at these specialized points of contact. Nerves are bathed in a sea of information chemicals (transmitters, peptides, hormones, factors and protein ligands), which bind to receptor sites on nerve cells and trigger nerve function.[22]

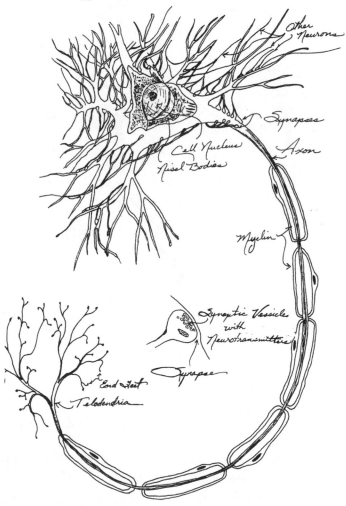

Figure 2.2: Motor Neuron

Some neurotransmitters or information chemicals are excitatory, increasing message transmission by lowering the membrane potential, or ionic polarity across the membrane. Others are inhibitory, decreasing message transmission by raising the membrane potential. Membrane potential and specific neurotransmitters will be discussed later.

Synapses are the sites of action for most drugs that affect the nervous system, and many psychiatric disorders result from disruption of synaptic communication.[23]

Messages are transmitted chemically across synapses at the cell body and electrically down the axon of the nerve fiber to the end feet of the telodendria. To give you a better picture of the process, here is an outline of events that occur when you accidentally place your foot on a sharp rock. Dendrites in the pain receptors in the sole of your foot take in the stimulus. Messages from dendrites are transmitted across the cell body and along the axon to the telodendria and end feet. From synaptic vesicles, neurotransmitters are released across the synapse, which activate receptor sites on the next neuron, usually an intermediate neuron in the spinal cord. This neuron then connects, via synapse, with a motor neuron whose axon carries the message to muscles in the foot so they don't step down hard on the rock. Simultaneously the intermediate neuron connects with another intermediate neuron taking the impulse to the sensory cortex of the brain where the whole idea of a sharp rock under your foot is realized.

This is the body's way of communicating between the external and internal environment. This constant molecular communication can be restructured, depending on usage, undergoing coherent, synchronized change as learning occurs. The wondrous flexibility of our nervous system accommodates a large diversity of skills. We may develop nerve nets to support the fine muscular control and musical sense of the pianist or the spatial acuity of the painter. It is largely up to us. In a sense, we custom design our own nervous systems to meet the choice and challenges of our interests and livelihoods.

NERVE NETS

During the processes of thinking, remembering and being mentally and physically active, new dendrites are grown from proteins synthesized in the Nissl Bodies in the cell body of the neuron. These new dendrites vary from less than twelve to more than a thousand per nerve cell. They act as contact points and open new channels of communication with other neurons as learning occurs.[24] Their role is absolutely essential because, as Solomon Snyder observes, "communication between cells or groups of cells is crucial for the survival of every multi-cellular organism."[25] Nerve net development is seen graphically in Figure 2.3.

Dendrites create increasingly complex interconnecting networks of neural pathways, through which reactions and thoughts travel in the form of electrochemical impulses. These ever branching pathways are in a continual state of becoming. As long as stimulation continues, more dendritic branching occurs. If the stimuli stop, the branching stops. These pathways alter from moment to moment throughout our lives.[26] Ultimately they form only a few permanent connections at the synapses with particular target cells. Experience can further modify these synapses as well. Many synaptic connections are made as new learning occurs. Later, these linkages are pared down in a specific way that increases efficiency of thought.[27] Neurons may have anywhere from 1,000 to 10,000 synapses and may receive information from 1,000 other neurons. Neurons with the most connections, an average of 300,000, are located in the cerebellum, the primary movement center of the brain, again pointing to the importance of movement and experience to learning.[28]

THE GREAT INTERMEDIATE NET

With our current understanding of the great intermediate net, the brain, we might liken it to an unstructured, freeform information network using simultaneous, parallel processors. While electrical impulses travel through computer circuits a million times faster than electrophysiological pulses travel in neurons, the computer is currently limited to a single processor. A single processor, no matter how fast, is eventually overwhelmed by information, and bottlenecks occur. Even attempts to circumvent these bottlenecks using high-capacity parallel processors run eventually into information management problems. It is very difficult to design programs that can avoid the bottleneck effect, i.e., causing some circuits to be too busy and others idle.

The great intermediate net has no such limitation. Through the complex interconnection of neurons, even with slow moving impulses, a true freeform information network is created, making all information within the brain available at any time from any point. The comparison and manipulation of information is truly simultaneous with no naturally occurring bottlenecks.

A more typical information database, a mailing list for instance, collects all applicable data (a "subset" of the total available information), compiles it into a single collection and stores it on a library shelf alongside other databases. The only way pieces of information can be shared among databases on

Figure 2.3: Nerve Nets (Newborn and 2 Months Old)

the shelf is to compile them separately into all other pertinent databases. As long as the information inside the various databases remains accurate there is no management problem. When a database becomes outdated, however, new data must be manually collected and re-compiled with the existing collection to create a new database. This would have to be repeated for all other pertinent databases, and so the process of collecting and compiling continues unabated in the face of incoming information.

The great intermediate net, however, is a true, free-form information network moving this way and that, depending on how experience pushes it, even in old brains. All information, not just one or more subsets, is instantly updated and made available for manipulation, learning and growth. PET scans and MRI's done just a week apart show changes in how the brain works on the same situation or problem.[29] Take the simple example of meeting someone new at a dance. All of the available information — name, appearance, content of conversation, body movement during dancing, environment, emotional context, etc.— is stored throughout the great intermediate net in free-form association with already existing information. Meeting the same person later immediately updates the network with new information. The great intermediate net is so immensely flexible that it really doesn't resemble a computer at all. The programming of the brain is so agile and adaptive that there are normally many alternate pathways for processing information.

Looking more closely at the neurons within this great information processing system, we see how much more flexible the brain is than even the most advanced computers. Within a computer the smallest possible memory location is either a 1 or a 0 (on or off). In the brain however, the smallest possible memory location (neuron) represents a computer in and of itself because so much information comes into that single point. And, the neuron is not only a computer, it is an adaptive computer that is constantly changing with new input.

The nervous system is very complex, both because of the number of connections within it and because some synapses inhibit while others excite the target neuron. The specific balance of forces and information determine how this exquisitely organized society of neurons operates. With an estimated one quadrillion nerve connections within the brain, at any one time the possible combination of messages jumping across the synapses exceeds the number of atoms in the known universe.[30]

If we compare nerve networks to a network of people, specialization results from the specific connections (who your contacts are) and the type of synaptic interactions (what your contacts tell you and what you let your next in line know about what you have been told).[31] The brain is a system of systems. Neurons organize into local networks, which are integrated into regions and structures in the brain, which in turn work together as systems.

BUILDING BASE PATTERNS

To graphically illustrate how we form base patterns of neurons and build on these all of our lives, let's examine how artistic skill develops. We start by becoming sensorially aware of nature, laying down neural patterns in the brain that represent this awareness. These patterns elaborate as we take in our world through touch, sound, smell, taste and finally sight. The areas of the brain that receive sensory input from touch begin to connect, through association areas, with those areas that receive sound and sight. These contacts allow us to cross-reference our experiences, giving us our familiar, base understanding of nature and our unique, subjective reality.

As we develop our motor skills, our sensory reality can now be translated into a movement of the whole body or a specific movement of the hand. From our internal images and direct sensory input, we begin to draw what we experience.

Our first drawings may be blotches of color that represent our sensory awareness and emotions. Simultaneously, through hand-eye coordination, our hand guides our eyes in a dance that embodies our tactile, kinesthetic understanding of the world. Later we explore line and draw the people and things in our environment, always referring back to our base understanding of size and space. This understanding comes from base patterns established though our experience of gravity and our tactile and proprioceptive senses, integrated finally with vision.

Our knowledge expands as we overlay our understanding of a three-dimensional world with learned techniques that allow us to represent perspective. It is elaborated further as we develop more nerve endings into our hands and gain fine motor coordination. The eye now becomes the trusted window to understand our world as the base patterns become more integrated. The eye then guides the hand through eye-hand coordination as we draw what we see, referring to our acquired reality instead of to our hand.

The ultimate artistry comes when we can incorporate all the base patterning from our knowledge of the world with our senses, emotions, movement and technical skill — to create something beyond and different from our reality. It is from this place of play, where the integrated brain, rich with base patterns, looks for novel possibilities, that the artistic within us reaches its pinnacle.

As nerve networks continue to build upon and change our base patterning throughout life, our proficiency and complexity increases. Yet even as great artists, in our later years we continue to refer back to the base patterns we developed as young children, through which we take in and understand our world.

The development of a skill, like all learning, starts with the establishment of our basal understanding of the world, through our senses, emotions and movement. Upon these basal patterns, we continuously add new learning in the form of more and more complex nerve networks. The base patterns provide a framework of information from which new nerve networks elaborate to increase our understanding and abilities throughout life.

Most neural pathways develop through stimulation and experience gained from interaction with the environment. This is especially true for people open to experiencing new and novel ideas and situations throughout their lives. As Michael Merzenich observes, "whenever we engage in new behavior, the brain remodels itself."[32] The brain retains this capacity even into old age. "In a healthy brain," Deepak Chopra writes, "senility is not physically normal."[33] The more active learning a person does, the less likely they are to show symptoms of Alzheimer's disease.

Physical and intellectual activity develops surplus brain tissue that compensates for damage. The more you use the body/mind system, the more it will grow. Learning or repairing nerve damage simply entails strengthening connections between neurons by creating more connections as well as by enhancing each neuron's ability to communicate chemically.[34]

I had the good fortune to meet Brandy Binder, who at the age of 6 had the entire right hemisphere of her brain removed due to severe seizures. Between ages 6 and 18, she spent a lot of time with OT's, PT's, and Brain Gym® consultants, in very active sensory-motor integrative play and stimulation. At home with her family, there was a lot of rough-and-tumble play, support and love. At the age of 18, this beautiful, highly literate girl, was able to easily dance, sing, ride horses, walk and hike without a limp and appeared as normal as any other 18 year old. She had won two major art contests without a right hemisphere, and had successfully graduated from high school with many friends and good grades even though some memory processing was slower then normal.[35]

In a stroke, even where the neurons in the affected part of the brain are permanently damaged, PET scans show that the victim may recover.[36] According to Stanley Rapoport, chief of the Neurosciences Lab at the National Institute on Aging, older brains actually rewire themselves to compensate for losses. They can shift responsibility for a given task from one region of the brain to another.[37]

The plasticity and exquisite organization of the nervous system gives us a window on the potential for life-long learning and healing. As Amy and Brandy began actively and consistently using all of their senses and integrated movement, they were able to reorganize their neural networks in more complex and efficient ways. What looked to be two girls with major physical and learning disabilities, became girls with only specific learning difficulties. As they overcame each challenge, the complexity and efficiency of their nervous systems grew. They have the neural hardware and the integrative tools to facilitate continued growth and reorganization throughout their lives. Amy and Brandy remind me that everyone is in the process of becoming. So why limit anyone with labels like "learning disabled," "emotionally handicapped" or even "mentally retarded"?

3

Sensory Experience

Learning is experience. Everything else is just information.
— *Albert Einstein*

It may be a long time, if ever, before we are able to unravel the wondrous mysteries of the human mind, mysteries of thought, emotion, learning, imagination, creativity, and the many marvelous capabilities that every person possesses. But there are many things we do understand thanks to the cascade of neuroscientific observation and research in recent years. These new insights help point the way to the fullest development of our capacities.

One area of research that is yielding particularly far-reaching discoveries has been the investigation of the brain's development and its total interdependence with the rest of the body. Our knowledge of this development has been illuminated by our ability to observe it, even before birth, in ever finer detail. The story of the brain's development is intriguing in itself, but even more fascinating for what it tells us about the evolution of the capacities of the human mind.

What we know, feel, learn, and think is shaped by how we know, feel, learn, and think. How we do these things is in turn dependent on the sensory-motor systems through which all our experience of the world and of ourselves is mediated. These sensory-motor systems shape our experience, and are shaped by it. So the story of how these systems unfold is a vital key to understanding learning.

SENSATION AS INFORMATION

Thought, creativity and learning arise from experience. As we experience, we bring in information and build the neural networks that allow us to use that information so we may better understand the world and how to thrive in it. A major component of experience is sensory input from our environment via our eyes, ears, taste buds, nose and skin; and from our bodies via nerve receptors on each muscle and organ.

Our whole body is designed as a fine tuned sensory receptor for collecting information. The sensory organs (eyes, ears and nose) that pick up distant signals, are perched high atop the trunk of our body which serves as a stable bipod. The receptor systems sit on the bipod, meeting the environment straight on. The parabolic ears reflect sound into the ear canals, the eyes take in the periphery as well as the broad forward expanse, and the nose detects minute chemical messengers in our air. Augmenting these are the taste buds which monitor dissolved chemicals at the gateway to the gullet, and a vast array of touch receptors.

Every square inch of skin has receptors for touch, pressure, heat, cold and pain, with more on the lips, hands and face. Through these receptors, our spacesuit skin can gain an accurate reading of our external environment while protecting us from water loss. And internally, every movement sends a wild array of impulses speeding toward the brain to keep it informed of all changes in position and of where the body is in space.

Besides the normal 5 senses we tend to think of, Rivlin and Gravelle have discovered 14 other senses that we have known receptor sites for, such as the sense of magnetic orientation, atmospheric pressure, airborne ionic changes, UV, sense of wet and dry, etc.[1] All of these sensations give us images of ourselves and our world and provide the essential raw material from which knowledge, thought and creativity can emerge.

SENSORY EXPERIENCES BUILD NEURAL NETWORKS

Our sensory apparatus is so vital to learning that it begins developing in utero with the embryo's response to sound at only 23 days after conception.[2] We first learn about gravity through our vestibular system, which is stimulated directly by sound and movement and is considered the entryway (vestibule) into the brain even before birth. Hearing, smell, taste and touch build on our gravitational sense to give us our first images of the world. Only later are we able to put these increasingly complex sensory images together to accommodate sight.

Nerve networks grow out of our unique sensory experiences, laying down intricate patterns that govern all our higher level brain development. Experience determines the shape and intricacy of these patterns. They are laid down in accordance with the activities we experience and all of our environmental circumstances.[3] The richer our sensory environment and the greater our freedom to explore it, the more intricate will be the patterns for learning, thought and creativity.

Images derived from our sensory experience are the stuff of thought and creativity. Images — in the form of shapes, colors, movements, feelings, tones, spoken or unspoken words — arise from our acquired patterns throughout all areas of the brain: color and shape patterns from the occipital lobe, tones and words from the temporal and frontal lobes, emotional experiences from the limbic system, and movement patterns from the basal ganglion of the limbic system. When we hear the word truck, all our experiences with trucks are instantly available to us as images — a heavier vehicle, noisy, dangerous, big wheels, diesel smell, sense of riding in one, how they feel as they pass us on the road, even the emotions of trucks as extensions of our power. From these images we make sense of new learning, tie remembered images together in different ways and come up with new ideas. Broad-based knowledge depends on these intricately woven, yet separate multi-sensory complexes of images that have been put together and reworked over and over again from our sensory experiences.

Consider, for example, the way we learn and incorporate new words into our vocabulary. Each sound, word, and phrase is supported by an elaborate internal image display. Whenever we read anything, the brain is actively putting the words into known sensory images so we may understand them. Notice that when you can't get an image of something you have read, it is difficult to determine the meaning.

Our sensory experiences, both external and internal, shape our way of imaging and, therefore, our thinking. New learning occurs as new sensory experiences modify, change and make ever more complex our images of our world and our selves. Our bodies are fully involved in this quest.

DEVELOPING OUR SENSES

In order to understand how essential sensory input is to learning, thought and creativity, we must explore how the brain grows and matures, beginning with its earliest structures and functions.

Dr. Paul MacLean, Chief of the Laboratory of Brain Evolution and Behavior at the National Institute of Mental Health in Washington, DC, developed a theory that postulates three distinct areas of the human brain. According to his Triune Brain Theory, the three parts are somewhat delineated biologically, electrically and chemically and are based on developmental patterns and evolved functioning. He named these three areas: 1) the brain stem or reptilian brain, 2) the limbic or early mammalian brain, and 3) the neocortex or neo-mammalian brain.[4] The reptilian brain or brain stem is the first area to develop. This is the oldest evolutionary part of the brain, developing between conception and fifteen months after birth. The job of this brain area is self-preservation. The reptilian brain monitors the outer world through sensory input and then activates the body to physically respond in ways that ensure survival.

Automatic and reflex reactions such as a baby's cry or its quick movement of the leg away from pain, are partially regulated by this area of the brain. It is also the part of the brain that takes over when we encounter danger or stress, because it initiates and regulates the body's fight-or-flight response. The reptilian brain oversees the body/mind's survival imperative, insuring that basic needs are met before other, higher functions can proceed smoothly.

The baby's first job is to satisfy its need for food, warmth, shelter and safety. So it learns to make appropriate responses that signal caretakers to provide for those needs. Eventually the baby learns — through its sensory systems — enough about its world, and about how to work its body, to master its environment and ultimately provide for itself.

The reptilian brain includes the brain stem, medulla oblongata, pons and cerebellum. All sensations go first through the brain stem and then are sent on from the switch-board (the pons) to the thalamus (in the limbic brain) and/or the neocortex for interpretation. Nerve nets must be developed first in the reptilian brain. The rest of the brain can then know what is happening in the outer world and respond to it. When we gate (close down) the reptilian brain, we are in a state of sleep and neither receive nor react with the outer world.[5]

The reptilian brain forms nerve nets encoded with our sensory-motor base patterns upon which learning, all the rest of our lives, will build. Nerves appear three weeks after the egg is fertilized and immediately begin to link up with other nerves. These forming nerve nets originate from the billions of neurons in the central nervous system.[6] As the reptilian brain forms, prenatally and in those first fifteen months of life, we develop an estimated 100 trillion nerve nets that link all our senses and muscle movements. These give us an understanding of the material world and our safety in it.

THE VESTIBULAR SYSTEM: SENSE OF MOTION AND EQUILIBRIUM

When we think about our senses, most of the time we only consider the five senses that take in information from outside our bodies: seeing, hearing, smelling, tasting and touching. However, just as important to our development and our lives is the integration of sensory input, which gives us information about gravity and motion, and about our body's muscular movements and position in space — the vestibular system and proprioception. These play a surprisingly significant role in our awareness of the world and also, as we shall see, in our ability to understand and learn.

The first sensory system to fully develop and begin myelinating by five months after conception is the vestibular system, which controls the sense of movement and balance. It is the sensory system considered to have the most important influence for everyday functioning — our ability to move and act against gravity. The vestibular system, considered the entryway into the brain, is the unifying system that directly or indirectly influences nearly everything we do. The first cranial nerve to develop, at five to six months in utero, is the vestibulo-cochlear or VIIIth cranial nerve, which stems directly from this system.

The vestibular system maintains both static and dynamic equilibrium. Static equilibrium refers to the orientation of the body, mainly the head, relative to gravity, for example when you are standing still. Dynamic equilibrium maintains body position, mainly the head, in response to sudden movements such as acceleration, deceleration and rotation when you are in motion, as when walking.[7]

Figure 3.1: Mechanisms of the Inner Ear

There are several small organs involved in vestibular sensation. From them we gather information about the head's position relative to the ground.

These are the most sensitive of all the sense organs, lying in the mastoid bone (the lump behind the ear lobe), and part of the inner ear. They include the utricle, saccule, semicircular canals, and vestibular nuclei of the medulla and pons.[8]

STATIC AND DYNAMIC EQUILIBRIUM

The utricle and saccule monitor the static equilibrium of the body. The walls of both the utricle and saccule contain the macula with hair cells, a gelatinous layer and otoliths (calcium carbonate crystals). Each time we move our heads the otoliths move, pulling the gelatinous layer, which pulls on the hair cells and makes them bend. This bending initiates sensory nerve impulses along the vestibular nerve to the brain. These impulses go through nerve tracts to the cerebellum that monitors and makes corrective adjustments in the muscle activities, including eye movements that originate in the cerebral cortex. This system connects directly or indirectly to every muscle in the body. This causes the motor system to increase or decrease its impulses to specific muscles, especially the core (torso) and neck muscles, to contract or relax. In this way our muscles adjust instantly so we don't lose our balance or equilibrium.[9]

With information from the utricle and saccule we are able to maintain a stable bodily posture relative to the ground. Traveling by car, air or water, however, can create a sense of disequilibrium that sometimes results in queasiness or nausea.

Information from the eyes contributes to the sense of equilibrium as well. "About 20 percent of the messages from the eyes, from the retina and extraocular muscles," as Homer Hendrickson points out, "go to areas of the brain concerned with balance mechanisms. Each of these subsystems must match and check with the other subsystems to produce consistent static and dynamic balance against gravity."[10]

Consider what happens when you read in a car. You are holding your eyes static as you read but the rest of your body is moving, especially the head. The system has to work very hard to keep the eyes level and static in a moving head. At the same time it is attempting to balance the rest of the body with the constant change of gravity, acceleration and deceleration. When no resolution to the confusion occurs, the body vomits, which may be its way of getting our attention to release the eyes. A similar thing occurs in IMAX theaters where the eyes have to move a lot, the body is static, and the communication between the two is confusing.

Children love to spin or ride for hours on hand-pushed merry-go-rounds, activating the vestibular system. But have you noticed that as an adult you would prefer to just watch? There is a reason for this. As we go through puberty, the endolymph fluid in the semicircular canals thickens in response to reproductive hormones. This thickening causes the hair cells to be bent for a longer time, thus causing the whole system to take a longer time to return to a comfortable equilibrium. Simple, regular vestibular activation through activities such as walking, swimming, bike riding, hiking, Tai Chi, sustained yoga postures or "The Elephant" (p. 140) are useful throughout life in maintaining balance and equilibrium in the body and keeping the brain awake, active and growing new nerve cells.

"Extreme sports" such as bungy jumping, hang gliding, and many amusement park rides really capitalize on stimulating the vestibular system by pulling it off balance and out of equilibrium. This causes not only a full body experience, but also an adrenalin "high." Adrenalin, our survival drug, allows for even more sensory stimulation and the added release of cortisol in the body. Fun as these activities may seem, they come at a certain cost since adrenalin and cortisol inhibit and destroy new nerve cell growth and development.

The three bony semicircular canals lie at approximately right angles to each other and maintain dynamic equilibrium by detecting imbalance in three planes. When the head moves due to rotation of the body, the endolymph fluid in the semicircular ducts flows over hair cells and bends them. Impulses from the bending hair cells follow the same pathways as those involved in static equilibrium.

According to Eugene Schwartz, even the slightest alteration of fluid and otoliths within the semicircular canals leads to changes in the muscles of the neck, trunk, limbs and musculature of the eye.[11] The vestibular system is already visible in a two-month-old embryo.[12] There is much activation of the head as the fetus moves in the amniotic fluid, then as the child goes from early movements and crawling to walking and running. The stimulation from these movements is crucial to brain processing.

The vestibular nuclei, a plexus of neurons lying in the medulla oblongata and pons, carries impulses from the semicircular canals and cerebellum to the Reticular Activating System (RAS) in the brain stem. The RAS is a nerve reticulum that carries impulses from the medulla oblongata and pons to the neocortex. Beginning in utero, the RAS "wakes up" the neocortex, increasing excitability and responsiveness to incoming sensory stimuli from the environment. This "wake up" by the RAS gets us ready to take in and respond to our environment, and to learn.[13, 14] The connection between the vestibular system and neocortex as well as the eyes and core muscles is highly important to the learning process. When we don't move and activate the vestibular system, we are not taking in information from the environment.

From conception to the first fifteen months after birth, the vestibular system is very active as the child gains a sense of gravity and knowledge of

Figure 3.2: The Vestibular System

the physical environment through movement. Every movement of the child stimulates the vestibular system, which stimulates the brain for new learning. From this sensory "wake up" and basal understanding of gravity a child is able to perform the most remarkable feats of balance. Beginning with only reflexive movement at birth, the child learns to stand, walk and even run in a gravitational field by approximately one year of age. Climbing and jumping on furniture, or in nature and eventually skipping, hopping, spinning, and walking on a narrow surface train all the muscles to work together, including the eye muscles which we so depend on for learning later on. In the Forest Kindergartens in Denmark, Sweden and Germany, I watched as children actively developed their vestibular systems. These 2 to 6 year olds rolled down hills, climbed over big rocks without help, climbed ladders and trees, walked on logs and spun around to folk songs as they sang.[15, 16] When they entered school, their bodies were fully ready to learn.

THE SENSE OF HEARING

The embryo and fetus are surrounded by the first patterns of sounds that will be absorbed by the nervous system. These include the mother's heartbeat, blood being pumped through vessels, her breathing, digestion and voice. By twelve weeks, the fetus moves in a more organized way to sound. Nerves, lungs and diaphragm begin to synchronize, exercising the lungs for the first breath after birth. At five months the fetus responds with movement, to phonemes of language (varying vibrations of sound such as the vowel sounds) that it hears through the amniotic fluid, spoken by the mother. There are approximately fifty phonemes in language worldwide. This sensory-motor response to phonemes allows the fetus to begin the process of learning language in utero.[17, 18]

By twenty-four weeks (six months), the fetus displays rapid eye movements during sleep, responds to music by blinking its eyes and moves as though dancing to a beat. By the seventh month, the fetus is thought to exhibit purposeful movements that are more than just reflexive.[19]

Once the amniotic fluid has dried out of the Eustachian tubes and outer ear canals, the sense of hearing becomes one of the most accurate and important to the newborn. For most of us, the sense of hearing is perfect at birth and goes downhill from there. The cochlea in our inner ear is made up of an elaborate mechanism of hair cells, set up much like the keys of a piano. These hair cells respond to specific vibrations by stimulating specific nerve endings. This elegant "inner keyboard" is able to pick up one hundred tones in its over 32,000 nerves, with the higher range of notes developing first in the cochlea.[20] We instinctively speak "parentese" (higher more vibrant speech) to babies because it's a greater stimulant to the cochlea and brain and elicits a more awake, alert, connected response from the baby.

Hearing is the baby's first line of defense. Babies will instinctively turn their dominant ear out when sleeping, to pick up sounds in the environment. If a sound is unfamiliar, loud or sudden, they will startle and then scream in an attempt to scare away the danger and to elicit help.

As adults, we still use this mechanism. If I am in an unfamiliar place, I will instinctively turn my dominant ear up while sleeping to alert myself to any danger. At home, where I feel safe, I usually sleep with my dominant ear down to block out incoming sounds. Since it is one of our earliest senses, hearing becomes important for alerting the brain to incoming learning, whether for protection or understanding, throughout our life.

Noise pollution (loud and/or constant sounds over a period of time) especially in the upper sound range, destroys these delicate hair cells of our "inner keyboard", thus reducing our hearing acuity. Dr. Tomatis discovered that these upper vibrations of sound also play an important part in maintaining alertness and energy within the system and tuning the muscles for good posture. He noticed, for example, some surprising consequences when monasteries in France dropped their Gregorian chanting in an attempt to modernize in the 1960's. These chants provided the upper register vibration and harmonics (overtones) that maintained alertness. As a result, the men in these monasteries needed more sleep, were less productive, were symptomatically depressed, and tended to get ill more often. Tomatis equated this to the experience of factory workers who had also lost the upper range of hearing because of constant factory noise, and similarly became listless, depressed and non-productive with stooped postures.[21] Overly loud sound above 85 decibels or exposure to constant repetitive sounds can cause damage.[22] Any damage to the hearing mechanism will result in inaccurate imitation of sound and difficulties with learning and speaking a language. Hearing loss in the range of 500 Hz (hertz) results in poor perception of the voiceless consonants (m, n, or p, t and f) that define language. This prevents children from learning easily and may be another source of confusion that fosters dyslexia.[23] Currently, loud rock concerts register at 150 decibels while lawn mowers, shop tools, truck traffic and subways typically run at 90 decibels. Twenty-eight million Americans have lost some hearing. Thirty-four percent of this loss can be blamed on excess noise.[24] Protecting our wonderful hearing mechanism is important, not only for survival and active listening, but to provide alertness, sound pattern understanding and a balanced posture — all of which specifically assist language development and learning.

THE SMELLS OF LIFE

Smell is also quite acute at birth. There are billions of tiny hair cells inside the bridge of the nose right under the frontal lobe of the brain. These stimulate olfactory nerve nets for every smell (chemicals in the air) known to man. Smell is strongly linked to memory and plays an important role in the baby's early learning and throughout life. Think of situations where you smelled something and the sensation brought back a flood of memories. A developmental expert in Germany claims that memory can be greatly assisted by rubbing the nose prior to learning something you really want to remember.[25]

Smell is also used to alert us to danger. When people or animals are afraid, they secrete pheromones that can be easily picked up by certain animals (dogs, for example) that will react to that fear. Like a dog, the baby or child may be able to pick up the sense of danger and fear felt within its immediate environment, and act to protect itself.

Our sense of smell also becomes important during puberty, as sexual scents increase. These are strong stimulants to the reptilian brain for display behaviors (grooming and preening), mating, and elimination of outsiders (protecting one's territory). Though our society does its best to override these natural urges, they still show up beautifully in our teenagers![26]

THE SENSE OF TOUCH

The skin is the largest organ of the body and is replete with nerve sensors for light touch, heavy touch, pressure, heat, cold, pain and proprioception. Proprioception is the sensation from muscles, tendons and the vestibular system that enables the brain to determine movement and the position of the body and its parts in space. All these sensations go through the brain stem to the thalamus and then to the somatosensory cortex of the cerebrum (parietal lobe).[27] With all these sensors, the skin becomes one of the primary organs for early environmental learning.

Just the act of being touched increases production of a specific hormone within the brain Nerve Growth Factor (NGF) that stimulates axon growth and nerve net development, helps maintain neuronal function and increases synthesis of acetylcholine.[28] Sensory neurons are stimulated by NGF during embryonic development. Later on, and into adulthood, NGF stimulates sympathetic neurons, which monitor sensory impulses for the autonomic nervous system — the instigator of fight or flight responses. When touch is lacking, children and adults exhibit depressed motor and mental functioning. There may in fact be a connection between lack of touch and lowered acetylcholine levels found in Alzheimer's patients.[29, 30]

Figure 3.3: Sensory Areas of the Skin

Jean Ayres also discovered a link between touch-sensitivity (inability to tolerate touch) and learning disorders in children.[31] Her highly successful program for learning disorders deals with waking up the sensory system by appropriately activating all the touch receptors. She uses light touch, pressure, fine brushes and balls rolled across the skin surface, especially on the arms, legs and back, all integrated with movement.

Touch, especially along the back, arms, hands, feet and face of the baby, stimulates growth of the sensory nerve endings involved in motor movements, spatial orientation, visual perception, and the stress response.[32, 33] If these nerve endings are not activated, the RAS (Reticular Activating System) that awakens the neocortex, will not operate fully. This leads to impaired muscular movements, curtailed sensory intake, overreaction to stress, and a variety of emotional disturbances and learning defects.[34, 35]

The absence of touch may so slow nerve development that essential bodily function development may not occur, and death ensues. In a study done in orphanages in France during World War II, orphans that were not touched exhibited high premature death rates. Even negative touch (spanking or beating) resulted in a much reduced death rate. Joseph Chilton Pearce talks of a program ("Project Kangaroo") in which premature babies are carried around in a pouch on the front of the nurse or mother, next to the skin. This constant touch has greatly decreased the mortality rate in these preemies. Touch alone stimulates sensory-motor growth, nerve net development and gives the baby a fighting chance at life.[36]

TOUCH AND LEARNING

Recent findings indicate that parent-offspring interactions that include a lot of touch, play and being fully present, may be crucial for cognitive development. The touch of closely bonded family members increases activity in the hippocampus, an important center for spatial and general learning and memory.[37] Adolescence can be a strange time, when the child is growing a greater skin surface and is more sensitive to light touch since those receptors take longer to develop. If we lightly touch our teenagers, they may be overly sensitive and move away with disgust. Parents are well advised to give their children of that age "bear hugs" with strong touch, or rough-and-tumble play with them so they feel the perimeters of their body. This helps to stimulate the growth of all the touch receptors in their new skin, and makes them less sensitive to our light touch. Panksepp discovered that rough-and-tumble play was the most effective way of stopping hyperactive behavior in adolescents.[38] Even adult learning difficulties and susceptibility to disease are associated with lack of early touch.[39, 40]

Besides the essential need to be touched, babies — and everyone else — need to touch in order to learn. There is a greater array of receptors for touch around the mouth and hands than in any other area of the body. This is shown in Penfield and Jasper's original mapping of the sensory and motor cortices of the cerebrum. (See Figure 3.4)[41] With a huge part of the sensory and motor cortices in the brain involved with the hand, the hand shapes our cognitive, emotional, linguistic and psychological development.[42, 43] Touch is an integral, natural part of life. Babies love to put things up to their mouths — not to eat them, though that may happen inadvertently, but to touch and fully sense them with the mouth and hands.

Figure 3.4: Mapping of the Sensory and Motor Cortices of the Cerebrum
(after Penfield and Jasper with Modifications from Phantom Limb Research)

Throughout our lives, using "hands-on" experiences or manipulatives during the learning process greatly increases learning efficiency. My college students have commented that just having clay available to manipulate during a lecture allowed them to more easily take in information. Whenever touch is combined with the other senses, much more of the brain is activated, thus building more complex nerve networks and tapping into more learning potential.

Touch is a strong anchor in behavior and learning. If children are gently touched on the shoulder while they are reading, the brain connects the encouraging touch with the reading and helps to anchor the positive experience. A Canadian elementary school teacher recently told me of an experiment with touch in the classroom that bears this out. The teachers focused on students that acted up in class and did not do or turn in their homework. Five times a day the teacher would catch these students "being good" and touch them on the shoulder while saying (in an accepting way), "I appreciate your doing your work." When they were acting up, the teachers ignored them. In all cases, within the first two weeks, all the students were behaving in class and handing in their homework.

Playful touch is profound in its ability to connect people together. Large areas of the brain are involved in playful touch, which stimulates dopamine production and activates more grace in movement and learning.[44] I realize there is a fear of inappropriate touching in our society, which has led us to avoid touching at a time when children (and adults) need it more than ever. It's time to relearn appropriate, supportive and playful touch and value it for its function in development and learning.

PROPRIOCEPTION

Proprioception, the body's sense of itself in space, is one of our most important ways of knowing. Charles Sherrington beautifully described it as "our secret sense, our sixth sense." As Oliver Sacks points out, proprioception is so much taken for granted that it wasn't until Sherrington "discovered" it in the 1890's, that we began to appreciate its distinctive role in our sense of ourselves.[45]

All of our muscles have proprioceptive receptors which sense the degree of stretch in the muscle. These stretch receptors let us constantly know everything

Figure 3.5: Proprioceptors

about our physical position and provide the feedback necessary for us to move and maintain our balance. As exquisite learning tools, proprioceptors allow us to explore our environment, understanding it through our muscle sense.

Developmentally, the proprioceptive system is intimately tied to the vestibular system that allows the balance necessary to move from an inert position. Babies begin moving from the core muscles, the inner muscles of the trunk. There is constant feedback from the proprioceptors to the motor cortex of the brain that allows more and more complexity of movement. So babies go from the belly wiggle, to rolling over, to sitting up, to standing up and finally walking.

Successful movement requires secure balance, which depends on a sophisticated proprioceptive system constantly aligning every part of the body. Proprioception gives the feedback necessary to maintain optimal muscle contraction and relaxation for balance in our environment. Thus the popular phrase "being centered" invokes the importance of the proprioceptive sense when doing yoga or the martial arts. These skills place emphasis on the core postural muscles where we first learn about balance and gravity through proprioception. When the feedback system between proprioceptors and muscles is well developed through use, balance is constantly maintained.[46] When stress interferes with the balanced activation of this system, then we become "uncentered" and lose our balance and our physical sense of ourselves in space. This is when accidents like scratches, bruises or broken limbs occur, because our proprioceptive awareness is concentrated on running from danger, rather than maintaining balance.

Parents and teachers often notice periods of physical awkwardness and lack of coordination in children who are in the midst of, or recently emerged from, growth spurts. What they are seeing is actually a lag between the body's growth and its proprioceptive sense of itself in space. When the proprioceptive sense adapts to the new sizes and proportions, the gawkiness disappears.

Our proprioceptive sense constantly sends feedback to the brain that readjusts the balance of our shoulder and neck muscles in order for the eyes to remain level while reading. It monitors our ability to sit in a chair, listen to information and take notes. It also lets us know what muscle choreography is necessary to walk on uneven ground without falling.

MIMICRY, MODELING AND REHEARSALS

Besides monitoring bodily balance, the sensitivity of the proprioceptive system also allows us to learn about our environment. If you have gone for a walk with a small child, you have probably noticed that when they come to something new and intriguing, they actually move their body to mimic the configuration of the object. Children are great imitators, acutely aware of and then modeling adult movements in their walking, talking, hand gestures, and other physical activities. This modeling on the body allows them to sense the world around them from within to understand it.

Children are great observers, spending hours watching and role-playing. Rich imaginations allow them to rehearse complicated movements like running, swimming, and even flying. This rehearsal requires more and more sophistication of the nerve pathways and builds the nerve networks necessary to master complex skills.

Adults do the same thing when learning a new skill. Beginning skiers, as they watch other skiers will actually make small modeling movements to entrain the sense of skiing upon their own muscles. Researchers have found support for the theory held by many sports trainers that athletes who mentally imagine and "rehearse" movements in advance will be more successful in accomplishing them.

Learning a motor skill by observing and mentally practicing it through visualization allows the brain to rehearse the neural pathways that control the muscles involved. These rehearsals involve minute muscle fluctuations that send a wave of sensory information from the muscle to the brain and strengthen the networks.[47]

SEEING TAKES MORE THAN OUR EYES

Touch, hearing and proprioception are important organizers of the visual aspects of learning. Vision is a very complex phenomenon, with only a small percentage (less than five percent) of the process occurring in the eyes. The other over ninety-five percent of vision takes place in the brain from association with touch, hearing and proprioception. As babies touch their environment, they learn dimension, texture, line and even color. Seeing the world with full acuity, color vision and binocularity takes over a year after birth to develop.[48] Touch is very important to vision. Listen closely to a child who is seeing something new. The child immediately reaches out to touch the object while saying, "Let me see that!" Touch is the major contributor to full understanding in vision.

Images coming in through the eyes, are turned upside down and backwards as they enter the optic nerve, and cross the optic chiasma. They are then funneled through the thalamus to the occipital lobe where primary vision is processed. For full vision to occur, information from all the cerebral lobes must be accessed. Information from the sensory and motor cortices associates the image with learned sensory and movement functioning. Gravitational and vibrational information from the temporal lobes relates the image to where we are in space. And, as noted earlier, approximately 20% of the messages from the eyes, retina and extraocular muscles, go to areas of the brain concerned with balance mechanisms. All the information together allows us to right the image and bring it into full context in the visual association areas.[49]

An experiment in which scientists fitted themselves with special pairs of glasses shows how our vision is educated to comprehend the world. These glasses had mirrors that turned the view of the world upside down and back to front. At first, the disoriented experimenters could barely move without bumping into something, but after a few days they adjusted and the reversed world came to look "right way up." Touch and the proprioceptive sense that guides vision had adjusted the new visual input to this new physical orientation. The fully intact vestibular system "knew" that the world had not gone topsy-turvy. This, together with touch and proprioception, provided feedback that allowed their eyes to adjust. The scientists could walk around without problems and saw the world just fine — until they took the glasses off at the end of the experiment. Then they had to go through a relearning process all over again, with several days of hitting and falling over things.[50, 51] This experiment demonstrates graphically that the brain has to assemble our visual world from learned pieces through our other senses, especially touch and proprioception.[52]

It's easy to forget, or ignore, how much of vision is learned. We have to train ourselves, through books, movies and art to see three dimensions in a two-dimensional space. We could call this visual literacy. Tribal people I have encountered in Africa and Australia who have never experienced books, simply cannot see a mountain scene in a picture on a two-dimensional page. They experience color and line, but no texture or perspective, because in actuality, there is none.

Linear perspective, which is so convincing that it seems natural, is actually an artistic invention that goes back only to the 1400's, a technique developed to bring more three-dimensional reality to art. Artist M.C. Escher used the eye's inaccuracy and dependence on inner brain images to master illusion in his art.[53] In the 1960's, Dr. Bella Julesz also explored the ambiguity of the eye using the first computer-generated 3-D images of randomly placed dots to study depth perception in human beings. From that work, Dan Dyckman and Mike Bielinski went steps further in their popular *Magic Eye* books. They used advanced computer technology to include a small visual defect or blip that the eye relays to the brain. The brain interprets the blip as meaning the situation is 3-D, so produces a 3-D image in the visual cortex, and we perceive three-dimensionality in the *Magic Eye* books.[54]

THE EYES IN MOTION

Our eyes are designed to move and accommodate for light, to give us as much sensory detail about our world as possible. The eyes must be actively moving for learning to occur. Many of the cranial nerves (coming from the medulla oblongata) connect to the eye, including the trigeminal, facial, abducens, oculomotor, and trochlear. These activate movement of the eyeball in all directions, contract or relax the muscles of the pupil to regulate light hitting the retina, and change the shape of the lens to accommodate for near or far vision. They also monitor proprioceptive stretch and touch sensations on and around the eye.

In a three-dimensional environment, such as outdoors, the eye is in constant motion gathering sensory information to build intricate image packages necessary for learning. The brain integrates these image packages with other sensory information like touch and proprioception to build a visual perception system. The eyes are equipped with different kinds of visual focus, of which three-dimensional focus is vital for learning, yet we emphasize two-dimensional focus in learning situations with books, worksheets, computers, and video games.

The retina, the sensory nerve layer of the eye, contains light-receptor cells of which approximately ninety-five percent are rods (so called because of their shape) and five percent are cones. The rods are distributed around the periphery of the retina and are stimulated best under dim light conditions. The cones, which give us color vision, are grouped in a small area of the retina called the fovea centralis and require bright light for stimulation. Major concentration on the fovea for reading in a two-dimensional field is called foveal focus. The combination of rods and cones allows for three-dimensional as well as two-dimensional focus, day and night time vision and peripheral as well as foveal focus.[55]

Considering the ratio of cones to rods, it strikes me that we were not designed to sit for long hours engaged exclusively in foveal focus activities, like reading, and watching TV or computer screens. The eyes need to actively experience the world as a whole for vision to develop fully. Active sensory and

Figure 3.6: The Eye and Light-Receptor Cells

motor functioning of the eyes helps to entrain the body on shapes and move-ment of natural forms, to develop the spatial awareness necessary for clear perceptions and assists in pattern seeing, essential for all learning.

THE IMPORTANCE OF SENSORY LEARNING

Even though each sense has a specialized receptor site and area within the brain, processing the senses is highly integrative. Vision is developed and continuously influenced by hearing and touch, allowing sensory information to be processed very fast in the neo-cortex as a complete experience.[56] Experi-ences and sensations constitute consciousness and learning. Sensations form the base understanding from which concepts and thinking develop. Sensory enriched environments are imperative to learning, as neuroanatomist Marian Diamond discovered in her work with rats. These enriched environments included playgroups of ten to twelve rats in large multi-level cages filled with a variety of bridges, ladders, swings and slides, assorted toys, and changing stimuli. Diamond discovered that compared with rats whose mobility and stimuli were restricted, rats in enriched environments actually developed structural changes in their brain, and exhibited behavior which could be interpreted as demonstrating improved intelligence.[57, 58]

In the New York Longitudinal Study, 133 subjects were followed from infancy into adulthood. It was discovered that competency in adulthood stemmed from three major factors in the early learning environment: 1) rich sensory environments, both outdoors and indoors, 2) freedom to explore the environment with few restrictions, and 3) available parents that acted as consultants when the child asked questions.[59, 60]

The importance and need for rich sensory and hands-on learning continues throughout our lives. However, many of our educational practices derive from the unexamined assumption that people will learn best if given lots of information in either lecture or two-dimensional written form. And in order to learn they must sit still, keep their eyes forward and take notes. We have only to look at the glazed eyes and vacant stares of students in a lecture hall or classroom to know that this is a belief that needs to be abandoned.

In general, our system of formal education relies too much on language as the medium of instruction. What's wrong with that? To answer that question I would like to refer back to Einstein's maxim, "Learning is experience. Everything else is just information." Consciousness researchers are now defining consciousness as our ability to have experiences.[61] Words, though important, are only bits of information. They are not experiential and only poorly substitute for the directness and freshness of hands-on learning.

Words can only be understood when they provoke some kind of image in the mind of the learner. If students cannot access the underlying images, the words are not comprehensible; there is no context or visual understanding. A lot of confusion is introduced when students miss the meaning of the teacher's words. Experiences, on the other hand are direct and real. They involve senses, emotions and movements and engage the learner fully. Real things happen when we experience with our senses, and in the experiencing we observe, relate to past experiences and notice patterns. Words are useful in this process, they help us to organize our thoughts about the sensations. But they are no substitute for the force and vividness of actual experience.

Learning occurred most easily for my college Biology students when we took field trips into nature, and then discussed scientific concepts as they were experienced. The next best was making sure every lab session was filled with rich sensory experiences and that lectures were short and became sensory-oriented discussions and hands-on activities.

Learning first comes in through our senses. As we explore and experience our material world, initial sensory patterns are laid down on elaborate nerve networks. These initial sensory patterns become the core of our free-form information system that is updated and becomes more elegant with each new, novel experience. These initial sensory patterns become our reference points and give us the context for all learning, thought and creativity. From this sensory base we will add emotions and movement in our life-long learning dance.

4

The Role of Emotions

My research has persuaded me that emotion is integral to the process of reasoning. I even suspect that humanity is not suffering from a defect in logical competence but rather from a defect in the emotions that inform the deployment of logic.
— *Antonio R. Damasio*[1]

It's not surprising that many of us believe emotion is somehow antagonistic to thinking. The notion that the best thinking occurs in the cool clear light of reason, high above the distraction and messiness of emotion, has a long history going back to Plato, Kant and Descartes. It has profoundly influenced our culture, particularly in the area of education.

People make distinctions between thought and emotion in the same way they make distinctions between the mind and body. However, despite our deeply ingrained assumptions, these distinctions don't actually exist. Body, thought and emotion are intimately bound together through intricate nerve networks, and function as a whole unit to enrich our knowing. And research in the neurosciences is helping to explain how and why rich emotional development is essential for understanding relationships, rational thought, imagination, creativity and even the health of the body.

Even computer scientists seeking to simulate human thinking recognize that artificial intelligence is limited and incomplete because it lacks emotion. Computer scientist David Gelernter makes this point emphatically: "Emotions are not a form of thought, not an additional way to think, not a special cognitive bonus, but are fundamental to thought." If we subtract emotion from thought, what remains is merely one end of a continuous spectrum — linear/logical thought — and to identify this narrow high-focus band with thought in general is entirely inaccurate.[2]

Gelernter goes on to assert that emotions, which are inseparable from thought, are also "inextricably tied up with bodily states. The bodily state is part of the emotion, feeds it and helps define it. This means that ultimately you don't think just with your brain; you think with your brain and body both."[3]

DEMONSTRATING THE LINKS BETWEEN REASON, EMOTION, AND THE BODY

Gelernter's insights are borne out by the growing cascade of brain research concerning the interconnection of emotion and thought. In a highly ingenious series of experiments, Antonio Damasio and his colleagues have demonstrated that when the emotions and the body were dissociated from cognition, rational behavior and learning were absent.[4, 5] The significance of this finding to our understanding of learning, and to educational theory and practice, cannot be overstated.

The subjects of Damasio's experiments were patients who had damage to the frontal lobe of the brain, particularly the area that connects directly with the substantia nigra of the limbic system, which processes emotions. Though the damage did not impair the patients' intellect or memory in any detectable way, it left them changed in two extraordinary and profound respects. First, they were unable to make reasonable decisions in personal and social matters — decisions that had been made as a matter of course before the damage to their frontal lobes. Instead they made foolish, imprudent, and irrational choices. Second, they were left with drastically reduced emotional reactivity. This sudden and momentous change was acknowledged by the patients themselves, when they recognized that they no longer reacted emotionally to things they "knew" would have affected them before the injuries to their brains.

Damasio and his colleagues set out to explore the underlying linkages between these two symptoms — irrationality and lack of emotion — caused by the damage to their patients' frontal lobes. In a series of experiments, known as the Gambling Experiments, subjects played a card game in which the cards were rigged so that a normal person could gradually learn to accumulate winnings. Rational choices, learned from the results of drawing the cards, were rewarded; irrational choices that ignored what could be learned from the game, were punished with losses. Frontal lobe damaged patients, even when they professed to be cautious, failed to learn from their losses. Normal subjects, even those who considered themselves high-risk gamblers, learned the low-risk successful strategy to win the game.

WATCHING THE BODY LEARN

The researchers then added an intriguing twist. They hooked up the players to a polygraph machine, which allowed them to continuously track the players' choices with their skin conductance responses. At first normal and brain-damaged players responded the same way to their wins and losses, the polygraph registering similar reactions following their turns of the cards. But after a few turns, the polygraphs of the normal players began to exhibit a striking new pattern. Before making a risky move, they showed a response on the polygraph. And as the game went on, each time they were about to make a risky decision, that anticipatory response grew larger. "In other words, the brains of the normal subjects were gradually learning to predict a bad outcome, and were signaling the relative badness of the particular [choice] before the actual card-turning."[6]

This learning curve, corresponding step by step with an emotional response expressed in and through the body, eloquently demonstrates the interrelatedness of knowing and feeling with the body. The critical element for learning — which is precisely what is missing in the patients whose emotions do not connect with their thinking — is this bodily alarm. When the emotions and bodily sense are dissociated from thinking, real learning does not occur.

EMOTIONS AND SURVIVAL

From these experiments, Damasio developed his theory that emotions provide the essential criteria on which we base rational decision-making for our lives. He believes emotions inform the thinking process about the right direction to go based on survival or social risk. Emotions are felt as bodily states and are the means through which the mind knows about how the body feels as a touchstone for cognitive survival.[7] When planning, strategizing, reasoning, and creating new ideas we rely on the stored knowledge that we have accumulated in our lifetime. For instance, suppose you have to decide whether or not to quit your job. A whole flood of past experiences and future projections will spring to mind. These experiences carry with them an emotional content. Memories of success or frustration in finding new jobs elicit the associated gut feelings that these memories produce.[8]

According to Damasio, this marking of experience with emotional value assures that we first and foremost promote our bodily survival. Qualities that are good or bad for us, as registered by the body, can be recalled and become the basis for predicting outcomes. This insures that our reasoning strategies advance our survival.[9]

Our capacity to emotionally mark and remember experiences is also important for the survival of our society. Emotions add the element of pleasure or pain to the learning of social behavior. This insures that each individual learns rules and values that advance the purposes of society and enable it to function. Without healthy emotional development of individuals, humans could not adequately become socialized and the values, rules and wisdom of the society would be lost.

How, then, do emotions develop, and what conditions promote healthy emotional growth?

THE LIMBIC SYSTEM

Emotions meet at the intersection of body and mind. This is almost literally true since most emotional processing occurs in the limbic system, the area that lies between the reptilian brain and the cerebral cortex. The limbic system has links with the neocortex allowing for emotional/cognitive processing. It also works in concert with the body to elicit the physical signs of emotions like the flush of embarrassment, and the smile of joy. Limbic system emotions also determine the release of neurotransmitters that either strengthen or weaken our immune system.

The limbic system consists of five major structures in the brain: the thalamus, hypothalamus, basal ganglia, amygdala and hippocampus.[10]

The thalamus acts as a relay station for all incoming senses, except smell. It also relays motor impulses from the cerebral cortex through the brain stem and out to the muscles. In addition, the thalamus interprets pain, temperature, light touch and pressure sensations, and it functions in emotions and memory.

The hypothalamus controls the pituitary gland and normal body temperature, food intake, thirst and the waking and sleeping states. It is also the center for mind-over-body phenomena, allowing enormous feats of strength and endurance during emergencies. In addition, the hypothalamus is involved in rage, aggression, pain and pleasure.

The amygdala has links to brain areas involved in cognitive processing, as well as those involved in bodily states related to the whole gamut of emotions from powerful reactions of grief or pain, to pleasure and joy. These emotions produce memories and biochemically control the routing and migration of monocytes that are pivotal to our immune system. This seat of emotions is the focal point of receptors for neuropeptides from throughout the body, making us conscious by helping us sort out sensory information for understanding the situations we are confronted with in our environment.[11] It is involved with the recognition of facial expressions and body language. It allows us to assess a situation by coordinating bodily reactions that serve as internal warnings so we respond appropriately with fear and anxiety or happiness.[12]

The hippocampus, where new nerve cell growth occurs throughout life, uses sensory input coming through the thalamus, movement coordination in the basal ganglion and emotions in the hypothalamus to form short-term memory. Short-term memory, with nerve net activation in the hippocampus, can then enter permanent storage as long-term memory throughout the brain and the rest of the body. During sleep, researchers see bursts of electrical activity in the hippocampus that stimulate the brain area that handles sensory information. This discovery supports the notion that communication between these areas during sleep as well as awake, fortifies our memories.[13]

The basal ganglion connects and orchestrates impulses between the cerebellum and frontal lobe, thus helping to control body movements. It facilitates the fine motor control in our facial and eye muscles necessary to communicate our emotional states to others and in learned, motor-based memory like learning to play the piano.[14] The basal ganglion is one of the areas connected with the frontal lobe through the substantia nigra that coordinates thought involved in planning the order and timing of future behaviors.[15] (See Figure 5.7.) This ties in to Damasio's findings that emotion, body and reason are physiologically inseparable.

The intricate wiring of the limbic system shows that in order to learn and remember something, there must be sensory input, a personal emotional connection and movement. As we experience the world, the collage of images and our responding actions are all run through an emotional filter in the limbic system that determines the value, meaning and survival potential of the experience in light of past experience.[16] Socially, everything we do stems from our need to be accepted within our group so we may survive. Emotions interpret our experience and help us to organize our view of the world and our place in it.

All of our emotional/cognitive processing appears to be biochemical. How we feel about a situation triggers specific neurotransmitters. Objectively speaking, to the body/mind every experience is simply an event. The way we choose to perceive that event, colored by our emotions, determines our response to it and our potential for learning from it. At least 80% of what we perceive in our lives takes shape in our mind dependent on where we focus our attention. We can change our reality by changing what we focus on and pay attention to.[17]

If we perceive the event as a disaster, the neurotransmitter adrenalin is released and the body/mind responds with a series of survival-oriented reactions. With increased adrenalin we also produce the neurotransmitter cortisol that decreases our ability to learn and remember.[18] If instead we choose to

Figure 4.1: The Limbic System

perceive the event as a learning experience, an adventure, other neurotransmitters like dopamine, GABA, acetylcholine, nerve growth factor, interferon and interleukins are released.[19] These increase our ability to establish or reorganize neural networks so we may effectively think and remember. We will be returning to the subject of neurotransmitters in a later chapter. The point here is that emotions, and the release of neurotransmitters that they elicit, are intimately intertwined with cognitive function.

WHAT DOES THIS MEAN FOR EDUCATION?

We have given social and emotional development a back seat, and
that's doing a great disservice to kids and to our society.
— *Rachelle Tyler, Prof. of Pediatrics at UCLA*[20]

The implications of these insights are enormous, especially in the realm of education. Elizabeth deBeauport brings this home succinctly when she writes: "What's missing from all our educational efforts? The feeling brain. Affection was the first characteristic of mammalian growth. When we began to care, we agreed not to be like reptiles and simply slink away."[21]

The emotional environment is a critical element of growth and learning from the very beginning. In utero, neural and chemical characteristics of the mother's emotional state affect the developing embryo and fetus. After birth, maternal separation, deprivation or rejection will cause an over-stimulated stress reaction in the infant. This will likely cause later cognitive deficits (85% of children with impaired caregiver-child attachments have significant behavior and language problems) and increased susceptibility to disease (especially heart disease) in both children and adults.[22, 23, 24, 25, 26, 27]

When we, as embryos, fetuses, children or adults experience trauma or neglect, the developing brain becomes hardwired to expect these types of problems. This can be seen in children with autism who show enlarged emotion and memory areas of the brain in Magnetic Resonance Imaging (MRI) scans.[28]

Developmental experts agree that the only factor shown to optimize children's intellectual potential is a secure, trusting relationship with their parents and/or caregivers. Time spent cuddling, playing, being fully present and consciously communicating with children establishes a bond of security, trust and respect on which the entire child-development pyramid is based.[29] School children must also feel safe, accepted and included in order for learning to occur. One of the most important things a teacher can do, especially with students with disabilities, is to bond with them. CAT scans show that children process information through their emotions first, and information that is the most emotional and emotionally relevant to them, is what students will learn. On the other hand, insecurity and fear can bring learning to a screeching halt by shutting down higher brain connections.[30]

Our body/mind system learns through experiencing life in context, in relationship to everything else, and it is our emotions, our feelings that mediate that context. In order to learn, think or create, learners must have an emotional commitment, otherwise, education becomes just an intellectual exercise.[31] Yet schools by and large deliver knowledge in piecemeal, segregated subject areas, in an unemotional, unsocial environment. The connection to the student's own personal concerns or future survival is usually remote. Most school lessons expect students to settle down to serious, intellectual business, devoid of social or emotional content. And teachers complain of having to be disciplinarians, instead of educators, in their efforts to put a lid on the social, emotional interactions among members of the class.

Students who feel safe, respected and loved are highly motivated to learn, already possessing an emotional commitment, and will learn because they love to learn. Others will do well because they have come to understand the personal survival importance of education to societal success and therefore approach learning with some emotional/survival commitment. But those who do not feel emotionally safe will lack an emotional commitment to the current educational curriculum, and those who cannot appreciate its application for their lives, may fail miserably in school.

Education would be more effective if homes and classrooms became learning societies, actively engaging emotions and social relationships in the service of knowledge acquisition. The Danish school system comes pretty close to this ideal in many respects. (Some of the features of the Danish system are described in Chapters 5 and 15).

DEVELOPING EMOTIONS

Exploration and expression of emotion is necessary for development of the limbic system and its connections to other brain areas. As with sensory development, we are not born into the world with this capacity fully formed. We must develop the neural networks that support emotional processing through social experience and expression.

Our first emotions have to do with safety --- babies who have loving, committed caregivers feel safe to explore the world without the need to constantly worry about survival. By approximately fifteen months of age, the limbic system begins the process of adding more complex emotions to the base patterns for sensory input and learned motor functioning. Out of this union, relationships between the individual and its world are discovered and stored first in short, and then in long term memory.

If you put two one-year-olds in a room together, they will hardly notice each other as they go about their sensory-motor job of understanding the material world. But at about fifteen months of age, they pay attention to each other for the first time and interaction begins. With this interaction comes the awareness of the child's place in the world as a unique, separate individual who is connected to others by common lineage, emotional bonds, language and specific cultural paradigms. Between ages two and three, children realize they are separate from their mother and the concept of "I" develops. From this newly found point of separation a child recognizes that this is "my mommy, my daddy, my toy". Through this recognition the child bonds with its parents, siblings, and caretakers. The social and family sense of concern or protection through bonding that assures societal survival is anchored in the emotional development of the limbic system.

Music is shown to be a strong developer of emotions, even before birth. Newborns are able to recognize the music their mothers' listened to during pregnancy. Babies, as young as two to six months old, prefer consonant sounds to dissonant ones and maintain a state of calm attention when sung to in a consonant way. Consonant sounds activate the corpus callosum and the area of the frontal brain that has to do with reward and pleasure. Research has shown that both children and adults enjoy music because it elicits emotions and feelings, including thrills, laughter and tears, thus assisting the development of the limbic system and it's connection to high-level reasoning and memory. The earlier children are introduced to music, via listening, singing, exploring musical instruments and dancing, the more their brains develop and the more able they are to feel and responsibly express emotions in a healthy way.[32, 33]

LEARNING BY IMITATION

In these early developmental years, exploration takes on a whole new dimension. Children begin to imitate the people in their world, gaining a physical and emotional understanding of significant persons and social relationships. Researchers have discovered there are mirror neurons in the premotor cortex and other brain areas that could be the neuronal substrate of our ability to mimic others; to sense what others are feeling and thinking; and to visualize a plan of action in empathy with them. [34] By fourteen months of age, infants are master imitators, but not merely as indiscriminate copycats. They sometimes opt for a simpler way to do what an adult shows them. This flexibility signals a budding capacity for evaluating the sensibility of others' behavior.[35] This may be the core of teaching and learning from childhood throughout life.

What we call "terrible two's" behavior is simply the child's exaggeration of our movements and emotions to gain a full sensory-motor understanding of them. The child is intrigued by the physical sensations of these newly found emotions, and great theatrics often occur. We may label these outbursts as temper tantrums, when they are simply emotional, physical, multisensory learning activities. Expression through movement is very important to the learning of emotions. At this age, the child has no cognitive or manipulative thought directing the emotion. They simply become the emotion! If parents understand this, they can be entertained by a wild and wonderful performance/mirror of themselves instead of seeing the two's as terrible. The amount and frequency of "terrible two's" behavior will diminish when the child's caretakers become aware of the importance of the modeling they are presenting to the child.

This physical/emotional link continues throughout our lives as our bodies continue to be the primary vehicle for expression of feeling. Notice the "goose bumps" you have when you experience a deeply moving scene in a play or great music that speaks to the soul. Notice the movement of choir members who are emotionally absorbed in their singing. Notice your own movements as you express a deep emotion. It is literally impossible to express emotion without motion. The major sensory areas of the face and hands are usually very active in the process. Hand and facial expression of emotion stimulates large areas of the brain for more sophisticated connections between emotion and thought.

Between ages fifteen months and four years the child explores the emotional richness of its world. The initial exploration involves emotions generated by the hypothalamus and amygdala which include states of rage, fright and aggression. These are linked directly to the reptilian brain for their expression and so become raw reaction without any cognitive control or understanding. As the nerve networks develop and link into the cortical centers in the temporal lobes for thought and higher cognitive functions, emotions such as anger, sadness, happiness and frustration emerge. This neural link-up with cognitive areas allows these gross emotions to reach conscious awareness and for stories, historical events, media presentations and observations to affect us emotionally.[36]

WHY WE NEED TO EXPRESS EMOTIONS

The exploration and expression of these gross emotions is essential to the later development of the refined emotions of love, altruism, compassion, empathy and joy, as nerve networks link into the frontal lobes of the cerebrum. Our emotions then provide us with the passion and action to live fully.

When emotions are connected directly to survival and fear, their expression may become an explosive reaction centered in the sympathetic nervous system and the brain stem. This reactive kind of emotion, though natural for a two year old, has long been feared in adults because it often leads to violence. Given this fear of violence, children are often restrained from any expression of strong emotions, even when they are just discovering them.

When we encourage people to express emotions, even anger and sadness, we show respect for their feelings. Because the person feels valued, the emotional response is usually linked to reason. Children who are taught through example and allowed to naturally and responsibly express emotions are better able to constructively or creatively use them throughout life. Talking about feelings is of particular benefit as we engage thought and reasoning processes to comprehend and verbalize the emotional experience. This helps to strengthen the important emotion-cognition link.

On the other hand, when people are given no outlet for emotional expression, they may start to doubt their personal value. The suppressed emotions lose their links with conscious awareness and this state of denial becomes linked with the survival centers. As a result, the emotion is then connected to fear and self-doubt. When the emotions are finally expressed, they can often emerge in a violent, explosive outburst. If they remain suppressed or denied, they precipitate a chronic release of adrenalin and depress learning, memory and the immune system, which can possibly lead to life threatening cancers and heart disease.[37] Encouraging children and ourselves to express our emotions in human ways allows us to connect safely and honestly with each other. This safe connection is paramount to learning, and is also important to our longevity and health.

In the 1940's, Harvard University began a longitudinal study that consisted of students (in their late teens and twenties) answering a battery of questions. Over the years, these students were followed to see if the perceptions they held in the 1940's affected their later lives. At the age of sixty-five, this group was assessed for heart disease, (because that is the number one killer in the U.S.) and to see if their answers as young people showed a correlation to their current heart health. The researchers discovered that ninety-three percent of the sixty-five year olds who felt they didn't have loving parents when they were in their twenties had heart disease, compared with thirty-five percent who felt they had one loving parent and only twenty-five percent of those who felt they had two loving parents.[38] The sense of connectedness a person feels, and the emotions elicited by that connection are key to health and also learning.

While visiting and teaching in a variety of other cultures over the past sixteen years, I have often been deeply impressed by enlightened societal attitudes towards the expression of emotion. Among the native people of Botswana and Lesotho, I have experienced great joy and passion. People from these cultures are not afraid to express emotion from their whole being, whether it be anger at injustice, sadness or joy. Joy was their main expression, coming from their whole body and mind. It would manifest in song, in a brilliant smile that went on forever, or in a deep embrace. They readily expressed joy in the simple act of meeting me, or enjoying a harvest, or watching a child, or waking to a new day.

In our culture, the expression of anger is more common than the expression of joy, and often does not even appear odd. On the other hand, a person expressing joy on the street may actually be considered mad. Why is it that in our culture we are much more attuned to and respectful of — and perhaps skillful at — expressions of anger than of joy? Could it be that fear of expression of one has made us wary of the other, and led us to discount and intellectualize away anything that might be construed as "emotional"? However, as science itself now affirms, our emotions, motives and thoughts are inextricably linked.[39] Emotions are part of thought. Once found they are always there. When we respect this inseparability and affirm a productive place for emotions in all educational environments we cultivate fertile ground for lifelong learning, thought and creativity.

I felt such fulfilling emotions among the all-embracing relationships of African communities, and with people in Poland and Russia — countries where honesty and struggle are a major way of life. These sojourns have confirmed my belief in the importance of emotion to the health and well being of any society. Passion, meaningful relationships are a large part of what we are missing and looking for in our own society. Encouragement and acceptance of rich emotional development are essential to our lives as individuals and as a society.

EARLY ALTRUISM

In the early years, the developing limbic system enables the child to form relationships and social bonds. This is the perfect opportunity to teach children about behavior toward other people and how to take care of other children, pets, objects and the environment. Signs of the development of altruism and empathy appear around three years of age. These qualities are ultimately important for the survival of the species.[40]

The development of altruistic behavior begins with showing concern and awareness for another's needs. The child moves from the possessive relationship to the idea of caring for the possession: "this is mine and I must take care of it." Taking the extra time to tend to a pet when your three year old discovers the pet needs food, even if you are already ten minutes late, honors altruistic learning and will last a lifetime.

Being willing to show concern and search for a lost toy rather than saying "we'll buy a new one," instills a sense of value in the child. Telling your child when you feel sad, and allowing the child to comfort you teaches empathy and nurturance. Altruistic learning is crucial in our society where concepts of "restore, reuse and recycle," are having a painful time germinating. It may be that our landfills, hospitals and mental institutions are overflowing because the early seeds of altruism weren't germinated during limbic development.[41]

Learning to control our emotions is also an appropriate task for this relationship brain. In order to avoid conflict we often give children what they want, when they want it. This deprives them of the opportunity to learn about delayed gratification. A painless way to assist this important learning process might be to play a time game. When a child asks for a snack, say "Sure, and I will give it to you in three minutes." Then set an egg timer and ask the child to let you know when it's time. Then give the child the snack. The time period can be lengthened with the learning. When children know their needs will be met, they easily develop a sense of time and learn delayed gratification. This lesson will serve them well the rest of their lives.[42]

EMOTION AND MEMORY

What is the connection between sensory physical awareness and emotion that gives us our memories? If you ask people to recall their earliest memory, they will usually go back to a time after the limbic system starts to mature. As the limbic system gears up, nerve networks connect the sensory and motor base patterns to emotion and memory is established.

Take a moment to recall an early memory. What were the colors, the sounds, the smells, the tastes, the emotions? What do you remember about your physical movements, who else was there and what did you feel about them? Memory is usually rich with bodily sensations of sight, sound, smell, taste, emotions and movements. The neural relatedness of these gives us our remembered pictures.

My first memory was of my mother swinging me on a small back yard swing strung between the house and a tree. I distinctly remember it was cool, probably Autumn, with clear, bright colors in the air and on the trees. The smells were crisp and pungent Autumn smells. I remember feeling secure watching my mother's face with her blue scarf as she talked and laughed at my giggling; the feeling of my body going back and forth, first very gently, then feeling it in my stomach as the swing went higher. It is a very physical, sensual memory and I see it now as in a movie clip. Imagination, dreams and cognition arise from this intricate interplay within the limbic system.

The limbic system allows us to see things in context for the first time. This newly found awareness is used to understand ownership, our relationship to everything else and our place in society. "It" becomes more than just something that we eat for survival. It is now recognized as "spaghetti," wiggly, the color of my shirt, mine instead of my sisters, and I can make a story with it.

This is also an important time for physical imprinting, the development of body memory. As children encounter new information, they will move to embody it on all their muscles and senses. Allow yourself to be guided on a walk with a three-year old child. When they come to something new, they will actually move their bodies to conform to the physical configuration of the new object to better understand it. Movement facilitates the entrainment process in understanding relationships physically.[43]

BASE PATTERNING AND MEMORY

The nature of memory has long been a subject of conjecture and debate. There is a growing consensus among brain scientists that memory is not stored in a single location in the brain. Instead, memories are constructed from neural pathways that fire together as patterns throughout the entire body, with experts like Candace Pert relating memories to a "hologram" of our entire system, where every part is connected to every other part.[44] These networks are constantly subject to modification and elaboration so we may link ideas and memories in infinite combinations.

The base patterns of memory form as we experience our sensory environment in greater and greater detail. Different sensory areas of the brain realize specific sensations. Patterns develop that allow us to recall those different sensations together as a single memory. These patterns are associated with the specific brain areas where that specialized sensory information is processed, for example, the occipital lobe for visual sensations, the temporal lobe for sound. So that when you recall a memory of your mother on a particular day, the images, sounds, words, smells, movements, emotions arise from different places in the brain but are linked neurally and thus can form a single memory.

Which of course may lead you directly to another memory because neural networks are so complexly interwoven.

According to this model, that is how we integrate new learning. Evolving patterns become base reference points to understand new information. As we are presented with new learning, the brain recalls past experience and provides an image display of base patterns from each area of the brain simultaneously. New information can then be integrated into existing base patterns, thus changing and enriching the nerve networks and giving us a more complex worldview.

Information starts as short term memory in the limbic system where sensory images are combined with emotional components that add important survival information. If the information is valued and practiced, it becomes the template for reorganization of previous patterning. This reorganization of base patterns becomes long term memory in the free-form information system throughout the body/mind system. We continue to elaborate and modify the patterning throughout our lives. The base patterns, ninety percent of which are acquired within the first five years of life, give us the template on which to attach all future learning.[45]

PET scans show that a cellular information highway speeds through all parts of the brain to coordinate memories for personally experienced events, called episodic memories. In a study at the University of Toronto, participants showed a stronger memory for words analyzed by meaning, as compared to words perused on a letter-by-letter basis. Episodic memories (or the meanings of words, as this Toronto study shows) have an added emotional component, which appears necessary for complex memory development.[46] Image displays and memory in the brain are ubiquitous and appear to be triggered more by episodic experience than just straight line rote processing. The memory function is more than a linear library system. Memory appears to be a free form information system that facilitates information retrieval from all bodily experiences instantly and simultaneously. Therefore, in order to most efficiently remember something, it is best to connect it to sensory, emotional, physical episodes.

Each person's patterns are specific and unique. The number of possible base patterns is infinite. These base patterns determine the way we process and act upon our learning. As templates, these base patterns can be modified, reorganized and pruned for more efficiency as knowledge increases.[47] They provide the basis of our beliefs, which in turn can be transformed by new information and broader insight. "The somatotropic map in the brain is modified by experience," Eric Kandel observes, "learning can lead to structural alterations in the brain."[48] Limbic brain development, with its rich emotional connections to all brain areas allows us to constantly enlarge our database. The base sensory, motor and emotional patterns become the template for new learning. Each step makes it easier for the system to learn, process, re-organize information and grow in greater understanding and complexity.

THE LIMBIC JEWEL — IMAGINATION

Imagination is more important than knowledge, for while knowledge points to all there is, imagination points to all there will be.

— Albert Einstein

As the limbic connections elaborate, all of the elements come into place for the development of imagination. Imagination will naturally spring from the sensory-motor patterning in relationship with emotion and memory. This is a process you can actually see unfolding if you observe how children respond when you read to them. As they concentrate on listening to you read to them, they are absolutely quiet. In their brains they are elaborating internal pictures and emotions connected to their already acquired understanding. They are actively forming new nerve networks.

When you have finished reading the book, the child immediately says: "read it again," and "again" and "again"! The repetition allows them to elaborate and myelinate the new nerve paths. If you happen to say the wrong word as you are reading, they will let you know. This consistency is important to the integrity of their imaginative pictures. They will then tell you the story to embody it in movement and sensation through speech. Finally, they will play act it. The physical play gives them the sensory understanding of the concepts and anchors all the parts together.[49]

As the child grows older and you are able to read more complex stories, books without pictures or few pictures are more desirable in assisting the imaginative process. Also, it is always good to encourage children to make up and tell you their own stories.

PLAY

In the early formative years, play is almost synonymous with life. It is second only to being nourished, protected and loved. It is a basic ingredient of physical, intellectual, social and emotional growth.
— Ashley Montague

The value of make-believe cannot be stressed enough.[50] The child can take its world, and through play and familiarity organize it into more and more complex mental and emotional patterns. The time from ages two to five is a crucial stage for children's cognitive development as they learn to process information and expand it into creativity. Interactive communication and play, when children are learning from each other's imagination, accelerates the process.

These marvelous changes unfold naturally, and happily do not require adult supervision and meddling. Unfortunately, however, these days there seems to be less time and opportunity for children to simply play. Even play-groups seem to be organized and structured. There appears to be an assumption that children need to be entertained and their play orchestrated. I see it a lot in organized sports for children. Adults are in charge and competition is the goal. Rarely do you just see children initiate "pick up" games that were routine when I was a child.

Some of my greatest learning occurred while playing with the neighborhood kids in the big vacant field behind our house. It had a tree smack dab in the middle with gullies, rocks, sandy areas and bushes from which to make hideouts or bows and arrows. There was enough room to ride our imaginary white stallions and play cowboys and Indians. Hours and days slipped by as we concocted one idea after another. We made our own toys from sticks, feathers, stones, chalk, string, glue, big packing boxes, our parents' old clothes — anything. Spontaneously co-creating toys with a playmate enhances brain development exponentially. Play provides the emotional spark which activates our attention, problem solving and behavior response systems so we gain the skills necessary for cooperation, co-creativity, altruism and understanding.

Dr. Paul MacLean ties the process of imaginative development to the development of play that becomes the essence of creativity and high-level reasoning. He feels the link between the emotional limbic brain and the frontal lobe of the neocortex allows for the ultimate expression of human creativity and development.[51] Our primary emotions (happiness, surprise, fear, disgust, anger and sadness) are not often activated in our consciously controlled society. But when we truly play, these emotions are allowed to surface in a safe way that insures us a richly motivated and passionate life.[52]

Play represents full body/mind integration, with masses of neurons being devoted specifically to the generation of rough-and-tumble play. These specific myelinated pathways exist between the thalamus of the limbic system, the sensory area (parafascicular complex and posterior thalamic nuclei) in the parietal lobe, the cerebellum, and motor cortex of the frontal lobes of the neocortex. Rough and tumble play, especially during early adolescence when the child's body is changing so radically, and they need that heavy touch more than ever, effectively reduces hyperactivity and the symptoms of ADHD.[53]

When we play, dopamine is released which induces elation, excitement, and orchestrates nerve net development and alignment all over the brain.[54] When we are able to take in our fill of sensory stimuli, process and integrate it with richly developed base patterns, and express new insights in a creative way, both physically and verbally, we are then truly at play. The human urge to create comes from the play impulse. Play on words, punning, and wit have contributed to creative thought in literature and drama throughout the ages. Composers, choreographers, and artists of all kind express their integration through play. The exhilarating play of modern science spills over into mathematics, paradoxical puzzles and language.[55]

As teachers, parents, human beings, we become much more effective in our relationships when there is play and heart to heart connection. Current research around the hearts' role in play and successful learning is greatly elaborated in my book: *Awakening The Child Heart, Handbook For Global Parenting.*[56]

Interestingly, the National Education Association is discovering the importance of the arts, especially drama/theater and music in assuring greater success in math and reading as well as a decrease in behavior problems, improved attendance, and greater focus and readiness to learn. Drama/theater and music allow students to express emotions through play and learn via the entire sensory-motor system. Students who play with the arts score on average 40 to 60 points higher on verbal and 15 to 40 points higher in the math parts of the SAT's with low income minority and academically vulnerable students gaining the most from regular arts instruction. Student who participate in the arts outperform those who don't on virtually every measure. Successful schools are integrating the arts into all aspects of the curriculum, thus providing more entry points of learning to those students who learn in a more gestalt context.[57]

We are finding that "play" also helps to stitch individuals into the social fabric that is the staging ground for their lives. It assists the vestibular system in growing brilliant, creative, healthy brains through cross-lateral, spiral movements that also increase the levels of dopamine important for neural plasticity and optimal learning. Play provides the touch necessary for nerve growth factor to assist the growth and health of massive interconnected nerve networks throughout the body, and the production of oxytocin which assists learning, focus and a sense of safety.[58] And, play teaches us how to be with each other in a way that fosters belonging and safety at all levels.[59]

With the massive increase in autism, (In California alone, there was a 273 percent increase in autism cases between 1987 and 1998)[60] play has been found to be the "relationship building" agent to assure the most success. The University of Michigan Play Project trains parents to play with their children for at least fifteen hours a week, taking cues from the children to shape the play interaction. More than 62 percent of those children whose parents played with them more than fifteen hours a week made good or excellent progress, compared with only 20 percent of those whose parents spent less than ten hours.[61]

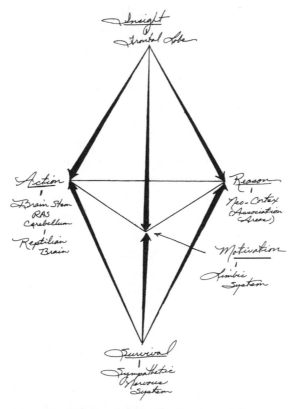

Fig, 4.2: Trowbridge Model of Balanced Functioning

Play at the simplest physical level as well as the furthest reaches of the intellect, depends on a balance of all the elements of our humanity. As Anthony Trowbridge has shown in his elaboration of Paul MacLean's triune brain theory, emotion is one of the key elements of that balance.[62] When the emotions are brought into dynamic equilibrium with reason, insight, action and even survival, learning becomes a rational, creative process. If any part of the brain processing is left out of the learning process, integration of patterning, and appropriate action are limited. When dynamic equilibrium is lost, learning and creativity suffer.

TV AND IMAGINATION

Television, computers, or automated toys often occupy time in children's lives that they would use less passively if they had fewer such props to fall back on. If children are given space and encouraged to create, they naturally will entertain themselves without sophisticated equipment or adult intervention. A lot of creativity comes from just being in a place where it is allowed to happen spontaneously. I strongly agree with Joseph Chilton Pearce's stand and Jane Healy's suggestion that TV be banned before the age of eight so that imagination and language skills have a chance to be established.[63, 64]

CAUTION:
CHILDREN NOT AT PLAY.

Figure 4.3: "Caution: Children Not At Play."
(From the American Heart Association)

This diagram from the American Heart Association says a lot. TV has preempted physical movement, interactive communication, play, motivation, use of more than two senses, problem solving, curiosity and productivity. And we could add to this the developmental lack of imagination that demands full sensory, motor, emotional, and human interaction/intercommunication practice.

Daydreaming and imaginative play promote the child's perceptual maturity, emotional growth and creative development. TV inhibits the process, and interferes with kids'learning how to play. Children naturally learn by doing and through interaction with other people. In that sense, learning via TV is unnatural. Learning also requires time for reflection, and for absorbing and processing experience. A study has shown that students who were heavy TV viewers (more than six hours a day) were more likely to have low IQ's than light viewers (two hours or less a day). "TV gives children stunningly complex pieces of information," Kate Moody writes, "but this knowledge is largely unintegrated and lacks sufficient context and meaning."[65]

TV bombards viewers with a constantly changing stream of pictures, words, and movement that are too fast for the young brain to assimilate. The child may be able to repeat what he has heard, but without any depth of understanding. It's that depth of understanding — which comes from the integration of new experience with the child's developing body/mind patterning — that leads to imagination and creative reasoning. The child is left passive without the internal mental, emotional, and physical involvement necessary for cognitive development.

The child's ability to process is exhausted by over-stimulation in an attempt to follow what is happening on the TV screen. This causes the child's eyes to go into ocular lock (staring) and disassociative hearing (no connection between words and pictures). The body goes into a stress mode that inhibits learning and memory and leaves the child irritable and fearful.[66, 67, 68]

It's important to emphasize that the act of watching TV itself, regardless of the content, has a lasting impact on a child's learning. Ages two to five are a crucial time for brain development. The brain is primed to learn how to take in and make relationships out of information. When children watch TV, they are habituating to a learning state that lacks physical, emotional and even some sensory (smell, taste, proprioceptive) involvement. This habituation will affect life long learning patterns.

The Henry J. Kaiser Family Foundation reported that of children ages two and younger, forty-three percent watched an average of two hours of TV on a typical day. During those two hours, the toddlers were not exploring, playing, learning or interacting with people who loved them and could teach them how to be imaginative and creative. In "heavy TV households", thirty-four percent of children ages four to six can read compared with fifty-six percent in homes where the TV is on less often. The study also found that twenty-seven percent of four to six year olds use a computer each day with twenty-four percent of boys playing video games compared with eight percent of girls. Girls do far better in school than boys.[69, 70] I hear over and over from teachers today that children are more irritable, lack imagination and have a more difficult time learning. Even with guidelines and suggestions, many of these children lack the basic neural networks to play with ideas and be creative.

John Rosemond, director of the Center for Affirmative Parenting in Gastonia, North Carolina cites a study that shows preschoolers who watched a lot of Sesame Street tended to do less well in school than children who watched no TV.[71] Stephen Hinshaw at Berkeley, concerned about the elimination or limiting of recess for these "TV grown" children, states that: "Even more vital than early reading, is the learning to play skills, which form the foundation of cognitive skills.[72]

DREAMS

We get a chance to experience our imaginative richness in our dreams. The limbic system is the area of dreams — our inner imaginative expression. The limbic system is dependent on the Reptilian Brain for imaginative expression during wakefulness. But when the Reptilian brain is gated (shut off) in sleep, the limbic system gives us our internal expression in dreams. Most dreams are full sensory experiences with strong emotional overlays.

Dreaming is important for the processing of emotional events and even appears to assist in the release of emotionally stressful situations. This is shown graphically in a study, in which REM (Rapid Eye Movement — Dream) sleep was associated with a surge of adrenalin that more than doubled during REM sleep.[73, 74] The elaborate connections of the limbic system, that forms the bridge between the body and the neocortex, supply the emotional elements imperative to live and relate at our highest level.

SUGGESTIONS FOR HEALTHY DEVELOPMENT OF
THE LIMBIC SYSTEM IN CHILDREN

A. Bond with your child, take time and be present. Encourage spontaneous imaginative play, either alone or with parents/caregivers and other children. Spend time playing, climbing, splashing, crawling and spinning with children in nature, allowing them to lead the play process. Rough-and-tumble play is good for both child and parent. Allow children to create their own toys. Steer clear of non-creative, fully constructed commercial toys.

B. Read and participate with full attention when with a child. Encourage creative, imaginative story making and play-acting.

C. Encourage and allow full emotional expression moving to rational dialogue between the ages of 3-5 years.

D. Expose children to good, consonant music. Sing and dance with children. Encourage them to explore musical instruments and musical styles.

E. Encourage lots of movement and interaction with other children to develop playground rules, sharing and the beginnings of altruistic behavior.

F. Honor care of other people, pets and objects.

G. Encourage a sense of time and delayed gratification.

H. Discourage any TV, video games or computers until at least age 8.

I. Provide a loving, low stress environment, and model rich emotional expression and stability. Model JOY.

J. Control caretaker's stress with movements like Brain Gym® (Hookups), yoga, Tai Chi, walking, swimming, and other integrative movements daily.

*Figure 4.4: Playground interaction shows the
beginnings of altruistic behavior*

5

Making Connections

When we try to pick out anything by itself we find it hitches to everything in the universe.

— John Muir

I had a human brain in a jar when I first began teaching college years ago in Colorado. I always felt a sense of awe and reverence when I took it out of the jar to explore it with students. Here lay a part of the whole universe of this person in my hands — part of their genetic and cellular memory, their life story, their pictures and understanding of the world, their feelings of love and hatred, the controls for the way they moved and interacted with the world, their passions and sacred dreams. Here in my hands was the physical record, the neural relationships of a unique individual, a being unlike any other that has ever been or ever will be. I still feel this awe and wonderment when I truly AM with another human being, of whatever age. This unique and unlimited person can be the doorway to worlds I might never otherwise visit.

During the same teaching stint, I teamed up with a geologist to teach field courses in the desert every Spring. Experiencing the desert through the eyes and minds of twenty-eight students turned out to be a great learning adventure. Each individual drew from a unique developmental background, emotional understanding and specific way of processing new information. Each had synthesized their understanding into skills and thought patterns uniquely their own. Each made the desert new and fascinating with their unlimited ways of experiencing and perceiving it for the first time. And each became a rich resource of new insights for me.

The unique set of connections which each of us makes from the very first moment we encounter the world, shapes our understanding of the world and of ourselves. Indeed, these connections are our selves, constantly moderating our experience of the world, constantly changing as experience is integrated with connections we have already made. And they are expressed and embodied in the knowledge, competencies and skills that make every human being unique and irreplaceable.

All our experiences begin with the brain stem, go next through the limbic system which incorporates emotions and monitors the sensations and finally are consciously realized in the neocortex, which associates the world for us. The neocortex is the most plastic area of the brain, it's the novelty brain that loves fresh input and as much variety as a lifetime can present. Like other parts of the brain, the neocortex is totally interdependent with the body as a whole, but at the same time follows its own timetable in unfolding and developing. Understanding this process gives us a much clearer view not only of our enormous capabilities — particularly in the area of learning — but also of the ways the development of these capabilities can be impeded or helped to flourish.

INTRODUCING COMMAND CENTRAL

The largest structure of the human brain is the cerebrum, where Command Central resides. To get a sense of its size, put your hands together in very loose fists with your two thumbs pointing up in front of you. Covering the cerebrum like a thin peel that covers an orange, is the cortex, or neocortex. The word neocortex refers to its evolutionary advancement over the non-mammalian brain. The neocortex is composed mainly of three types of neurons in a thin layer 2 to 5 mm. thick that covers the surface of all the convolutions of the cerebrum. It contains ten to twenty billion or more nerve cells, mainly the Great Intermediate Net of association neurons, or what I consider to be Command Central.

Command Central neurons are held together by eighty to one hundred billion neuroglia (glial) cells. Glial cells form a supporting meshwork by twining around nerve cells or lining structures in the brain and spinal cord. Some bind nervous tissue to supporting structures and attach the neurons to blood vessels.

If spread out, the neocortex would cover five hundred square inches of surface area. It uses one and one half pints of blood every sixty seconds and burns four hundred calories every day. The neocortex constitutes only one fourth of the brain's total volume, yet it has approximately eighty-five percent of the total neurons in the brain.[1]

The neocortex is made up of grey matter, the unmyelinated cell bodies of neurons, which have unlimited ability to form new dendrites and reorganize dendritic patterns from new experiences throughout life. It is estimated that the nerve nets within the neocortex of an adult have over one quadrillion (that's a million billions) connections in a normal brain and are able to process one thousand new bits of information every second. This means that at any one time, the possible combinations of signals jumping across the synapses in the brain exceed the numbers of atoms in the known universe.[2]

The white matter is composed of myelinated axons extending from or going to nerve cell bodies in the neocortex. These axons quickly carry sensory information to the neocortex, and carry its motor commands to the body.

Figure 5.1: White and Grey Matter of the Cerebrum

This very second as you read these words, your brain is monitoring the light, heat, cold, sounds, and smells around you. It monitors the functioning of all your organs, and every touch and pressure on your body. It knows who and what is in the room with you. It knows where every muscle in your body is, and which are relaxed, and which contracted. It constantly makes muscle adjustments to keep your body, especially your eyes, aligned to the book. It moves the muscles of the eyes to track across the page, adjust for distance and adjust for light. And it visually takes in the words on the page, integrates them with specific remembered images, sounds, and movements in your life, to understand each word and meaning in your special context so that you may evaluate the relevance of the text, judge its correctness, consider the ways you might implement it — amazing!

At birth the neocortex weighs 350 grams (about 12 ounces), which is twenty-five percent of its adult weight. It grows by increasing dendrites and glial cells, at the rate of 1 milligram every minute to fifty percent of adult weight by six months, seventy-five percent by two and a half years and ninety percent by five years of age. From these figures, we could assume that ninety percent of base neural patterns form before a child even goes to school. By five years of age the child has mastered gross motor control over gravity, learned a world of information through its senses, put these together into language, music and art, and become socialized enough to interact with family and strangers in culturally acceptable ways. This amazing feat of neural development — taking in sensory experiences and creating mental models — will continue to be refined and augmented constantly throughout a lifetime.

FROM SENSORY EXPERIENCE TO UNDERSTANDING

As sensory experience floods our system, it travels through the brain stem and the reticular activating system and on to the thalamus of the limbic system. All pathways from the sensory nerve endings to the neocortex pass through the thalamus, except for smell. The thalamus not only monitors sensory input and adds emotional context to the information, it has direct connections with all areas of the neocortex. This close association, from the thalamus to the neocortex and then from the neocortex back to the thalamus, is called the thalamocortical system.

These subtle, invisible transactions among sensory/emotional/motor areas of the brain allow us to create meaning from our experience. In the process of developing the base patterns which organize our experience, different lobes of the cerebrum are involved: the occipital lobe for visual understanding, the temporal lobe for hearing and gravitational understanding, and the parietal lobe for touch, pressure, pain, heat and cold sensations and proprioception all over the body.

The linkages among these areas give us the images that comprise our memory. You might, for example, remember a time when you dropped a ball and it bounced with a rubbery sound. You might also remember a glass dropping and shattering. Out of remembered experiences like these, we build concepts like: all things fall, glass things break, rubbery things bounce. Through our base patterning we construct models of the way things work, make predictions, organize physical responses, and come to more complexity of understanding as we assimilate new learning.

MAPPING THE CEREBRUM

Curiosity about how each area of the brain works has probably existed since Aristotle's time. But ever since Wilder Penfield began exploring the brain during surgery, we've been driven in our attempt to specifically map all the areas and functions of the brain. In the 1930's, Dr. Penfield discovered that the brain itself has no pain receptors. This made it possible for him to perform brain surgery using only local anesthesia on a fully awake patient. During the course of an operation, Penfield was able to use an electric probe with a mild current to stimulate the neurons of a live, fully conscious brain and talk with its owner about what was happening. To each stimulus, the patient would give a physical or verbal response, or have a memory flashback that he could describe as a coherent recollection of an earlier experience.[3]

In this way, Penfield was able to begin identifying the function of different brain areas. Today we can use the PET Scan (Positron Emission Tomography), MRI (Magnetic Resonance Imaging) and SQUID (Superconducting Quantum Interference Device) to assist in our pursuit to understand brain function.[4]

The PET Scan measures the rate at which the brain burns up glucose, its primary fuel. Volunteers receive injections of minute amounts of a radioactively labeled glucose compound that their brain cells absorb. PET scans then chart where more glucose is being used during specific activities.[5]

Each hemisphere of the cerebrum contains four lobes that are shown in Figure 5.2.[6] A very elementary overview of the four cerebral lobes' functions follows:

Occipital Lobe: Primary Visual Area (receives sensory impulses from eyes, interprets shape, color and movement); and Visual Association Area (relates past to present visual experience, recognition and evaluation of what is seen).

Temporal Lobe: Primary Auditory Area (interprets basic characteristics of sound, pitch and rhythm); Auditory Association (Wernicke's Area) interprets speech; Vestibulo Area (sensations from semi-circular canals — gravitational sense, balance and vibrational sense); Primary Olfactory Area (sensations related to smell). These tie directly into the memory centers of the limbic system.

Parietal Lobe: General Sensory Area (touch, pressure, pain, cold, heat and proprioception);[7] Somesthetic Association Area (integrates and interprets sensations — shape and texture without visual input, orientations of objects, relationship to body parts, and past sensory experiences); Gustatory Area (taste: sensation of sweet, salt, sour and bitter).

Figure 5.2: The Four Lobes of the Neocortex

Frontal Lobe: Primary Motor Area (controls specific muscles all over the body);[8] Premotor Area (concerned with learned motor activities of complex, sequential nature — skilled movements); Frontal Eye Field Area (voluntary scanning movements of eyes); Broca's Area (translates thoughts into speech and development of inner speech as described by Luria).[9] Researchers have found a link between good academic performance and a greater density of neurons in the frontal lobes.[10]

All of these lobes accept external stimuli and information from the opposite side of the body, via the brain stem and limbic system. This information is then integrated, organized and reorganized with sensory-motor memory in the association and gnostic areas of the neocortex (The Great Intermediate Net), so that new experiences can be understood in light of past experiences.

The association areas occupy the greatest portion of each lobe and are concerned with memory, emotions, reasoning, will, judgment, personality traits and intelligence. The gnostic area is the common integrative area collecting information from all four lobes. It is located among the somesthetic, visual and auditory association areas. This area also receives impulses of taste and smell, sensory information from the thalamus and impulses from the lower portions of the brain stem. It integrates sensory interpretations from the association areas and impulses from other areas so that a common thought can be formed from the various sensory inputs. An example of the integrative image that emerges might be: "this cold red apple is soft, but it smells fresh and sure tastes good." It then transmits signals to other parts of the brain to cause the appropriate physical response to occur, again via the limbic system and brain stem.[11] This response might be "bringing the apple to the mouth, opening the mouth and biting into the apple again."

The occipital, temporal and parietal areas partially develop along with the brain stem and limbic systems, but exhibit a major growth spurt at approximately age four. It is not until approximately age eight that we get a major growth spurt in the frontal lobes.

PUTTING IT ALL TOGETHER

To get a snapshot of the complex functioning that occurs when we put all the building blocks together, we have only to look at what happens during the act of seeing the first violets bloom in the Spring. In order to see the violets, the body and eyes must move into position and focus. This act requires gross motor integration in the brain stem, orchestration through the basal ganglion in the limbic system and fine motor coordination in the frontal lobe of the neocortex. Further movement occurs as the iris muscles contract to accommodate for light, and the ciliary muscles on the lens accommodate for distance.

Light reflected from the violets registers on the photosensitive cones and rods of the retinas of both eyes. The cones and rods send specific neurological messages via sensory neurons to the primary visual area of the occipital lobe of the cerebrum. This allows us to "see" the violets.

The frontal eye field coordinates eye teaming, allowing us to track our eyes over the violets. The lines and shape are integrated into structure and three-dimensionality through associative images with the proprioceptive areas of the sensory cortex of the parietal lobe. From there, the impulses diffuse out across nerve net pathways, pulling together information from associative areas in the parietal and temporal lobes.

The combined images from throughout the brain give us a concept of violets including their name, function, where and what they are doing in this

Figure 5.3: Schematic Representations of PET Scans of Lobes and Function [12, 13]

time and space, how they smell and taste and some memory of their physical and emotional relationship to us. From this memory we can make new associations, like gathering the violets and making cards from the pressed flowers, extracting the dye, putting them in a salad, drawing them, or figuring out how many are in an area of lawn. These new associations can stimulate us to solve a puzzle, make a decision, create something new or physically employ the object in our lives. The brain can then prompt various muscular responses, like picking the violets, pressing them in a book, eating them, jumping over them, etc.[14]

The activation of all the brain areas in an associative, integrative dance allows us to play with the violets (or any object) in our minds, thus generating new, creative ideas of what can be done with and to the object.

THE IMPORTANT HEART-BRAIN CONNECTION

In 1995 when Smart Moves was first published, my understanding of how we learn centered on the importance of the brain and movement. Since then there has been a flood of research showing that the brain is actually regulated by the heart. It appears, the heart, via nerves, hormones and other information chemicals (neurotransmitters) to the brain, determines health and whether learning will be easy and natural, or difficult and forgettable.[15]

There are more nerve fibers going from the heart to the brain, than the other way around and the heart beats on it own without innervation from the brain.[16] The nerve fibers between the heart and the brain, connect with the amygdala, the thalamus and even the pre-frontal cortex, thus connecting emotions with the senses and putting information together for learning. Also, as measured by a SQUID (Superconducting Quantum Interference Device), the heart generates an electro-magnetic field that is at least one thousand times greater than the field produced by the brain and extends a measurable distance of eight to sixteen feet from the body.[17] Since our heart fields overlap within eight to sixteen feet of one another, I feel the saying "come from your heart" is intrinsically relevant in being with, teaching and parenting the people in our lives.

All of the information chemicals found in the brain are also found in the heart.[18] Two very powerful hormones secreted by the heart, ANF (Atrio natriuretic factor) and ICA (Intrinsic Cardiac Andrenergic) directly affect brain function. ANF affects the regions of the brain that regulate our emotional state, influence our learning and memory and balance the body's hormones via the pituitary gland.[19] ICA regulates the synthesis and release of dopamine and adrenalin, which either assists or decreases learning and memory.[20]

When we are peaceful, committed to learning, relaxed, enthusiastic and appreciative, the heart exhibits a very coherent heart rate variability pattern (using the R lead of an EKG, the wave pattern of the heart is fairly uniform). In this state, the heart sends a neural message to the amygdala that causes it to function in a parasympathetic state (relaxed, receptive, safe and secure). A message also goes from the heart to the thalamus, which stimulates it to easily take in sensory information from the environment. In this coherent state, new nerve cells are being produced in the hippocampus of the brain. A message also goes to the pre-frontal cortex of the brain, setting up a coherent pattern, which allows us to fully understand the sensory information coming in so we can learn and remember it. In this coherent state, ANF and ICA are assisting optimal hormonal function throughout our bodies and we are healthy.

According to researchers, in order to correctly perceive, learn from and remember our experiences, there must be coherent activity of clusters of neurons, especially in the pre-frontal cortex in order to render unified scenes and meaning from all the diverse sensations in our environment.[21]

When we are stressed, feel fear or frustration, the heart exhibits an incoherent heart rate variability pattern (the wave pattern from an R lead is erratic). In this state, the heart sends a neural message to the amygdala that causes it to function in a sympathetic state (the survival state of fight or flight). A message from the heart causes the thalamus to shut down to any incoming sensory information that does not relate directly to survival, and the message to the pre-frontal cortex of the brain is incoherent so we don't learn or remember. In this incoherent state, cells within the hippocampus lose their dendritic connections and die off resulting in poor memory, fuzzy thinking, and lack of creativity. Also, ANF and ICA are inhibited, thus throwing off our hormonal balance and affecting our health. [22, 23, 24]

Rhythm provides important patterning that allows the brain to take in the sensory-motor patterns of our world. Rhythm begins in utero with the sounds of the mother's heartbeat, breathing and her moving patterns. If coherent, they form the important coherent patterns in the pre-frontal cortex to take in the patterns of language, visual patterns of light, and rhythmic patterns to nurse, crawl, walk, run, skip, and jump. As children mature, rhythm becomes even more important as they begin to put together words in language, reasoning, logic/time sense, and mathematical functions. Our important learning is directly connected to coherent heart-rate variability patterns, produced by safe, connected relationships in our world.

The heart research is elaborated in much greater detail in my book, *Awakening The Child Heart, Handbook For Global Parenting*.

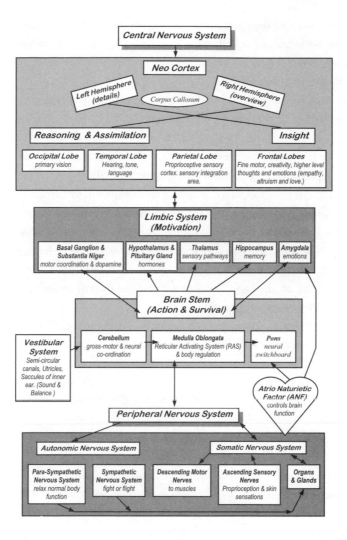

Figure 5.4: Map of the Territory

THE BRAIN'S TWO HEMISPHERES

The cerebrum contains two hemispheres, each with the four lobes described above: occipital, parietal, temporal and frontal. The two hemispheres are connected by white matter — connective motor and sensory axons — in a structure called the corpus callosum. Interestingly, the cerebrum has a crossover pattern such that each side of the body communicates with the opposite hemisphere. Information coming into the left ear goes to the right temporal lobe of the cerebral cortex, while the right hand is controlled by the left motor cortex of the cerebrum. All sensory-motor functions on the right side of the body are either realized or controlled by the left hemisphere. And all sensory-motor functions on the left side of the body are realized and controlled by the right hemisphere.

Though our understanding is constantly changing due to new research, it appears that each hemisphere of the cerebrum develops and processes information in a specific way. To put it in simple terms, the logic hemisphere (usually the left) tends to deal with details, the parts and processes of language, and linear patterns. By contrast, the gestalt (usually the right hemisphere) — meaning whole processing or global as compared to linear — tends to deal with images, rhythm, emotion and intuition.[25] Because some people are transposed and process the logical functions on the right and gestalt functions on the left, I will use the terms logic and gestalt instead of right and left. The corpus callosum then acts as a superhighway allowing quick access to both the linear detail in the logic hemisphere and the overall image in the gestalt hemisphere for integrated thought.

Following is a very simplified summary of the basic differences between these two hemispheres.[26, 27, 28]

LOGIC	GESTALT
Starts with the pieces first	Sees whole picture first then deals with pieces
Parts of Language	Language Comprehension
Syntax, Semantics	Image, Emotion, Meaning
Letters, Sentences	Rhythm, Flow, Dialect
Numbers	Image, intuition
Analysis — linear	Intuition — estimates
Looks at differences	Looks at similarities
Controls feelings	Free with feelings
Planned — structured	Spontaneous — fluid
Sequential thinking	Simultaneous thinking
Language oriented	Feelings/Experience oriented
Future-oriented	Now-oriented
Technique	Flow and Movement
Sports (hand-eye/foot placement)	Sports (flow and rhythm)
Art (media, tool use, how to)	Art (image, emotion, flow)
Music (notes, beat, tempo)	Music (passion, rhythm, image)

Figure 5.5: Summary of Differences between the Brain's Hemispheres
Both hemispheres contain all functions until specialization starts to

occur. This specialization develops at a different rate in each individual. However, on average the gestalt hemisphere exhibits a growth spurt of dendrites between ages four and seven and the logic hemisphere between seven and nine years. Under normal circumstances, complete hemispheric specialization is in place between nine and twelve years of age. The more that both hemispheres and all lobes are activated by use, the more dendritic connections form and extend across the corpus callosum and myelinate. The more myelination, the faster the processing between both hemispheres and the rest of the brain.

When fully developed, the corpus callosum carries four billion messages per second across the two hundred million or more mostly myelinated nerve fibers connecting the two hemispheres of the brain. This integration and quick access leads to full operational thinking so that ideas and concepts can be manipulated, resulting in formal reasoning.[29, 30, 31]

Recent research shows that two regions at the front of the corpus callosum in ADHD (Attention Deficit Hyperactive Disorder) are markedly smaller than those of non-ADHD people.[32] It has also been found that females have ten percent more fibers across the corpus callosum than men.[33]

These differences may not be genetic. I believe that the experiences necessary to develop full sensory-motor-emotional patterns have been more limited both for those labeled "learning disabled" and for men in our society. These people may have missed interactive relationships that include rich dialogue and emotions. My guess is that with more activation of both frontal lobes and acceptance of emotional experience and expression, this corpus callosum discrepancy would vanish.

CONNECTING THE HEMISPHERES

The differing functions of the two cerebral hemispheres has by now become such a familiar part of popular lore about the brain, that it's not uncommon to hear people described as left- or right-brained. In fact all of us do have a certain degree of hemispheric dominance. People may exhibit a preference for either analytic or global processing, particularly in times of stress as it becomes a more efficient pattern to just react, without the need to use both hemispheres.

But the more we access both hemispheres, the more intelligently we are able to function. Actually, it is necessary to use both hemispheres of the brain to be maximally proficient at anything.

Creativity, for example, is not exclusively a gestalt hemisphere function. It is a whole brain process that requires technique and detail from the logic hemisphere and image, flow and emotion from the gestalt hemisphere. Similarly, ease with language requires the words, verbalization and proper sentence structure from the left and the image, emotion and dialect from the right. This integration allows ease of reading and writing as well as comprehension and creative access.

Cross lateral movements, like a baby's crawling activate both hemispheres in a balanced way.[34] These activities work both sides of the body evenly and involve coordinated movements of both eyes, both ears, both hands and both feet as well as balanced core muscles. When both eyes, both ears, both hands and feet are being used equally, the corpus callosum orchestrating these processes between the two hemispheres becomes more fully developed. Because both hemispheres and all four lobes are activated, cognitive function is heightened and ease of learning increases.

When learners, and teachers, take advantage of this simple way of increasing the brain's efficiency, learning is bound to be more engaging and successful. I've been delighted to see math, for example, being taught in new ways that utilize both hemispheres of the brain. Times tables were deadly for me — endless hours of memorization. Teachers are now setting up cooperative learning groups in their classrooms that are responsible for coming up with a rap that those students then teach to the rest of the class. The numbers from the logic side and the rhythm and image from the gestalt side provide a winning combination for ease of learning.

WHAT CAN THE BRAIN DO — AND WHEN CAN IT DO IT?

In describing the functions and anatomy of the neocortex, I've mentioned several developmental turning points. These are very important landmarks for anyone who wants to know what we are capable of doing, and, equally important, when we become capable of doing it. Failure to recognize these landmarks, and thus to accommodate each individual's specific learning pace is a root cause of many problems in education today.

The first areas of the brain to mature are those with the most basic functions, such as processing the senses and movement. Areas involved in spatial orientation and language in the parietal lobes follow. Areas with more advanced functions, such as integrating information from the senses, reasoning and other "executive" functions in the prefrontal cortex mature last. The brain's center of reasoning and problem solving is among the last to mature with such "high-order" centers as the prefrontal cortex not fully developing until young adulthood, and more influenced by nurture than heredity. There are times of overproduction of grey matter in the cerebral cortex during the first eighteen months of life followed by a steady decline as unused circuitry is discarded. A second wave of overproduction of grey matter occurs just prior to puberty, followed by a second bout of "use-it-or-lose-it" pruning during the teen years.[35] The following chart gives a "ballpark" rather than exact developmental picture. We all naturally develop at our own pace in our perfect time.

AGE   DEVELOPMENT

Conception - 15 months   Reptilian Brain
Basic survival needs — touch, food, shelter, and safety
Sensory development starting with vestibular system, then hearing, tactile, smell, taste and finally seeing — rich sensory activation
Motor development moving from reflexes to core muscle activation, neck muscles, arms and legs leading to rolling over, sitting, crawling and walking — motor exploration

15 months - 4 ½ years   Limbic System / Relationship
Understanding of self/others, self/emotions, self/language
Emotional exploration; Language exploration/communication; Imagination; Gross motor proficiency; Memory development; Social development

4 ½ - 7 years   Gestalt Hemisphere Elaboration
Whole picture processing/cognition,
Image/movement/rhythm/emotion/intuition
Outer speech/integrative thought

Boys have a slower growth period during the following stages than girls, usually around 2 years difference, and need a longer period of time with gestalt hemisphere elaboration especially through movement and emotional development.[36, 37, 38, 39, 40]

7 - 9 years   Logic Hemisphere Elaboration
Detail and linear processing/cognition
Refinement of elements of language
Reading and writing skills development
Technique development — music, art, sports, dance, manual training
Linear math processing

8 years   Frontal Lobe Elaboration
Fine motor development — skills refinement
Inner speech — control of social behavior
Fine motor eye teaming for tracking and foveal focus (2-dimensional focus)

9 - 12 years   Increased Corpus Callosum Elaboration and Myelination
Whole brain processing

12 - 16 years   Hormonal Emphasis

Learning about body, self, others, community, and meaningful living through social consciousness

16 - 21 years   **Refining Cognitive Skills**
Whole mind/body processing, social interaction, future planning and play with new ideas and possibilities

21 +   **Elaboration and Refinement of the Frontal Lobes**
Global / systems thinking
High level formal reasoning
Refinement of emotions — altruism, love, compassion
Insight
Refinement of fine motor skills

*Figure 5.6: Landmarks of Cerebral Neocortex Development
(Ages Are Approximate)*

We must get away from the notion that we simply experience the world until we go to school at the age of five and then we learn. Learning is a progressive, constantly changing process that serves to enrich and expand our understanding throughout life. The neocortex is always growing and modifying neural networks linked to the brain stem and limbic system, developing the neural connections that enable it to become the integrator of knowledge.

Even at the age of about twenty-one, there is a growth spurt of nerve net development in the frontal lobes. It's the time when people realize their parents are smarter than they thought, as emotional refinement allows for insight leading to altruism and love. There is also another spurt of growth at approximately age thirty with further refinement of muscle movement, especially of the hands and face. Increased fine motor coordination leads to greater achievements for musicians like pianists and violinists who can move their fingers with more agility. We also see it in vocalists who are now able to command a greater range with their vocal cords (muscles). And we see it dramatically in character actors who can now control their facial muscles with such subtlety that they express any emotion with just their faces.[41]

READING AND WRITING — WHAT'S APPROPRIATE?

In the usual course of development, children are accessing gestalt function at the time they traditionally begin attending school, at about five years of age. The gestalt hemisphere begins development and enlargement between the ages of four and seven, while the logic hemisphere doesn't enlarge until ages seven to nine.[42] The most natural way, then, for children to learn when first in school at age five and six is through use of all the senses, image, emotion, rhythm, verbalization and movement.

Under normal circumstances children at the age when they first enter kindergarten already have wonderful imaginations and a very large vocabulary. The British curriculum of education, from which ours is derived, however, begins alphabet and number recognition immediately, with reading following in quick order. This might not be a problem if we involved image, emotion, and movement, and built on the student's imagination and vocabulary. Strangely, we do just the opposite. We teach children to "sit still," learn letters and numbers in a linear fashion (that includes printing, a very linear, logic hemisphere process), and read books with simplistic vocabulary, no emotion and few images.

By age four or five children naturally love to "write" stories — very elaborate stories. They usually write in a pretend cursive style, because they are mimicking grown-up writing, and because the natural rhythm and flow of it is easy for them. This process is anchoring learning in a holistic way and could be an excellent point of departure for new learning.

HOW THE DANES MAKE IT EASY FOR THEIR CHILDREN TO LEARN TO READ

The Danish school system, respecting natural brain developmental patterns, does not start children in school until six or seven years of age. They teach writing and reading from a holistic, gestalt processing format and then move to the details later, around age eight, when the logic hemisphere is ready to handle it. Reading is not taught until age eight — and Denmark boasts one hundred percent literacy. [43, 44]

Children in Denmark are given the freedom and encouragement to write stories. Though the teacher cannot decode them, the child can, so the children read their stories. The stories are rich in elaborate, image-based vocabulary. As the child reads his or her story, the teacher notices which images are emotionally important to the writer. The teacher makes use of this information, for example by saying: "It sounds like 'dinosaur' is one of your favorite words. Would you like to see how I write that?" The children almost always want to know how adults write words. So after the teacher writes out the word "dinosaur" in cursive, the next story the child writes will have the usual undecipherable scrawl with the word "dinosaur" interspersed. The child has learned the whole word without effort. Because the child then reads his story to his friends, they see the symbol for "dinosaur" and it shows up in their writing also — and the process of reading is underway.

For reading, the teacher asks for a favorite song, that she writes in cursive and then has the children follow the words as they sing. This establishes an emotional-relational connection, so important to the memory process, since memory is closely linked to emotion in the relational limbic system. There is a lot of movement and rhythm play in each learning process.

I can vouch for the effectiveness of this approach by recalling my own experience of learning the alphabet. It took singing the alphabet song to help me finally learn my ABCs. I still find myself singing it when I have to file papers in alphabetical order.

In contrast to the Danish system, I remember my first reading book having a lot of words like "the" "and," "yes," "can." Just recently a child brought me a book she was working on in kindergarten. The name of the book was: *Yes I Can*. Now, what kind of image do words like these elicit? To learn something new it is imperative that we tie it into something familiar and — at this young age — something with a concrete image. Teachers give students three letter words because they appear simple, but in reality they are far more difficult than "dinosaur" because they hold no internal image or emotion.

BLOCK LETTERS AND WRITING BLOCKS

Another unnatural challenge has to do with learning to print block letters as the first step in writing. Printing is a highly linear process that takes us away from the more continuous rhythmic flow of language, both as it is experienced in the mind and as it is expressed through the hand — as in cursive script. In many European schools they never teach printing, and find children have no difficulty going from writing in cursive to reading block printed text, usually at the age of eight. I am surprised there hasn't been more research done on the comparative effects of the ways writing is introduced in different school systems worldwide. Educators in Germany have told me they are finding that students are now having more difficulties with language since they have switched over to teaching block printing as the first step to language.

Part of the problem is the lack of hand development, and asking children to perform the complex process of printing, way too early. In order to print the child must first crawl for a good long time with hands forward, to develop the bones in both the hand and to gain upper arm strength. As the child matures, they need to further strengthen the upper arm and hand by pulling themselves up on furniture, ladders, rocks and trees. They must also lift and manipulate objects of different weights and textures like blocks, sticks, pots and pans, etc. If you look at an X-ray of hand development, you will notice that the very intricate bones of the area near the wrist — the carpals, are not fully developed until about age twenty. The more developed these bones, the easier to hold a pen or pencil to print. If the child has had a lot of sensory-motor activation of the hand, printing can more easily be taught at about ages eight to ten.

If you hold the carpal area of your hand while doing cursive writing and printing, you will notice how much more bone movement is required for printing. The development of the hand is intimately linked to brain development — the rich supply of nerve receptors that develop are not only essential for grasping, they are important for conscious perception.[45, 46]

In the American school system we follow the British lead and teach children to print at age five. At this early age, children have to work very hard at printing since it defies the natural development of the hand as well as brain functions. I believe this premature introduction is a major causative agent in the writing blocks many students and adults experience. After age eight, when the hand is developed enough to accommodate the discrete and linear operations necessary for printing, we then teach them cursive. It is a crazy game that only serves to maintain high stress levels in the child and leads to "learned helplessness." This learned helplessness occurs when the person decides that whatever they do will be wrong, so they make only a marginal effort, or just give up.[47]

This is not the only example of learned helplessness resulting from a pedagogical strategy that sacrifices long term gains for short term, illusory results. The excessive use of lower level skills tests, usually of rote memory, and usually timed — as often as two or three times a week right up through college is a graphic example. Rote memory is a straight line process requiring none of the depth of understanding that comes from whole brain activation. In short, rote memory does not require thinking. These tests induce learned helplessness by promoting situations and habits where students only study for the tests, and students with test anxiety end up in a state of perpetual stress.[48]

Under these circumstances there is no time or space to develop deep understanding of concepts, test out new ideas through verbal and written action, or develop deductive reasoning skills. The long-term educational effects are as predictable as they are unfortunate. The National Science Foundation analyzed not only the six most widely used national stadardized tests, but also the tests designed to accompany the four most commonly used science and math textbooks in fourth and eighth grade and high-school classes.

These tests were found to focus on lower-level skills (primarily rote memorization and application of routine formulas), instead of problem solving and reasoning which curriculum experts say should receive the greater emphasis. The study also noted that since states judge schools and determine teacher assignments based on students' test scores, these tests inadvertently set the agendas of many teachers.[49]

Research done by Herman Epstein shows that formal reasoning has not been a natural outcome of our current educational process. He discovered that at age eleven, only five percent of the population is at a formal reasoning level. Only one quarter have reached this level by age fourteen, and in adults he found only half are fully functional formal thinkers.[50]

FROM KNOWLEDGE TO MEANING

The final goal of any learning experience should be the creation of meaning. Real knowledge occurs as we take in our rich sensory environment and piece it together in our own unique way to give us a picture of our world. This becomes our reality. Each new experience refers to this picture; each new experience reorders and expands it.

Figure 5.7: Thinking and Memory Orchestrated by Neural Connections from Key Movement Centers of the Brain

From this reality, we are able to make decisions and take actions that explore, test and anchor our beliefs and our understanding. The process by which we integrate our experience into a growing understanding of the world should be the prime concern of the educational system. Demonstrating that understanding, through work assignments that require thinking, should be an indispensable part of any learning experience.

Skills manifest as conscious physical responses demonstrating knowledge acquisition. Thinking itself is actually a skill dependent upon the whole, integrated body/mind system. The whole system must be active in order to take in information, select what is important about that information, integrate it with existing patterns and finally, to anchor it with movement. Thinking and learning are anchored by movement.[51, 52] Actions such as doodling, eye movements, speaking aloud to oneself or to others, writing things down, are familiar movements that occur during thinking. Without movement of some kind, you don't get conscious thought. The final outcome of this process is meaning.

USE YOUR HEAD — AND YOUR BODY

Real learning — the kind of learning that establishes meaningful connections for the learner — starts with movement in response to a stimulus, then creates a context or experience to understand the sensory input. Finally, learning is not complete until there is some output, some physical, personal expression of thought. Much of learning involves the establishment of skills that enable us to express our knowledge. Speaking, writing, computing, drawing, playing music, singing, moving gracefully in dance and sports: the development of our knowledge goes hand in hand with the development of the skills that support and express that knowledge.

As we build these skills we use the muscles of our bodies, establishing neuromuscular routes as well as their ties to cognitive routes. Learning is not all in your head. The active, muscular expression of learning is an important ingredient of that learning. This point may seem obvious when you think about it, but not many people are used to thinking about muscles in this way. We tend to relegate muscles to the domain of the body, not the mind. But it is through expression that we advance and solidify our understanding. This can be seen in the research showing that students who take drama, or music where a lot of expression is encouraged, do far better on standardized tests than students without experience of these arts.[53, 54]

Usually this expression takes the form of speech (or sign language in the case of deaf people) or writing, which of course use a great deal of very highly coordinated muscular actions. Language is an indispensable and distinctly human capacity that serves to integrate knowledge and facilitate thought. Humans have other means of expression and integration as well: pictorial, symbolic, musical, gestural, to name a few. And of course there are mediums that blend all or several skills into a unified expression of meaning. Drama, for instance, integrates words, visual elements, bodily demonstration and very often music. Artistic expressions — in drama, music, dance, visual art, literature — represent highly skilled use and integration of body, thought and emotion. Artistic expression is immensely valuable to overall personal development and cognitive understanding.

The same could be said for sports. Athletic activities integrate many different kinds of knowledge with skilled muscular coordination — knowledge about space and time and human dynamics like teamwork, motivation, goal seeking. Educators should not lose sight of their value. Arts and athletics are not frills. They constitute powerful ways of thinking and skilled ways of communicating with the world. They deserve a greater, not lesser portion of school time and budgets.

I am happy to see that with the widespread interest in Howard Gardner's Theory of Multiple Intelligences, schools are including more varied skills and activities in the classroom. According to Gardner's theory, we have seven kinds of intelligence: logical/mathematical, linguistic, visual/spatial, bodily kinesthetic, musical, interpersonal, and intrapersonal.[55] Schools have always emphasized the linguistic and the logical/mathematical intelligences, but often they have neglected the other important ways that we know and learn. Inclusion of the other intelligences in the school curriculum is a positive step toward creation of higher level skills and greater integration of knowledge.

HOW LANGUAGE INTEGRATES BODY, MIND, AND EMOTIONS

Language ... is the source of thought. When the child masters language he gains the potentiality to organize anew his perception, his memory; he masters more complex forms of reflection of objects in the external world; he gains the capacity to draw conclusions from his observations, to make deductions, the potentiality of thinking.

— Alexander Luria[56]

Language is perhaps the most spectacular example of integrative processing that engages body, mind and emotion. Through language we powerfully orchestrate and develop our capacity to think. As with other human capacities, understanding how language develops can also help us to understand both how it can be undermined and how it can be encouraged to flourish.

The sensory and motor networks that enable language begin to form very early in life. The natural progression of language occurs as the child moves from a sense of vibration and rhythm in utero to tone and hearing as a toddler. The intricate combination of all these elements leads to speech. The child mimics the intonation and cadence of her models and delights us with the ability to intone first and then to speak. As the child plays with sounds, she develops nerve nets and myelinates nerve fibers to the muscles of the voice box (larynx). She is able to synchronize the tonal vibrations she is hearing with the sounds she makes by learning to contract or relax the muscles of the larynx. Higher tones are produced by more contracted vocal fold muscles, while the long wavelength lower tones depend on lengthened or relaxed muscles. Playing with sounds, even crying, is essential for this motor development.

Movement, through the motor cortex, is very much a part of verbal expression. In Figure 3.4 you will note that almost one quarter of the motor cortex deals directly with vocalization. The motor cortex stimulates muscular movements of the larynx, tongue, mouth, jaw, facial muscles and eyes that form and give expression to the words. Muscular memory of how to form the words appears to be housed in the basal ganglion of the limbic system. Within the basal ganglion is a specialized area called the substantia nigra, which connects the basal ganglion with the frontal lobe — significantly, with those areas that control vocalization and thought. The basal ganglion, especially the substantia nigra, is actively involved in movement, thought and speech. It orchestrates gross motor movements from the cerebellum and fine motor movements from the motor cortex of the frontal lobe to accommodate movement based on thought, including speech.

The neural connections between the motor cortex and the formal reasoning area of the frontal lobe underscore the importance of movement to thought processing. Most people need to discuss, write or draw a picture of new ideas in order to anchor them in the body with movement for memory and clarity of thought.

Language acquisition entails several essential steps. The ability to discriminate rhythm and tone along with the newly found ability to form words, allows the child a greater sensitivity to dialect or accent. This heightened awareness makes learning a second language easier for children than adults. In order to learn to speak accurately, we must be able to hear the full tone, including the higher harmonics that occur in normal speech. This only occurs when children are directly communicated with, because TV, computers, tapes and CD's are digitized (compressed) so that part of the harmonics and over-tones are lost — often including the consonants that help to define language. If the child doesn't hear the analog of the sound (another real human voice), he can't speak it or later symbolize it to read.[57]

When these capabilities are impaired, language acquisition suffers. Some observers believe this is actually a widespread problem in our society. According to Jane Healy, "Children are not speaking properly because they're not hearing words pronounced slowly. TV is too fast."[58] Children with recurring ear infections in the first years of life may miss these complex tones, and therefore be more at risk for later specific hearing and speech difficulties.[59]

Children between ages fifteen months and four years gain a functional sense of objects and people from the language modeling of their caregivers. Words become playthings to label the world with. The child and caregivers engage in a game of vocabulary building that puts a name to each object. If we go beyond just the name to the object's function, the child can broaden his understanding even more. An example would be: "I can put this on to keep warm," rather than "This is a shirt." Understanding the function of an object, rather than just its name, creates a far broader context of the child's relationship with the object. This relational approach accommodates optimal development of the limbic brain that searches out relationships. Since speech and language help us to define our world and our thinking, more open-ended speech may strongly facilitate greater creative thought processing.[60]

Parents should be aware that prior to age four, even though language is progressing, the child is taking most of its behavioral cues from what it sees, not from spoken commands. The parent may have told the child not to do something, but the physical stimulation is so compelling that the sensory fascination overrides the verbal command. The child may even be able to tell the parent what it was told not to do, but without full comprehension of the meaning. My daughter's fascination with the cat, for example, overrode my constant warnings about the cat's justifiable retaliation. Many warnings and scratches later, she finally understood the connection.

Broca's area of the left neocortex of the brain enlarges after age four, insuring the ability to produce clear speech. Wernicke's area also enlarges in the left neocortex, assisting language comprehension that is connected to higher reasoning. This development helps children to override the motor enticement to perform actions even when told not to. At approximately four years of age parent/child talks begin to become meaningful and effective.

OUTER, STREAM OF CONSCIOUSNESS SPEECH

Once speech is in place, the child will process thought through outer speech until about age seven. I distinctly remember ages four, five, and six as being very verbal times for my daughter. I got to a point where I would cringe every time I heard "Mommy, what ...?" or "Mommy, how ...?" or "Mommy, why ...?" and I found myself looking for a moment of quiet so I could think. The child may talk continuously as she discusses her world and all the new relational insights she is gaining.

Stream of consciousness speech is the problem-solving tool of the four to six year old, and "Why?" becomes the generator of that process. This stream of consciousness speech, in varying degrees, is essential to language and thought development. Inner speech development doesn't normally occur until around age seven, so children literally think out loud. I'm sure that children of this age wonder if adults ever think because we are so quiet.

So insistent is the need for outer speech, to hear one's own voice and thoughts, that silent reading is ineffective before the age of seven. A whole classroom of children can be focused on reading aloud to themselves or sharing their stories with another person without bothering other classmates.[61]

WHY CHILDREN NEED TO SPEAK

The translation of thought into speech or into the written word is a very complex task. It involves sensory areas, primary auditory, auditory association, primary visual, visual association, motor speech and gnostic areas of the neocortex.[62] Movement becomes a vital part of language as integrated thought patterns are transmitted to the vocalization areas of the motor cortex and basal ganglion of the limbic system to bring thought into the formation of words, first in speech and later in writing.[63] The neocortex is the novelty brain that loves challenges, and language can become a great adventure as it unfolds from age four on.

In Figure 3.4 mapping the functions related to the sensory and motor cortices of the parietal and frontal lobes, you will note the large area of the brain dedicated to sensations and motor function of speech and vocalization. There are more nerve endings going across the temporal-mandibular joint (TMJ) — from sensory neurons or to motor neurons activating muscles of the face — than at any other place in the body. These muscles give us facial expressions that amplify our words and the meaning behind them. They give our eyes expression and they move the tongue, mouth and jaw for enunciation.[64] The concentration in this area of muscles and nerves related to verbalization and expression suggest that it is a prime site for exercises that can enhance communication.[65]

Hand action is also very important to speech. Compare Figure 3.4 with Figure 5.3 for speaking. You will notice that the hand area is actually the primary area for speaking, with the verbalization area being secondary. Talking (or signing in the case of deaf children) while using hand gestures is essential to language development and to thinking. Hand gesturing while speaking appears to tap into different parts of the brain dealing with visual and spatial subject matter, making demands on other memory stores that allows the speaker to free up cognitive resources and remember more.[66] In most African cultures, children are encouraged to tell stories and repeat myths of the clan as well as to communicate their ideas in the family circle. In our culture, particularly with the advent of TV, computers and video games, children have even less opportunity to interact verbally in a meaningful way.

The Paul Rankin study done in 1928 set daily communication times as 45% listening, 30% speaking, 16% reading and 9% writing.[67] In 1975 Elyse K. Werner did a similar study showing that listening had increased to 54.93%, speaking decreased to 23.19%, reading to 13.27% and writing to 8.61%.[68] In the 1993 American's Use of Time Project, TV took up 38% of our free time while reading a book, newspaper, or magazine accounted for less than 10% or fewer than three hours per week.[69] While the percentage of speaking time was not addressed in this study, my guess is that it accounted for no more than 10% and the figures today would be even lower for interactive communication time.

We have become a listening society where conversation is becoming a lost art. The importance of talking to a child in full sentences is paramount. This activity allows the child to hear and then mimic full ideas. Books also lay out ideas in complete sentences, thus assisting full thought development. Monosyllabic, incomplete speech patterns, as exhibited in the sitcoms on TV, model and foster incomplete speech patterns even in adults. We begin to think in incomplete sentences, which carries over to incomplete idea development. We can hear it in the typical teenage communication of "You know?" "It's like ... you know?" etc. This incomplete language development shows up graphically in students' inability to think and write. "The culprit," Jane Healy maintains, "is diminished and degraded exposure to the forms of good meaningful language that enable us to converse with others, with the written word, and with our own minds."[70]

Parents, teachers, and caregivers who wish to ensure the proper development of all their children's communication skills, need to engage them in full, conscious dialogue. This assists them in developing and trusting their ability to communicate valuable information, creative thoughts and intimate feelings. One of the best gifts a person can give to another person is conscious listening and communication. It becomes reciprocal as both parties learn.

When new ideas are presented, if students are able to verbalize and "flesh out" the ideas with other students, or work together on group projects, the thought becomes anchored in understanding and memory. And yet, how much opportunity do students have to develop and express full ideas in the classroom?

Unfortunately, activities that permit children to talk through their ideas are often seen by teachers and administrators to be merely disorderly. However, pedagogical exercises that require quiet, orderly classrooms may actually be inefficient and inappropriate ways of eliciting thinking and understanding. Typical classroom activities that are supposed to promote quiet thinking such as silent reading, filling out worksheets, drills on lower level skills and the like, often seem designed more for the purposes of crowd control than education. And sometimes this is the message the children get. As one child recently told me, the activity that teachers in her school call "SSR," (for sustained, silent reading) is universally interpreted by the students to mean "sit down, shut up, and read!"

INNER SPEECH

The frontal lobe is the final lobe to develop, elaborating greatly at about age eight. Broca's area of the frontal lobe is the area for development of inner speech. Inner speech naturally occurs and allows a person to process information internally at a much faster rate than verbalization would allow.

As a young child says a word, the movement of that word becomes memory in the basal ganglion and a language pattern is developed. Language elaborates as more and more such patterns are developed. These language patterns correspond to inner images and gestures related to specific sounds. So that when a child hears the word (sound) "NO," it gets an inner image that allows it to stop a certain action. The child starts to use these sounds in outer speech to control its own movements and behavior.

When this language patterning has strengthened, the child can begin to connect the image with a non-verbal sound inside and use inner speech for the control of movement and behavior. These tools are closely linked and necessary to develop reasoning as well as self-management skills.[71]

Inner speech develops in the same area of the brain that controls skillful movements of the hand. As we evolved into problem solving, tool using animals, the frontal lobe became the center for fine motor coordination, pattern recognition, simultaneous processing of information, high level planning and global thought.[72]

Inner speech also controls social behavior by allowing a person to think of all the consequences of an action before acting. Historically, as people began to band together, increasing complexity and specialization of culture led to self-awareness and monitoring of one's behavior with respect to social norms. We police our minds for antisocial or disruptive impulses through the self-talk we do with inner speech.[73]

In Chapter 4 we discussed the important contribution that emotions make to reasoning and thinking. The frontal lobe is able to synthesize thought with emotion through the thalamocingulate ganglion of the limbic system to give us compassion, reverence for life, unconditional love and all-important play. The link-up of the frontal lobe with the limbic system and social behavior influence the development of altruism and empathy. Because of its connections with the medial dorsal nucleus of the limbic system (that connects to the stomach), the pre-fontal cortex receives a strong impulse from the great visceral nerve coming from the stomach area.[74] This feeling in the gut —"Gut Feeling"— is presumably necessary for an individual's identification with the feelings of others and for the "insight" to feel concern for the future of others as well as the self.

It is the full activation and balance of all parts of our body/mind system that allow us to become effective, productive thinkers. With the full development of the neocortex and its integration with the rest of the brain's structures, we are able to creatively play with ideas, use fine motor skills to present them to others, and reach out as human beings to the world at large.

6

〜

Movement

"We have a brain because we have a motor system that allows us to move away from danger and towards opportunity. Educational systems that reduce most student movement to one appendage writing sequences of letters and digits on a playing field the size of a sheet of paper don't understand the significance of motor development."

— *Robert Sylvester*[1]

The more closely we consider the elaborate interplay of brain and body, the more clearly one compelling theme emerges: movement is essential to learning and to the manifestation of life itself. Even in seeming stillness, our whole body teems with movement: the digestion of food; the expansion and contraction of our lungs and muscles; the beat of our hearts; nerve impulses; and blood moving rapidly throughout our body.[2] Movement awakens and activates many of our mental capacities. Movement integrates and anchors new information and experience into our neural networks. And movement is vital to all the actions by which we embody and express our learning, our understanding and ourselves. So in this chapter, I will focus on movement, particularly on the part it plays in learning. Is what we now know about this subject reflected in the ways we raise our children and the ways they are taught in school? What happens when it isn't?

Movement within the womb gives us our first sense of the world and the beginning knowledge and experience of the laws of gravity. The rhythmic movements of our mother's walking, before and after birth, her rocking, breathing, heart rhythms, all set up coherent patterns that assist us to understand the patterns within math, language and natural science. We build on movement to shape our vision, to explore the shape and form of our environment, and to interact with the people and forces around us.

Every movement is a sensory-motor event, linked to the intimate understanding of our physical world, the world from which all new learning derives. Movement of our head aligns our sensory organs (eyes, ears, nose and tongue) to environmental input. Subtle movements of the eyes enable us to see at a distance, experience three dimensions, sense our periphery and focus on small letters on a page. Refined movements of our hands allow us to touch, play with and manipulate our world in infinitely complex ways and communicate our emotional nature and inner self. Movement aligns us to pick up smells that will key our memory to events, or sounds that will form internal images for protection and/or understanding. Movement allows us to experience the wind upon our face, just for the learning of it.

Imprinted on the muscular/memory structure of our bodies is not only the knowing of how to sit, stand, walk and run, but where we are in space and how to move with grace and reason — and even to create something beautiful and exquisite in the process. Movement gives our faces the ability to express joy, sadness, anger and love in our very human quest to be understood.

Every number and letter has movement to it. It has a shape felt and imprinted on the musculature so it can be repeated and elaborated through the movement of writing. Through years of learning (movement integrated with sensory input) we are able to play with, reassociate and create new understanding. Through movement we can put thoughts and emotions into words and actions and enrich the world with our creative ideas.

Every time we move in an organized, graceful manner, full brain activation and integration occurs, and the door to learning opens naturally. Howard Gardner, Jean Ayres, Rudolf Steiner, Maria Montessori, Moshe Feldenkreis, Glenn Dolman, Neil Kephardt and many other outstanding innovators in the field of learning espouse the importance of movement to the learning process.

KINESTHETIC INTELLIGENCE

Part of my purpose in this chapter is also to question a societal prejudice that tends to downgrade physical achievement and minimize its importance in "serious" endeavors like work and school.

Howard Gardner, in his delineation of the Bodily Kinesthetic Intelligence[3] points out that rather than considering motor activity as subservient to "pure" thought, we might follow neuroscientist Roger Sperry in reversing our perspective and consider thinking as an instrument directed to the end of executing actions. "Rather than motor activity as a subsidiary form designed to satisfy the demands of the higher centers, one should instead conceptualize cerebration as a means of bringing 'into motor behavior additional refinement, increased direction toward distant, future goals and greater overall adaptiveness and survival value.'"[4]

Learning involves the building of skills, and skills of every manner are built through the movement of muscles — not just the physical skills of athletes, musicians, dancers and artisans, but also the intellectual skills used in classrooms and workplaces. Storytellers entertain, teachers teach, scientists research, doctors and nurses practice and politicians lead through the complex muscular expressions of language, speech and gesture.

MOVEMENT ANCHORS THOUGHT

To "pin down" a thought, there must be movement. A person may sit quietly to think, but to remember a thought an action must be used to anchor it. We must materialize it with words. When I write, I'm making connections with thought by moving my hand. I may never need to read what I wrote, but the movement is necessary to gain the thought — build the nerve networks. "Our hands are central to our psychology as they continually switch between executive, exploratory and expressive activity."[5]

Most people find that talking anchors their thinking. Talking is very much a sensory-motor skill, requiring fine motor coordination of millions of facial, tongue, vocal fold and eye muscles, as well as all the proprioceptors in the face and hands. Talking allows us to organize and elaborate our thoughts. When we talk about what we've learned, the physical movements internalize and solidify it in nerve networks. That is why, after presenting new material to a class, I ask them to grab someone and share verbally how the information relates to them personally.

Acetylcholine, a neurotransmitter, is released across synapses of activated neurons to stimulate muscle function during talking. Increased and consistent release of acetylcholine at these nerve endings stimulates and attracts dendritic growth in the area, thus increasing nerve networks. In people with Alzheimer's disease, acetylcholine levels are low. However, people who dance frequently or play a musical instrument dramatically decrease their chance of getting Alzheimer's or dementia[6] — another strong affirmation that movement assists brain growth and health for a lifetime.

Many of us have a distinct tendency to think better and more freely while engaged in a repetitive, low concentration physical task. I've heard people say they think best when they are swimming laps in a pool, taking a walk, or while shaving. An older woman student in one of my classes spent a whole semester knitting through my lectures, never so much as lifting a pencil to take a note, and finished the course with an A as well as nine sweaters. I myself like to chew, especially crunchy things like carrots, when I'm deep in thought. I realize that movement is actually helping my thinking.

If we consider that consciousness is actually experience in the present moment, then movement and being conscious to learning are synonymous. Almost daily, new research is illuminating the strong neural links between areas in the brain involved with movement and those involved with cognitive activity. In the 1990's, research revealed that the frontal lobe areas, important in coordinating thought, are directly connected to the motor control areas of the brain as seen in Figure 5.7.[7]

The cerebellum, long thought to only control gross motor movement, has more neurons than any other part of the brain, with an average 250 – 300,000 synaptic connections per nerve cell. The cerebellum appears to be the main sensory system in that it examines, evaluates, and integrates sensory input from the vestibular system, and relates it to motor function by relaying information sequentially forward to the rest of the brain via the hippocampus, substantia niger, basal ganglion in the limbic system, and the motor cortex of the frontal lobe. The cerebellum possesses the fastest conducting pathways between itself and the neo-cortex, adding 5 – 10% to the speed with which the cortex can put together information and reason. Thus moving while learning increases the learning!

The cerebellum is responsible for guiding all learning of movement including how we move, the timing and dynamics of movement for coordination, and how the muscles adjust for maximal benefit during resting and active periods. The cerebellum even adjusts our constant head movements, to keep our visual field fixed on the retina of the eye as we move. It's connection to the hippocampus provides memory retention for motor learning, like learning to roll over, sit-up, crawl, walk, run, jump, skip, ride a bike or a complex dance sequence. [8, 9, 10]

So important for higher cognitive function, the cerebellum and basal ganglia via the thalamus, activate the part of the prefrontal cortex that has to do with spatial working memory and reasoning. This gives us the knowledge of how far to step when walking up stairs, or how far to lean when riding a bike around a corner, or how to set up complex architectural designs. Computer imaging shows the cerebellum is the most active part of the brain during learning, while in non-learning processes, such as watching TV, it is almost inactive. [11, 12]

The cerebellum's link with the substantia niger that produces dopamine is responsible for linking sensory-motor experiences with taking coordinated actions. Dopamine is our motivational chemical that sensitizes us to look for patterns, and sparks us to physically explore and learn from our environment and each other.[13]

HOW MOVEMENT LEADS TO LEARNING

To understand the basis of this movement-thought link, we must return to our earliest brain development. The baby undergoes a miraculous feat of strength and coordination as it goes from inert lying to walking in its first year. That feat is matched only by the massive elaboration of nerve networks established through the practice of each new movement. Early movements are reflexive (reflexes) and change from those vital for survival like the Moro Reflex, which develops in utero at 9 weeks, to more elaborate reflexes that allow the newborn and infant to grasp (the palmer reflex), lift its head (the tonic neck reflex) and eventually roll-over, sit-up, crawl and stand. Reflexes prepare us for voluntary movement and assist the development of all the senses. They don't disappear, but integrate with the higher nerve centers in the vestibular, limbic, and sensory-motor systems of the cerebrum. In children with autism, aggression, and phobias, the reflexes may not have integrated with the higher functions, and thus the child is reactive, reflexive, hyper-vigilant and often labeled ADHD. [14, 15]

As a baby's repertoire of movements grows, each development places the sensory apparatus, especially the ears, mouth, hands, nose and eyes in an increasingly advantageous place for environmental input. The vestibular system is tied to the core muscles of the abdomen and back and it is these muscles that first work to lift the head — a very liberating accomplishment. As the neck muscles strengthen, the child is able to lift the head to hear the world with two ears and start to see it with two eyes. Being held upright with its belly against the caregiver's back or front, as well as lying on its belly on the ground, allows the baby to actively work and strengthen its neck muscles.

Incidentally, this leads me to question the wisdom of excessive use of the popular baby carrying seats that double as car seats. These seats keep the baby at a forty-five degree angle that inhibits active muscular movements either of the neck or core muscles. The same is true of jumpers and carriers where the baby is facing out, away from the parent. Even though the baby's eyes are forward, because movement is inhibited the baby is not as actively developing vision.

The baby explores feet and hands with its mouth bringing the appendage muscles into play. The ears assist baby's first attempts to roll over as it follows a sound with its ears and uses the core muscles to move the whole body. The core muscles then come into play as the baby strengthens the shoulder girdle area, by lifting the shoulders as well as the head, in response to sensory stimuli.

As the nerve nets to the core muscles elaborate and myelinate from use, the baby is able to hold itself up to sit against gravity and to creep. With practice, first with one end of the body and then the other, the baby goes from scooching to finally being able to crawl. Again, this is highly dependent on core muscle activation so the shoulders and pelvis work together.[16]

We have known for years that children who miss the vitally important crawling stage may exhibit learning difficulties later on. Crawling, a cross-lateral movement, activates development of the corpus callosum (the nerve pathways between the two hemispheres of the cerebrum). This gets both sides of the body working together, including the arms, legs, eyes (binocular vision) and the ears (binaural hearing). With equal stimulation, the senses more fully access the environment and both sides of the body can move in a more inte-grated way for more efficient action.

A special education teacher told me of her concern as her son went from creeping to walking. She had read all the literature on the importance of crawling to eye teaming development for reading, and definitely didn't want him to miss this stage. So she would crawl over him, not letting him stand up for a good two months. I've occasionally wondered if she didn't replace dyslexia with claustrophobia!

When my daughter came along, I still hadn't read the literature on the importance of crawling. At seven months old she was given a nifty bright green walker with a round bumper bottom that allowed her to run all over the house and afforded my husband and me a great deal of entertainment. Unfor-tunately, our fun preempted her crawling for longer than a few weeks. When she began having difficulties learning to read in first grade, which demands cross-lateral hand eye coordination, we felt it might have been linked to her lack of crawling. I suggest parents read: Caution, Save Your Baby, Throw Out Your Equipment, by Laura Sobell, which explains why we need to get rid of the jumpers, walkers, car-seats when not in the car, etc. in order to allow our children to grow their brains.[17]

Ultimately, with all this motor development, the child stands against gravity and learns to balance enough to walk, and very shortly run. It is a mammoth undertaking. The beautifully coordinated and graceful children of rural Africa as they run for long distances or balance nimbly on a rock ledge, provide a magnificent glimpse of the inherent intelligence and beauty of movement.

MOVE MORE, LEARN MORE

Exercise is really for the brain, not the body. It affects mood, vitality, alertness and feelings of well-being.[18]
— *John J. Ratey, MD, Harvard Medical School*

It is essential to the learning process to allow children to explore every aspect of movement and balance in their environment, whether walking on a curb, climbing a tree, or jumping on the furniture. A Navajo teacher and mother told me that when she was a child, she and the other children would explore the mesa from early morning until after sunset. Neither she nor any of the other children were ever seriously hurt in this adventure, and she felt it was essential to her total learning process. Yet with current perceptions that the world is a dangerous place for children, she has never allowed her children to go up on the mesa. Without the mesa to explore, the children had made TV their favorite pastime. She admitted her children had movement and balance difficulties. She thought these might also relate to the learning difficulties, especially reading and writing, that they were experiencing in school.

Research shows that muscular activities, particularly coordinated, balanced movements, appear to stimulate the production of neurotrophins, such as dopamine, natural substances that stimulate the growth of existing nerve cells and increase the number of new nerve cells, and neural connections in the brain.[19] As we learn and master movements and skills, our brains require less energy and function more efficiently.

The California Department of Education completed an interesting study that matched scores from the spring 2001 SAT-9, with results of the state-mandated physical fitness test, known as the Fitnessgram, given in 2001 to students in grades five (353,000 students), seven (322,000 students), and nine (279,000 students). Key findings of the study showed much higher academic achievement was associated with higher levels of fitness at each of the three grades.[20] Executive functions of thought associated with frontal lobe and hippocampal regions of the brain are sustained and enhanced in people with higher levels of fitness.[21]

In the U.S., boys earn 70 percent of the D's and F's that teachers dole out and they make up two-thirds of the students labeled "learning disabled" and eighty percent of attention deficit disorder diagnoses. They also account for eighty percent of high school dropouts and are less likely to go to college now than ever before.[22] We have discovered that boys need more movement time than girls for brain growth and development. The stress that comes from lack of movement in boys early on and during the learning process has inhibited important pattern development necessary for inner speech, formal reasoning and the ability to succeed in our current school curriculum.[23]

In a study of more than 500 Canadian children, students who spent an extra hour each day in gym class performed notably better on exams than less active children. Similarly, men and women in their fifties and sixties, put on a four month aerobic training program of regular brisk walking, increased their performance on mental tests by ten percent. In another study of 13,000 adults and children labeled with dyslexia in Australia, South Africa and America, a twice daily for ten minutes program of standing on a cushion and throwing a beanbag from one hand to the other, or balancing on a "wobble board", freed all participants of dyslexic symptoms within six months.[24] And in a close look at thirteen other studies on the exercise/brainpower link, exercise was found to stimulate the growth of developing brains and prevent the deterioration of older brains.[25]

There are many teachers that are learning the importance of movement in the learning process. One brilliant teacher from New York City, gives her inner city high school students a "rhythm break" when she senses their lack of attentiveness. She points to one student who stands up and begins tapping or clapping out a rhythm and moving in a coordinated, cross-lateral way. Everyone in the class then attempts to match that rhythm and movement and even adds new rhythms to the set for about 2 minutes. Then she signals, they all sit down and are attentive again, usually for the rest of the class period. Because the brain is a pattern recognition organ, engaging students in a movement activity that has a distinct pattern like Brain Gym® or a "rhythm break," every 30-60 minutes keeps the brain awake, alert and helps increase attention span.[26] Teachers might want to get the book *S'cool Moves for Learning*, that contains a wealth of ideas for movement breaks in the classroom.[27]

MOVEMENT AND VISION

Vision is very much a bodily function. In an active learning situation, the external eye muscles are constantly moving the eyes up and down, side to side, and all around. The internal eye muscles constrict or dilate the pupil for proper lighting and the ciliary muscles on the lens either lengthen or broaden the lens for far and near vision. When our eyes stop moving, as with staring, visual input also stops. Notice that when you stare, you miss what is happening in your environment.

Figure 6.1: Internal and External Muscles of the Eye

When the body and head move, the vestibular system is activated, and the eye muscles strengthen as they move in response. The more the eyes move, the more the muscles of both eyes work together. Efficient eye teaming enables the student to focus, track and concentrate when reading. As the eye muscles strengthen and move more in concert with each other, more connections to the brain are developed and available.[28] This occurs because eighty percent of the nerve endings in the muscles have a direct connection, via proprioception and the vestibular system, with the motor nerves to and from the eyes.[29]

I often find that children with learning difficulties experience distress when I ask them to focus on my thumb as I move it through their entire visual field. Their eyes jump, they complain that it hurts, and they have difficulty maintaining their focus. This visual stress, when the eyes don't focus effectively or track together efficiently, is due to inadequate muscular development in the eyes, often caused by lack of integrated whole body movement and vestibular system development.

Babies start out following the movements of their hands or feet with their eyes. In time, specific nerve networks elaborate and hand-eye coordination develops. The baby is able to bring the objects of the world to the eye for scrutiny and learning. Hand-eye, foot-eye coordination then allows the infant to accurately move in response to objects in its environment. With practice and maturation of the networks, a shift occurs and eye-hand coordination develops. The eye now leads the hand movements, so that the vast array of internal knowledge becomes the template for movement. We can now learn to connect movement with sight as Amy, described in Chapter 1, did with the soccer ball. This connection is essential in writing, drawing, playing an instrument, learning a sport or dancing.

The muscles of the eye also play an important part in classroom learning. Light passes across the body of the eyeball onto the retina where 137 million receptors (nerve endings) take in the information. Ninety-five percent of the receptors, the rods, are for peripheral vision, while only five percent are cones for foveal focus, which is what we use for up close, two-dimensional paper work. Before entering school, three-dimensional and peripheral vision allow the greatest environmental learning. They integrate the visual with the kinesthetic to understand shapes, movement of natural forms and spatial awareness. When children enter school, they are often expected to quickly develop their foveal focus in order to see small, static, two-dimensional letters on a page. The transition from three-dimensional and peripheral to foveal focus is very abrupt and in many cases unnatural.[30]

Before approximately age seven, the ciliary bodies (muscles that shape the lens of the eye) are short, causing the lens to be thin and elongate. With the lens in this shape, the incoming image is spread out across the retina, bringing into play maximum rod and cone stimulation. This lens shape easily accommodates three-dimensional, peripheral and distance vision. At about age seven, these muscles start to lengthen, allowing the lens to round out and more easily focus the image only on the fovea centralis of the retina for natural foveal focus.[31]   Children who have looked at books in the home may have already acquired some foveal focus if the process was their choice and free of stress and pressure to perform, however, most children are not physically ready to read at age five as is now mandated in our schools.

We need only look at the recent past situation in Singapore to understand how we may be unintentionally damaging our children's vision.   In Singapore, children were expected to sit still and do seat work (reading and some writing) by age three or four. Because of this, eighty-five percent of their five year olds had myopia and needed glasses, and by age ten, almost one hundred percent needed glasses. This progressive country that cares greatly about the health and learning of their children has now changed the curriculum to include an equal amount of kinesthetic (play and manipulatives) to cognitive work in the learning process. We must let go of the belief that reading equals intelligence and allow our children's visual system to develop normally without the stress of early reading.

A TALE OF TWO CULTURES

As with many cultural expectations in the area of learning and child development, the norms of other societies can throw ours into stark relief and raise important questions about things we take for granted. A few years ago, I encountered a fascinating and tragic example of what can happen to learning when two different cultures intersect.

In South Africa, rural African children without available books absorb a rich oral tradition, and have excellent three-dimensional and peripheral vision. Traditionally they can speak three different languages, though they are usually not conversant in English. At the age of five when they first enter school, they have been found by occupational therapists in KwaZulu to be "far superior" to the white children on all but three of the pre-school tests.[32] At this point, they attend the British Standard Schools where they are expected to read the alphabet within the first two weeks, and read English within the first year. However, because their eyes have not yet developed the lens flexibility for foveal focus, they perceive only a blur when looking at a written page. The curriculum is not set up to allow time for foveal focus development. Though these children are highly motivated to learn and have strong family support, they experience humiliation and failure and 25.4% drop out in that first year of school.[33] Due to unnatural expectations, stress and lack of adequate time to develop foveal focus, South Africa has lost, and will continue to lose, a valuable resource in these children.

It's easy to see, when it's pointed out, where the Singapore and South African schools go wrong. But how well do our schools accommodate the natural evolution of children's movement skills and needs? And how well are our expectations and understanding of their development synchronized with the expectations and tasks we impose on them?

From the earliest grades, school children are taught not to move their bodies during class. They are also taught not to move their eyes beyond a blackboard or their desk. But these restrictions ignore the fact that seeing and "lens resiliency" are intimately connected with movement. The eyeball is not completely shaped with collagen fibers until approximately age nine.[34] Therefore, long periods of reading without relaxing the focus into the distance could possibly cause inflammation and the elongation of the eyeball leading to myopia or near-sightedness. At least twenty-five percent of the population of the U.S. has myopia with children tending to become myopic at the time they begin schoolwork.[35] Myopia has even been implicated in approximately 5.6% of blindness among American school children and a predisposition to retinal detachments, retinal degeneration and glaucoma later on.[36]

Much eyestrain comes from foveal focus overdependence, staring and lack of blinking. Blinking is important because it serves to keep the eye moist and healthy as well as to relax the focus. So it should be encouraged, and students should take breaks every seven to ten minutes so the eyes can reestablish three-dimensional and peripheral vision in a relaxed, natural way.[37]

Results of studies suggest that the nerve connections in the brain that influence vision can be greatly affected by the nature of our visual experience and environment.[38, 39] The two highest factors which contribute to myopia are genetic inheritance and doing close work.[40] F.A. Young demonstrated a significant development of myopia in monkeys who were forced to view objects at a distance of only 20 inches or less.[41] Other studies found that most men working in close quarters in a missile launch facility developed myopia. Myopia has also been related to high anxiety in the learning environment.[42]

The eyes need time to rest, without light stimulation, in order to function properly. Recently, there has been great concern over how artificial light impacts visual development in babies exposed to night-lights. In a study of 479 children ages two to sixteen, ten percent who slept in the dark developed myopia, while fifty-five percent exposed to night-lights at the age of two developed myopia.[43]

There are three areas of agreement among researchers regarding myopia:

1) significant amounts of myopia occur at an earlier age today than in the past, 2) myopia shows an increase in incidence and amounts as a child progresses from second grade through high school, and 3) today's incidence of myopia is higher than even 20 years ago.[44]

WHEN ARE THE EYES READY FOR READING?

By age seven or eight, as the frontal lobes of the cerebrum mature, fine motor coordination of muscles throughout the body, including the eye muscles, naturally develops. Before then, we have good peripheral and depth vision, but it is only when the frontal eye field of the frontal lobes matures that accurate enough eye teaming is possible for two-dimensional focus. Eye teaming occurs when the dominant eye tracks across a page of writing and the non-dominant eye follows the movements exactly and blends the information, giving optimal binocular vision. Because we have a nose between our two eyes, we will never have true binocular vision. Therefore, one eye takes the lead, as the dominant eye, to guide the movements of both eyes.

This laterality can be demonstrated by focusing both eyes on a vertical pen held at arm's length and aligned to a vertical structure in the room. Then alternate closing eyes, noticing which eye holds the image of the pen. That is the dominant tracking eye. Fine motor movements of the eyes and eye teaming ensure ease of information gathering and point to another physiological reason for not starting the reading process until age seven or, preferably, age eight.

VISION AND STRESS

In emotionally stressful situations, an interesting phenomenon occurs that makes it virtually impossible to track across a page of writing. As a reflex response to the sensation of danger, the eyes move peripherally so they can take in as much of the environment as possible. This makes it extremely difficult for the eyes to team and track across a page of writing. Attempt to read something right after you've seen a scary movie or been in a traumatic situation. I think you will find if very difficult.

When people live with continually stressful circumstances, their outer eye muscles may tend to strengthen, lengthening the inner eye muscles and making foveal focus and tracking even more difficult. Sexually abused or traumatized children exhibit what is called "wall eye" with both eyes in a sustained peripheral focus. When I work with children in special education classes, I find the eyes are always a factor. Just the act of having to track my finger back and forth causes their eyes to hurt and be jumpy. No wonder these children have problems reading and don't want to read. Their muscles hurt and must be retrained before they can comfortably read! As we shall see in the next chapter, movement activities provide a simple way to easily activate all the muscles of the eyes. The suggested activities discussed in Chapter 7, reduce the stress reaction and assist with ease of reading and comprehension.

Perhaps as much as ninety-five percent of learning occurs through direct, intimate sensory-motor experiences with the environment. Formal training may account for only five percent of lifelong learning.[45] Movement is an indispensable part of learning and thinking. Each movement becomes a vital link to learning and thought processing. Just as with our sensory systems, all of us must develop our own elaborate nerve networks of movement patterns, an "action encyclopedia." Thinking is a response to our physical world. In studying the brain, we can only understand it in the context of a physical reality, an action reality. Movement is an integral part of all mental processing, from the atomic movement that fires the molecular movement that orchestrates the cellular (electrical) movement, to the thought made manifest in action.

7

Moves That Improve

In 1986 I was asked to become part of a Hawaiian intermediate school as a Comprehensive Student Alienation Program (CSAP) counselor and tutor. The students I would work with had learning or emotional difficulties and therefore were considered alienated from the school program. It was an experiment for me. Here I was, a professor of biology at the University of Hawaii, having taught college biology for over twenty years, with no psychology or counseling background, asked to work with alienated, pubertal, intermediate kids. All this because I had successfully used accelerated learning techniques with my college classes, and I was just gutsy and curious enough to say "YES."

I had never worked with this age group before, so I spent three weeks during the summer of 1986 on the staff of Supercamp, an accelerated learning program for kids ages thirteen to seventeen, to gain understanding about students of this age and background. Some of these kids had been adjudicated in New York City and were on scholarships from the New York City Police Department. It was great training for me in being accepting, open, non-judgmental and capable of seeing the potential in every person. My daughter, who had just turned twelve, also consented to give me pointers. And so by the beginning of the new school year the stage was set for this strange experiment in my life.

MY INTRODUCTION TO BRAIN GYM®

Having an open and accepting attitude and a few Superlearning tools was not, however, the same as having an actual program for helping the troubled children I would face back in Hawaii. At this point, a Nurse Practitioner friend suggested I use Brain Gym® with these kids. It had been life-transforming for her son Todd, and I was open to anything that might work.

Todd, though bright and loveable, had been certified as learning disabled. As a sophomore in high school he still could not read though the family had spent thousands of dollars on learning programs. At age sixteen, Todd was six feet, two inches tall and the basketball team had recruited him to give them some height. But alas, he was clumsy, tripping over the ball as he attempted to dribble down the floor.

In that year his mother attended a Touch For Health conference in California where Dr. Paul Dennison first spoke of his work with learning disabilities and the Brain Gym® program. She returned home very excited announcing, "Todd, we're going to Cross Crawl." To get Todd to participate, the whole family did Cross Crawls and other Brain Gyms® every morning before Todd went to school and every evening before bed. Within six weeks Todd was reading at grade level. He became an important addition to the basketball team soon after.

All the pieces of learning had been there for over ten years, but Todd had been unable to integrate them. It took the Brain Gym® activities to finally fit the pieces together. A highly successful student, Todd has now completed college degrees in biology.

I figured if something so simple as Brain Gym® worked for Todd, it was worth a try. At first I played beat-a-second baroque music while simply following directions on how to do specific activities that were supposed to activate full mind/body function. I had no preconceived notions as to what would happen with these CSAP kids, but they seemed to enjoy the music and Brain Gym, and it fit in with my experiment.

Not knowing the protocol, I chose to work with these students without looking at their charts or past histories. What happened next surprised them, and me, and their teachers. They were finally succeeding and in charge of their own lives, emotionally, physically and mentally.

The principal was so impressed he had me make an inservice presentation to teachers, even though my training in the work was minimal. He also signed me up to give a four hour presentation to all the principals on the island. In an attempt to understand the shifts I was seeing in the students I took the Brain Gym® In-Depth training in November, 1986. With no satisfactory explanation of the physiology behind the shifts I was seeing, I began my search to understand the molecular, cellular, physical and neurological aspects of why simple, integrated cross-lateral movements work in assisting learning and life.

MICRO-INTERVENTIONS LEAD TO MAJOR CHANGES

We are all natural learners, born with a remarkable body/mind system equipped with all the elements necessary for learning. Various stressors, however, can introduce blocks that inhibit the learning process. (We will be discussing stress and its impact on learning in the third part of this book.) Hurried life styles, environmental factors, and physical ailments such as frequent ear infections are stressors that impact learning success. Though theoretically taking in all the information necessary to learn, still the stressed learner has difficulty assimilating and integrating new information to actually learn it, remember it and appropriately apply it to his or her life.

Brain Gym® and other movements, like walking, dancing, skipping, twirling, Tai Chi, Yoga, and even rough and tumble play appear to contribute the minor adjustments necessary to enable the system to proceed with the learning process. Dr. Dee Coulter, a cognitive specialist and neuroscience educator who has worked extensively with learning difficulties, refers to these minor adjustments as micro-interventions. She explains that these bring about major change because they supply the necessary integration and also reverse the expectation of failure.[1]

I have seen many such micro-interventions take place after using integrative movement. Once I worked with an eleven year old Down's Syndrome boy whose teacher had worked daily with him for three months in an attempt to have him learn his numbers one to ten. He had a chart that had the numerals in order on the top line, the numbers written out as words on the middle line, and pictures of objects on the bottom line (e.g., one apple, two shirts, three trees, etc.). His job was to take a laminated card and match it with the appropriate numeral, written number or figure on the chart.

As hard as he tried, he could not "get it." He would pick up a 3, say "seven", and place it on the ten. When reminded it was a 3, he would say "three," but then lay it down on a five. After using every technique she knew, both the teacher and the student had become extremely frustrated with the project.

I asked him if he would be willing to do a Brain Gym® activity called Dennison Laterality Repatterning, which he was pleased and excited to do. This series of activities took about fifteen minutes, after which he said he was ready to do his numbers again. He sat back down at the chart, picked up a 3, said "three" and placed it on the three in the chart. He immediately picked up a 7, said "seven" and put it on the seven, continuing until the whole chart was filled correctly. I felt the back of my chair shudder a bit and turned to see the teacher with big tears running down her cheeks.

The next day he drank water, did two minutes of Cross Crawls, Brain Buttons and Hook-ups and then sat down and correctly filled in the chart again. He was given another chart he had never seen, which had the numbers mixed up. He easily and correctly placed all the laminated chips on it. Somehow he had been taking in the information, but it took a "micro-intervention," the cross-lateral integrative movements of Brain Gym, to link the information up and make it useful.

These micro-interventions are seen on a regular basis by people who use this work for themselves and with others. The examples are simple but profound. Here is a graphic example of one first grade boy's immediate, demonstrable improvement in writing after a few minutes of doing some Brain Gym® exercises.

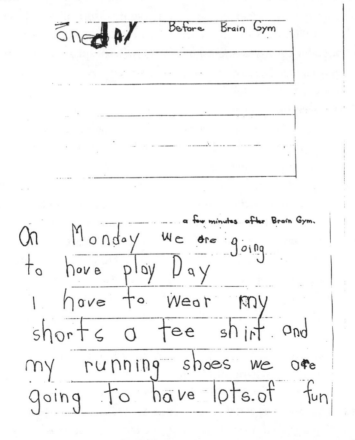

Figure 7.1: First Grade Boy's Improvement in Writing after Brain Gym®
(Penelope Mathes, teacher)

EVEN THOUGH IT'S SIMPLE AND EASY, IT DOES WORK

Our society today needs something simple and elegant to initiate and accomplish these micro-interventions. Every learning situation deals basically with the same steps: sensory input, integration, assimilation, and action. Simple integrative cross lateral movements which focus on sensory activation and balance, facilitate each step of the process by waking up the body/mind system, and bringing it to learning readiness.

The importance of movement in the learning process should be clear from the preceding chapters. As teachers in many cultures have intuitively recognized, numbers, letters and writing can all be taught effectively with lots of movement. Rudolf Steiner, to mention only one noteworthy example, believed in helping children to learn through the process of eurhythmia, which anchors learning with rhythm and specific coordinated movements similar to Brain Gym.[2]

The two greatest obstacles to full, widespread use of simple movement modalities is: 1) the strongly held misconception in our society that mind and body are separate, that movement has nothing to do with intellect, and 2), that physical activities which are simple, take very little time, and depend on no technologically associated assistance, can't be very useful.

In 1995, many of America's foremost brain researchers gathered in Chicago to examine the link between movement and learning. Since then, the research concerning the body/mind connection has been very prolific. Exercise, besides shaping up bones, muscles, heart and lungs also activates major growth of neurons and nerve nets in the basal ganglion, cerebellum and corpus callosum of the brain. Aerobic exercise increases the supply of blood and oxygen to the brain. But a coordinated series of movements, done slowly with balance, produces increased neurotrophins (natural neural growth factors) and a greater number of connections among neurons and even new nerve cell growth, especially in the hippocampus and frontal lobes of the brain.[3]

As we are able to step past our limited thinking, we are finding out that simple common-sense solutions often produce the most profound results.

SOME BACKGROUND

I applaud people like Rudoph Steiner, Newell Kephart, Jean Ayres (sensory-motor integration), Frederick Alexander (slow balanced reflex work), Glenn Dolman and Carl Delcato, George Goodheart, John Thie, Janet Goodrich (vision work), Paul Dennison and many others who recognized the importance of movement in the learning process. Even historically, the Greeks equated athletics with intelligence and Tai Chi has been used throughout Chinese schools to enhance learning from the inception of education.

Regarding Brain Gym, Paul Dennison drew from the work of these pioneers, adapting their research and his own, into quick, simple, task-specific movements and a simple balance format that would benefit any learner. The ease and simplicity of the work call for its natural inclusion in any learning situation. Many people from throughout the world have embraced the original Brain Gym® work, and vastly refined, clarified and enriched it with their knowledge of: developmental reflexes, psychology, physiology, Alfred Tomatis's work in hearing and language development, and even quantum physics.

Brigance Inventory
Reading & Comprehension

Math Scores

Figure 7.2: Changes in Brigance Inventory of Basic Skills Test Scores of Fifth Grade Special Education Students after A Year of Brain Gym®

Since establishment of the Educational Kinesiology Foundation in 1987, research projects using Brain Gym® have sprung up worldwide with remarkable results. My first attempt to quantify the effects of Brain Gym® occurred in 1989 with nineteen fifth grade special education students. Their teacher used the Brigance Inventory of Basic Skills test to pre- and post-test these students at the beginning and end of a one year school period. Each student did approximately five to ten minutes of Brain Gym® daily. As you will note from the graphs in Figure 7.2, the results showed a one to two year average gain for all students on the reading and reading comprehension test and an average gain of at least a year for more than fifty percent of the students on math. These results, especially in reading, were highly unusual for a whole class of special education students. The most surprising results were the remarkable improvements in self-esteem and in ability to focus on task.

BRAIN GYM® IN RUSSIA

In 1988 I was part of a guest delegation of twelve educators to the Soviet Union with the Association of Humanistic Psychologists (AHP) Soviet Project. Our job was to work with Soviet educators and introduce effective teaching technologies. I introduced Brain Gym® and left fifty Brain Gym® manuals with the Institute of Pedagogical Sciences, in Moscow and St. Petersburg (then Leningrad). One of these books made its way into the hands of Svetlana Masgutova, head of the Accent Institute of Psychology in Orechovo-Zoueva, Russia. In 1991, she asked me to come and meet with some psychologists and medical doctors that she had introduced to Brain Gym. At this time she told me of her extraordinary experiences with this body of work.

In 1989 there had been a serious train explosion an hour and a half from Moscow. Dr. Masgutova had been put in charge of working with the severely traumatized, surviving children. She used every professional tool she had with these badly burned children including art therapy. The pictures they drew were of charred, one-eyed monsters and burning horses depicted in dark tones. After three months, over half of the children had died. The rest were symptomatically depressed, continuing to draw horrifying pictures in their art therapy sessions.

At that time Dr. Masgutova discovered the basic Brain Gym® book and immediately started using the activities with the children and within several weeks the pictures they were drawing changed. Bright colors emerged along with rainbows, butterflies and children running through meadows. All of the children exhibited positive perspectives and were healing. This so surprised her, the medical doctors and the children's parents that at the end of six months she compiled her carefully kept records and wrote a professional paper.[4] Experts throughout Russia were interested and invited her to give talks.

When I arrived to teach in 1991, she had assembled fifty psychologists and medical doctors from the Moscow/St. Petersburg area and also from an institute in Tomsk, Siberia, that had been using Brain Gym. They shared with me their remarkable successes with people of all ages, with every problem imaginable. Currently, major cities throughout Russia are using the Brain Gym® work, with great success.

AND IN SOUTH AFRICA

In 1991 in Botswana, I was invited to work with trainees of the Botswana Insurance Company that were preparing for their Insurance exams. Though people had taken the exam each year, the pass rate had hovered at less than thirty percent. After my six-hour session with these people in February, they committed themselves to continue using Brain Gym® when they studied. Every single one of them passed the exam in May. One man named, Walks Tall, had worried the examiner by spending the first 30 minutes of the timed test doing Brain Gym. He was the first person in Southern Africa to receive one hundred percent on the Insurance Exam.

Brain Gym® even played a part in the emergence of a new South Africa. In late 1993, the Town Council of Verwoerdburg, Pretoria was developing a process to empower their semi- and illiterate trainees and decided to use Brain Gym® in a pilot study. An experimental group and control group of eight semi- and illiterate trainees were chosen by the Town Council. The experimental group was exposed to Brain Gym® activities over a three-day period by Andre Vermeulen, a Brain Gym® instructor with Destinatum Ltd. Two weeks after the experimental group had been exposed to Brain Gym®, trainers from the Affirmative Vision organization presented the same Life Skills course (Basic Orientation to Modern Society) to the experimental and control group in an identical manner in the same language, Northern Sotho (the mother tongue of the trainees). All variants including time spans, breaks, presenters, translator, content, tests, and workshops were kept the same.

Upon testing the content of the five day course, the evaluators found that the experimental group tested 27.7% better than the control group. They also found that the experimental group was much more confident, creative, attentive, relaxed during training, at ease during testing and involved in the workshops. They had more insights and also more positive attitudes, expressing their desire to learn. Because of this pilot study, banks and mining companies in South Africa began incorporating Brain Gym® into their training programs.

BRAIN GYM® ENHANCES PERFORMANCE TOO

Brain Gym® is also highly effective with sports, music, art and dance of every kind. In order to perform well in any of these, a person must be able to master technique and integrate that mastery with rhythm, flow, emotion and image in a spontaneous way. I have taught Brain Gym® to technically good musicians who found they could finally feel and express the passion in the music they played. Visual artists I have taught were stunned by the depth of expression they could achieve in their work. Brain Gym® is used in a course called Switched-On Golf that many golfers now consider their secret weapon.[5] Ron Langford uses Brain Gym® in his work with racecar drivers, a sport that demands calm, focus and integration.[6]

In Hawaii, I was invited to work with a soccer team of boys ages fourteen to sixteen who wanted to win the state championship. They were good players but all too often, they lost their "cool" during games, got penalties and lost. I did one Brain Gym® session with these boys as they focused on this goal: "we are calm, cool and collected and win the state championship." Until the tournament the boys voluntarily drank lots of water and did Cross Crawls, Brain Buttons and Hook-ups (the PACE program discussed below) before and in the middle of each practice and game. Their whole game improved and they qualified for the state championship play-off in Honolulu. There, they easily won the first two playoff games and advanced to the final championship game. The tension during this "make or break" game was very high and the boys began to lose their cool. During a time out, the boys spontaneously lay on the field and did Hook-Ups as the coach, parents and everyone else looked on in amazement. Then they returned to the game and won the state championship.

The tremendous contribution and appeal of Brain Gym® is its ease and utility. People can do the exercises at any time to enhance anything they do. It is simply movement, free and easy.

A BRAIN GYM® SAMPLER

I will go over a few of the Brain Gym® movements and their physiological mechanisms as I understand them from my research of brain function.[7] I will begin with PACE which stands for *Positive, Active, Clear and Energetic* learning. It is a learning readiness sequence that is usually done at the beginning of the school day, after recess and after lunch to effectively prepare the student for learning. I do it prior to any activity I want to be totally integrated for. It includes drinking water for energetic learning and then doing Brain Buttons, Cross Crawls and Hook-ups.

Brain Buttons are done by placing one hand over the navel while the other hand stimulates points between the ribs. The hand over the navel brings attention to the gravitational center of the body. Here lie the core muscles, important contributors to bodily balance. This action alerts the vestibular system, which stimulates RAS activation to wake up the brain for incoming sensory input. If a person is staring, this vestibular activation will get the eyes moving again so the brain has access to external visual information.[8]

The other hand gently rubs the indentations between the first and second ribs directly under the collarbone (clavicle), to the right and left of the sternum. This is thought to stimulate blood flow through the carotid arteries,

Figure 7.3: Brain Buttons

the first arteries out the heart that supply nutrients and freshly oxygenated blood to the brain. The Brain Buttons lie just above where the two carotid arteries branch. Baroreceptors (pressoreceptors) in the walls of the carotid arteries may account for the effects noticed when rubbing these points. Baroreceptor nerve cells are capable of responding to changes in blood pressure and (through the carotid sinus reflex) maintain normal blood pressure to the brain.[9]

I first realized the value of Brain Buttons when I was teaching an evening course at the University of Hawaii after working at the elementary school all day. The twenty-five minute drive home after class was deadly. I would find myself falling asleep at the wheel. My students had been doing Brain Buttons as part of PACE at the beginning of the class and I remembered their comments that it really woke them up and got them ready to learn even after their long work day. So I pulled the car over and did my Brain Buttons. It was as if a fog had lifted and I was able to stay alert for the rest of the drive. Many of my students have commented that it brings them back to focus when they are taking a test.

CROSS CRAWL

The Cross Crawl is simply a cross-lateral walking in place. By touching the right elbow to the left knee and then the left elbow to the right knee, large areas of both brain hemispheres are being activated simultaneously. Cross Crawling is like consciously walking, which facilitates balanced nerve activation across the corpus callosum. When done on a regular basis more nerve cells and networks form and myelinate in the corpus callosum, thus making communication between the two hemispheres faster and more integrated for high-level reasoning.

Infant crawling has long been known to be crucial for activating full sensory functioning and learning. Crawling involves movements that cross the body's midline and use both sides of the brain in concert. Our cross-lateral movements help us to build the capacities that allow full sensory access (auditory, visual, proprioceptive) from both sides of the body. (Later on, walking incorporates all of our early stages of development from infancy to toddling.) The Cross Crawl assists people who have missed or shortened this important step in development.[10] Drs. Dolman and Delcato coined the term patterning to describe the process of repeating a natural movement, like crawling, again and again to imprint it in the body's physiology even years after the developmentally appropriate time has passed. They have been instrumental in successfully assisting stroke patients to regain function through crawling.[11]

It's most effective to do the Cross Crawl movements very slowly. When the exercise is done slowly, it requires more fine motor involvement and balance, consciously activating the vestibular system and the frontal lobes. Children labeled hyperactive will have a hard time going slow, so engage them by first allowing them to go fast (which requires less balance), and then saying "Who can go the slowest? " There are many fun variations possible for all the activities I will present, with suggestions in two wonderful books: *Hands On, How to use Brain Gym® in the Classroom,* [12] and *S'cool Moves for Learning.*[13] As with the findings that running wheels stimulate the production of new nerve cells in the hippocampus of rats, cross-crawls are stimulating the same areas, thus it would make sense that they improve learning and memory.

Figure 7.4: Cross Crawl

This simple movement is elegant in activating full brain function and major diffusion into the frontal lobes. Whenever I get stuck, for instance, with writer's block, I Cross Crawl or take a walk, and the ideas begin to flow again. The simple act of walking uphill or on uneven ground helps strengthen the back and neck muscles, thus allowing the head to balance properly so the eyes can more easily team together. Having children walk or climb up and roll down hills is a great way to develop their learning system.[14] Robert Dustman, director of neuropsychology research at the Veterans Affairs Medical Center in Salt Lake City, Utah, found walking to improve mental performance in fifty to sixty year old men and women. He first administered mental and physical tests to a group of relatively inactive men and women in their fifties and sixties. He put the subjects on a four-month program of regular brisk walking. At the end of the four months, their performance on the same series of mental tests jumped by ten percent.[15]

HOOK-UPS

Hook-ups are done by first crossing one ankle over the other — whichever feels most comfortable. The hands are then crossed, clasped and inverted. To do this, stretch your arms out in front of you, with the back of the hands together and the thumbs pointing down. Now lift one hand over the other,

Figure 7.5: Hook-ups

palms facing and interlock the fingers. Then roll the locked hands straight down and in toward the body so they eventually rest on the chest with the elbows down. This complex crossover action has a similar integrative effect in the brain as the Cross Crawl. In a balanced way, it consciously activates the sensory and motor cortices of each hemisphere of the cerebrum, especially the large area devoted to the hands.

While in this position, rest your tongue on the roof of your mouth behind the teeth (hard palette). This action stimulates the tongue ligaments, which connect to the vestibular system, thus activating the RAS for focus and balance, and also helps to release a tongue thrust caused by postural imbalance. This complex balanced configuration equally stimulates both hemispheres of the brain, the entire motor coordination system and the vestibular system, thus stopping the survival reaction by bringing the system into coherence, and assisting focus, learning and memory.

As a counselor, I had a two-minute rule. When students (ages five to fifteen) were sent to me for being disruptive in the classroom, or following a playground fight, they had to sit in Hook-ups for two minutes before we talked. This consciously brought attention to the motor cortex of both frontal hemispheres and away from the survival centers in the reptilian brain, thus decreasing adrenalin production. Following the two minutes they were able to see both their own and each others' points of view more clearly. None of these students wanted to "get in trouble," and they were grateful to have a tool they could personally use, at any time, to control their own behavior.

This is one of my most frequently used Brain Gym® activities. Teachers often use it for themselves when their stress levels rise, and also to quiet and refocus students after changes like recess or lunch.

I invite you to do an experiment. Concentrate on a stressful or extremely challenging situation in your life. Notice where you tense up, where you feel muscles tighten, if the backs of your knees lock in the tendon guard reaction, and how you are breathing. Then sit, stand or lie down in Hook-ups for two to five minutes. Notice the differences in muscle tightness, breathing and outlook after this time. The situation is the same, but the whole body/mind system is being used to handle it more efficiently.

Following is a sampling of other Brain Gyms that work for specific skills development.

THE ENERGY YAWN

The Energy Yawn is done by massaging the muscles around the temporal-mandibular joint (TMJ) while yawning. The TMJ lies right in front of the ear opening and is the joint where the lower jaw meets the upper jaw. Across this joint run nerves from major cranial nerve trunks that gain sensory information from all over the face, eye muscles, tongue and mouth and activate all the muscles of the face, eyes and mouth for expression, mastication and vocalization.[16] This is also one of my most frequently used Brain Gyms, as many as 12 times per day because it activates so much for learning. Figure 3.4 graphically depicts the large area of the sensory and motor cortices these nerves supply.

The simple act of yawning also stimulates the tongue ligament, which helps to activate the RAS, waking up the brain and assisting focused attention.

Figure 7.6: The Energy Yawn

When we are stressed, the jaw tightens up and nerve function across this area decreases. (It's a protective reaction, so that if we are hit, the lower jaw won't be dislocated.) The Energy Yawn relaxes the whole facial area so the eyes, ears and facial muscles work more efficiently. It also facilitates more effective verbalization and communication.

When children are having difficulties with reading, tension in the TMJ may cause the eyes to not work well together due to stress. Tension in the TMJ may also make it difficult for children to hear clearly and verbalize, consequently affecting thought processing and memory. The Energy Yawn is remarkable in its effects. By relaxing the muscles and facilitating full nerve function across the temporal-mandibular joint, all the nerve functions to and from the eyes, facial muscles, and mouth are improved.

I used to enjoy watching Michael Jordan, a most amazing basketball player. He is grace in motion, *and*, his jaw is usually totally relaxed. This shows he is *playing* basketball, not stressed by it, which makes him a great basketball player. I have also seen this in Tiger Woods's beautiful, relaxed smile when he is *playing* golf.

The Thinking Caps exercise wakes up the whole hearing mechanism and assists memory. It is done by unrolling the outer cartilage of the ears from top to bottom several times.

Figure 7.7: The Thinking Cap

The link between hearing in the temporal lobe and memory in the limbic system appears to be very strong. My students at the University of Hawaii found the Thinking Caps to be very useful when needing to recall some technical information for an essay or exam. They'd also begin using this activity when I'd say "I want you to remember this information." Often, if I can't remember a person's name or the reference for an article, I do the Thinking Caps and the answer pops into my mind. The simple act of physically stimulating the tactile receptors in the outer ear, wakes up the whole hearing mechanism. (Acupuncturists identify over 148 points in the outer ear as corresponding to areas of the body, from the feet at the top of the ear to the head at the ear lobe.)[17]

It might be interesting for you to do this simple experiment: Close your eyes and listen for a few minutes. Are you hearing things equally with both ears? Does one ear seem bigger, or is it hearing more clearly than the other? Are any sounds muffled? If you are in a noisy environment, are you able to pick out individual sounds? Now, unroll your ears about three times on each side and close your eyes again. Notice the difference.[18]

X MARKS THE SPOT

The X is a very powerful symbol for the brain. Both hemispheres of the neocortex and the developed neural pathways of the corpus callosum are required in order to see the center of the X. The X lies in the center of the infinity symbol which, when used with hands, eyes, or body, in a smooth easy way going up the center and out assists integrated, graceful, coordinated movements of the hands, eyes and entire body. The X and infinity symbol are used a lot in the Brain Gym® activities, however, the infinity symbol is called a "Lazy 8", or an 8 lying on it's side. I will move between using the term "Lazy 8" and "Infinity Symbol" in the following text.

LAZY 8'S FOR WRITING

The Lazy 8 for writing is a pencil and paper activity specifically geared to improve written communication. Lazy 8's for writing are excellent for establishing the necessary rhythm and flow for good hand-eye coordination. To do a Lazy 8 you draw an infinity symbol (a sideways eight), with the X of the symbol right at the position of your belly-button (midline), in a flowing continuous movement. Start at the middle, draw counterclockwise first: up, over and around; then clockwise: up, over, around and back to the midpoint. *make sure to start up the middle*, which follows the midline of the body. Five or more continuous repetitions are done with each hand and five or more with both hands together.

The Lazy 8 is best done large at first (but within the visual field), to stimulate large muscles, and on a surface to stimulate tactile awareness. Especially with young students, I suggest this activity be done first in sand, birdseed, on carpet squares or textured walls with the full hand, rather than pen or pencil, to activate both hand areas in the motor and sensory cortexes of the brain. This action relaxes the muscles of the hands, arms and shoulders as well as facilitating visual tracking.

You can experience the integration this activity brings by thinking of something you need to communicate in writing. Notice the position and how tightly you are holding the pen as you begin to write. Now write a few sentences and notice if the ideas flow easily or if there is effort in communicating what you want to say. Do the Lazy 8 (infinity symbol) as big as an 8½ x 11 inch sheet of paper. Then write a few sentences again, noticing the position and how tightly you hold the pen, how clear your thoughts are and if you are now able to communicate with ease. Also notice your writing before and after, was the writing more fluid and easy?

Lazy 8's are very helpful to me when I get writer's block. Students also find them very helpful when taking a test. If they start to feel stressed, become confused and/or can't think of the answer, they simply do some Lazy 8's on their desk tops with their fingers and experience cross-lateral integration again. Then they can find the answers more easily.

Figure 7.8: Lazy 8's For Writing

The Lazy 8's also assist with art, graphics and playing any musical instrument. In South Africa, I had one of the nation's top artists draw a picture of a person we were with, and I gave him only ten minutes to do this. Then I had him do the Lazy 8's and gave him ten minutes to draw a picture of another person. He was astounded, as were we, at the difference in his ability to more closely and complexly capture the second person after just one or two minutes of Lazy 8's.

LAZY 8'S FOR EYES

Lazy 8's for eyes are similar to the Lazy 8's for writing except that the focus here is on eye movements and improving hand-eye and eye-hand coordination. These Lazy 8's are done by training the eyes on a moving thumb as it describes an infinity sign in the visual field. To do this, hold either thumb at eye level in the mid-field of the body at approximately an elbow length from the eyes. For maximum muscular activation the movements should be slow and conscious. Holding the head still, but relaxed, and just moving the eyes to follow the thumb, move the thumb directly up the center of the mid-field to the top of the visual field and then counterclockwise out around and down to the left side. As the thumb reaches the lower mid-field of the visual field bring it back up the center and clockwise out, around and down the right side. This should be continued in an even flowing movement at least three times with each hand. Then both hands should be clasped with the thumbs forming an X. While focusing on the center of the X, again follow the clasped thumbs through the Lazy 8 pattern.

Figure 7.9: Lazy 8's For Eyes

This activity effectively strengthens the extrinsic eye muscles, assisting network development and myelination from the frontal eye field area for fine motor tracking. It also sets up learning patterns that coordinate hand-eye and eye-hand muscle alignment.

The Lazy 8 pattern can also be drawn in a three-dimensional field close to and away from the eyes. In this version of the activity the plane of the figure 8 is shifted ninety degrees so that it is now perpendicular to the body. This exercise works the intrinsic muscles that hold the lens of the eye, thus activating near and far focus. Starting at the midpoint, move the thumb up and away from your body as you circle the outer loop, then move up through the midpoint and toward your eyes as you circle the nearer loop. Again, this should be done in a free-flowing pattern with only the eyes and hand moving.

People with glasses might want to take them off so the visual field is not pre-empted by the rims of the glasses. If done right, you should feel maximal muscle movement, equally in both eyes. This means you may feel like you've been doing push-ups with your eyes if the muscles are a bit weak.

This is often difficult for people who have been under a great deal of stress. One student I worked with, who had been in a sexually abusive situation for years, could only do a few of these at a time without pain in her eye muscles. It had been impossible for her to read, because in her chronic state of stress her outer eye muscles had strengthened for peripheral vision and her inner eye muscles were very weak. In this condition she was unable to bring her eyes into focus for two-dimensional foveal focus or to track across a page of reading. With persistence, over a month's time, the muscular movements of her eyes became stronger and more balanced so she was able to achieve foveal focus and finally read.

Lazy 8's are an important activity for me after working on the computer. I can start to feel the eye-strain setting in, which also causes my neck muscles to tighten and my shoulders to become sore. By doing the Lazy 8's for eyes, my eyes and shoulders relax and I'm able to continue with my work.

A wonderful variation is the infinity back massage that not only assists writing and eye teaming, but also the release of nerve growth factor (NGF) and oxytocin for increased calm, focus and learning. In a classroom situation, one student sits at the desk and rests his head on his arms, while another student draws the Lazy 8 on his back. The student drawing the Lazy 8 should be aware of his eyes moving with his hands and the feel of the fabric on his hands, which stimulates both the motor and sensory cortexes of the brain. Then they can switch roles. Done as a regular treat, at least once a day for several minutes, it greatly assists a sense of safety, calm, focus and learning for all.[19]

THE ELEPHANT

This is one of the most integrative of the Brain Gym® activities. It is done by placing the left ear on the left shoulder, tight enough to hold a piece of paper between the two, then extending the left arm like a trunk. With knees relaxed and bending with the flow, the arm draws a Lazy 8 pattern in the mid-field, again starting up the middle and out and around with eyes following the movement of the finger tips. For increased effectiveness, it should be done slowly three to five times on the left and an equal number of times with the right ear against the right shoulder.

The Elephant activates all areas of the body/mind system in a balanced way. The movement is mainly from the core muscles, activating the vestibular system, especially the semicircular canals. Hand-eye coordination is also involved, all orchestrated by the basal ganglion of the limbic system in conjunction with the cerebellum and sensory motor cortices of the cerebrum with emphasis on the frontal lobes. Visual input activates the occipital lobe and, if elephant sounds are added, the hearing mechanisms within the temporal lobes.

Figure 7.10: The Elephant

People who have experienced chronic ear infections find the Elephant extremely challenging, but see major results with improved balance and equilibrium within a few weeks. If done on a regular basis, the Elephant stimulates the whole vestibular system, re-establishing nerve networks that might have been damaged during ear infections. Elephants are highly recommended for people labeled ADD, as this exercise assists full activation of the Reticular Activating System, thus improving attention.

OTHER PROGRAMS OF INTEGRATED MOVEMENTS

The physiology of brain function that applies to Brain Gym, also applies to most yoga, Tai Chi, Alexander Technique, and other movement programs in which each posture and movement is done slowly, with maximal activation of both gross and fine motor areas of the brain in a controlled, coherent, cross-lateral way that stimulates whole brain/body balance and frontal lobe processing. This routine activation of the motor cortex elaborates nerve networks in the rest of the frontal lobe including the pre-motor and superior pre-frontal cortex.

Since these specific movements are growing and activating nerve networks throughout the brain, in both hemispheres simultaneously, they help build the hardware needed to assure success for life-long learning. I enjoy watching the people in China, in the morning as they gather by the hundreds to do Tai Chi in the parks. They are the vision of grace and beauty. Unfortunately, most of the participants are older people, sometimes very old. It seems the young people of China have turned to becoming Westernized with high stress jobs, sedentary lifestyles in offices, at computers or TV, and the resulting obesity never before present.

Figure 7.11: The Integrated Movements of Tai Chi aid learning

All these activities effectively optimize learning and performance at every level in all areas of life: cognitive endeavors, healthy relationships, communication, creativity, art, music, sports and dance and increased productivity in the workplace. Because they relieve and manage stress to help maintain brain coherence, they also contribute to overall health.

With the high pressure to perform academically in Singapore, two parents I met, Sumi Said and and Hadi Chua Muhd, decided to use Brain Gym® and other integrative movements in order to assist their own children through school. In their home they hung a rope ladder for climbing. They constructed a balance beam from 2 x 4 boards laid on blocks, provided balls to roll around on, throw, and do Brain Gym® activities with, and colleted a lot of manipulative objects for hand development. Their children spent much time in nature playing in streams and rivers, playing with sticks and rocks, climbing cashew and palm trees, rope structures, big rocks and even the sides of buildings. As you can see from the accompanying photographs, the children are barefoot. We are learning the importance of foot flexibility. The more children can go barefoot, the more they develop their sense of balance and their entire vestibular system, which in turn affects their hearing, attention, language, and all learning.

As their children succeeded in school, other parents became interested in what Sumi and Hadi were doing. The interest was so great that they opened sessions to other children. Currently they work with hundreds of children a week. The children coming to their center are labeled with learning and physical disabilities, many severe. Sumi and Hadi get them climbing, doing a variety of activities that demand strong balance, doing Brain Gym. They even take children on camping trips in nature for the fun of it. The play and joy these two people bring to those children has left each child functioning at high physical and academic levels, acknowledged by the media as outstanding, and they just started out as concerned parents.[20]

Figure 7.12: Brain Waves Educational Kinesiology Consultancy School, Singapore

Schools and all other learning settings from preschool to corporate training classrooms are obvious places to incorporate these simple activities. I have never worked with an age group or type of individual that failed to learn more effectively as a result of using integrated movements. They help the young to get ready to learn, and the elderly to maintain active thinking and memory. But perhaps the most profound improvements I have witnessed were with adults and children labeled "learning disabled," "Attention Deficit Hyperactive Disorder," "Emotionally Handicapped," Autistic, Dyslexic, Down's Syndrome. These activities are drug-free, simple and highly effective. They maintain a fine-tuned body/mind system; assist comprehension, and understanding; and promote more joy and enthusiasm in every area of life.

8

What Goes Wrong?

Every child has inside him an aching void for excitement and if we don't fill it with something which is exciting and interesting and good for him, he will fill it with something which is exciting and interesting and which isn't good for him.

— Theodore Roosevelt

If movement is essential for learning and thought, then why aren't "hyperactive" people, who move all the time, thinking and learning? If people have all the necessary elements to take in the world sensorially, to process and integrate information, and to demonstrate the skill of thought, why are some people labeled "learning disabled"? If the drive to learn is intrinsic to the human body/mind from before birth to death, why do some people have "attention deficit disorder"?

In the United States alone there are between three and four million school-aged children, mainly boys, who are labeled with specific learning disabilities. As many as five hundred thousand preschool children are also being labeled with learning disabilities, between one and one and a half million preschool children with speech and language disabilities, five hundred thousand preschoolers with emotional disturbances, seventy-five thousand with hearing impairments, and one hundred thousand with autism.[1] Every week, fifteen thousand American school children are being referred for assessment, and up to eighty percent of all American school children could be diagnosed with learning difficulties.[2, 3]

In my observation, based on years of work with schools and school children, the labels used for specific learning difficulties are generally arbitrary, based on behaviors and non-pathological. These labels include: Hyperactive, Attention Deficit Disorder (ADD), Attention Deficit Hyperactive Disorder

(ADHD), Learning Disabled, and Emotionally Handicapped. Efforts to help people with learning difficulties have often relied on the pigeonhole strategy: labeling a problem and thinking that greater understanding will follow from greater generalization. But more often than not, labeling leads to oversimplification and insensitivity to the very real, very unique people behind the label. Sadly, in some ways we have trapped these children — and adults — in a diminished view of themselves and their potential for learning.

In light of the amazing resiliency of the human body/mind system, I propose that we hold off such a judgment until a person has completed their learning, which will take a lifetime. How can we label someone who is still in the process of becoming, a process we all are engaged in until we die? Having said that, I hasten to agree that there are people with specific learning difficulties. However, if we must label them, why not label them according to the underlying core problems rather than just the symptoms? I suggest the label SOSOH: Stressed Out, Survival-Oriented Humans.

WHO ARE SOSOH?

What do I mean by stressed out, survival-oriented? I am referring to non-integrated, lopsided brain functioning, a tendency to operate reflexively and/or reactively from survival centers in the brain stem and the sympathetic nervous system. How does stress fit into the picture? Stress from various environmental, developmental, family and social influences is a trigger setting off events in the nervous system that produce and regulate survival-oriented behavior. We certainly know that chronic exposure to stress inhibits full brain development and learning. [4]

Stress necessitates an overemphasis on survival-oriented brain processing at the expense of rational, limbic and cortical functioning, especially within the frontal lobes. Consequently, stressed out, survival oriented humans have less opportunity to develop nerve nets into the frontal lobe and may exhibit learning difficulties as a result. In the next five chapters we will look at these detrimental effects of stress in greater depth. Here I wish to emphasize that stressors of various kinds, some obvious, some less visible, are causative agents for many learning difficulties.

As far as I can tell, my SOSOH label easily covers all the other labels we currently apply to learning problems. These familiar labels, including Fetal Alcohol Syndrome, have been attached to the following patterns of behavior:

Excessive activity — hyperactivity,

Difficulties in maintaining attention and focus on a task,

Disruptive behavior,

Learning difficulties,

Inability to control behavior in alignment with social norms,

Marked discrepancy between seemingly high verbal skills (constant talking) and the ability to communicate effectively,

Erratic, non-graceful, unbalanced or poorly controlled movements.

Insensitivity to the needs and feelings of others.

All these behaviors fall within the realm of frontal lobe functioning. The frontal lobes control fine motor movement, inner speech, self-control, and reasoning. I believe that people who exhibit these behaviors, my SOSOH group, have been exposed to stressors that require them to be concerned more with survival than reason. Because of this, they lack integrated nerve-net development and myelination into the frontal lobe area of the cerebrum.

HYPERACTIVITY AND THE FRONTAL LOBE

A study by Alan Zametkin and colleagues at the National Institute of Mental Health graphically demonstrated the frontal lobe/hyperactivity connection. Zametkin studied 25 hyperactive adults of childhood onset (who also had hyperactive children of their own). Using PET scans to measure these adults' cerebral glucose metabolism while engaged in an auditory-attention task, researchers found 8.1% less brain activity in the hyperactive group as compared to a normal control. The area of the brain with reduced function was the frontal lobe.[5]

Hyperactivity (and ADD or ADHD) is characterized by a lack of fine motor coordination, and constant, erratic, non-graceful adrenalin-initiated movements. Constant external chatter is also characteristic, pointing to a lack of inner speech development that controls social behavior. Exhibited also is a lack of deep feelings such as empathy, compassion and love for others and their needs and feelings.

The largest reduction of brain activity in the Zametkin study was found specifically in the premotor cortex and superior prefrontal cortex of the frontal lobes.[6] (See Figure 5.2, the four lobes of the neocortex.) These areas of the brain are crucial for the self-talk which controls behavior and planning, for fine controlled movement, for integrative thought, and for creativity and higher level emotions such as empathy and altruism. The prefrontal cortex, with its connection to Broca's area on the left side for motor control of speech, affects focused attention, motor activity and the ability to think before acting.[7]

When fully developed, in late adolescence or even adulthood, the frontal lobe takes all the information from the rest of the brain and synthesizes it into thought, creativity and action. These areas of the frontal lobe light up on PET scans when a person is thinking, and they link to the motor cortex which facilitates appropriate action in relationship to reasoning.[8] (See Figure 5.3 which schematically represents the brain areas involved in thinking) Jay Giedd implicates malfunction in the frontal lobes and smaller frontal areas of the corpus callosum in ADHD. A smaller frontal corpus callosum reflects communication problems between the two brain hemispheres.[9]

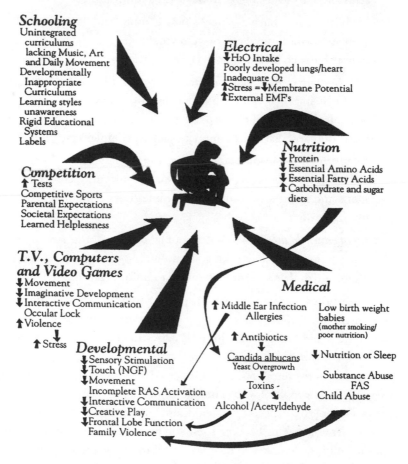

What Inhibits Learning

Schooling
Unintegrated
  curriculums
  lacking Music, Art
  and Daily Movement
Developmentally
  Inappropriate
  Curriculums
Learning styles
  unawareness
Rigid Educational
  Systems
Labels

Electrical
↓H₂O Intake
Poorly developed lungs/heart
Inadequate O₂
↑Stress =↓Membrane Potential
↑External EMF's

Nutrition
↓ Protein
↓ Essential Amino Acids
↓ Essential Fatty Acids
↑ Carbohydrate and sugar
  diets

Competition
↑ Tests
Competitive Sports
Parental Expectations
Societal Expectations
Learned Helplessness

T.V., Computers and Video Games
↓Movement
↓Imaginative Development
↓Interactive Communication
  Occular Lock
↑Violence
  ↓
  ↑Stress

Developmental
↓Sensory Stimulation
↓Touch (NGF)
↓Movement
  Incomplete RAS Activation
↓Interactive Communication
↓Creative Play
↓Frontal Lobe Function
  Family Violence

Medical
↑ Middle Ear Infection
  Allergies
↑ Antibiotics
Candida albucans
Yeast Overgrowth
  ↓
Toxins -
  ↓   ↘
Alcohol /Acetyldehyde

Low birth weight
babies
(mother smoking/
poor nutrition)
↓Nutrition or Sleep
Substance Abuse
  FAS
Child Abuse

Figure 8.1: What Inhibits Learning

SOME OF THE SOURCES OF STRESS IN OUR LIVES

So what are some of the stressors people face in their lives that limit frontal lobe development? I will attempt to categorize what I believe are the main stressors. Many are interlinked:

Developmental — lack of sensory stimulation, lack of movement, lack of touch (diminished Nerve Growth Factor), lack of interactive creative play and communication, unbalanced or incomplete RAS (Reticular Activating System) activation.

Electrical — inadequate water consumption, inadequate oxygen, excessive exposure to external EMF's (electromagnetic fields).

Nutritional — inadequate amounts of proteins, lack of essential amino acids and fatty acids, high carbohydrate and sugar diets.

Medical — low birth weight babies, chronic middle ear infections, allergies, medications, yeast overgrowth, inadequate diet or sleep, substance abuse, child abuse, poor vision or hearing.

TV, computers and video games — which can lead to violence, decreased imaginative development, less interactive communication, ocular lock, decreased motor development, decreased motivation, and linear thinking that lacks comprehension of complex systems.

Competition — inappropriate expectations (at home, school, work and self-imposed), pressures towards social conformity, competition in sports and in the arts, learning in a winner/loser rather than cooperative framework.

Rigid educational systems — developmentally inappropriate curricula, constant low-level skills testing, lecture/writing formats for quiet classrooms, unawareness of or inattention to unique learning styles.

Most of these stressors overstimulate the survival centers of the mind/body system. They cause nerve activity to be centered in the sympathetic nervous system and brain stem, with little activation of the rest of the brain, especially of the frontal lobes.

A review of the research shows strong evidence for a variety of effects of stress on SOSOH people. I will go into greater detail in coming chapters, but one more example may suggest the significant, complex links that neuroscientific research is establishing between stress and brain function. The hippocampus of the limbic system, key to memory and learning, is profoundly affected by stress. In research on rats, Solomon Snyder found that enkephalins, chemicals produced in the brain during stress to numb pain, also increase hyperactivity and decrease memory.[10] In addition, the stressed rats did not grow new nerve cells in the hippocampus (involved in memory) and lost more hippocampal cells than the non-stressed ones.[11] Furthermore, only the stressed rats lost cells in the part of the hippocampus that suffers selective damage in Alzheimer's disease in humans.[12] These results are thought to apply directly to humans, stress and aging. Adrenalin output rises during aging, rendering the hippocampus more vulnerable to neurological insults like seizures and strokes, especially in the presence of stress.

Many sources of stress can interfere with the learning process. In earlier chapters I have discussed the impact of various developmental factors on brain functioning and learning capacities. In the chapters ahead, I will do my best to address the rest of the list. Some, like malnutrition are well known inhibitors of learning and health. Others, like TV, competition and educational expectations exert less visible but no less serious influences on learning. We will take a look at them all. Armed with greater knowledge we can help ourselves and our children avoid situations and influences that pose a danger to brain development and to learning. That is why I have called the second part of this book, *Nurturing and Protecting Our Learning Systems*.

Nurturance and protection of the young are the primary roles of every family and every society. But as we look at our children, our schools, and our future, concerns mount that somewhere along the line we have gotten dangerously off track. We may be accepting far higher levels of stress than we can possibly manage and dissipate. In the following pages I hope to point us in a better direction.

9

Basics for the Brain: Water and Oxygen

How do we nurture and support the complex development, organization and reorganization of the learning-thinking process? What are the essential elements necessary to protect our body/mind system throughout life? How do we assure full, efficient functioning of these massive networks with their boundless potential for learning? How do we responsibly care for Control Central so it will take care of us?

Aside from giving the body and mind something new and exciting to work on regularly, we must also provide them with the fuel and safeguards they need in order to thrive. Fortunately, some of the most important building blocks of high performance are readily available. But we have to know what they are, and why they are so important. In this chapter, we'll begin with the most basic: water and oxygen, and their connection with the electrical systems within our mind and body.

COOL, CLEAR, WATER

For a substance that is so essential to life, water seems remarkably unremarkable: colorless, odorless, tasteless and ubiquitous. Yet, it is the magic elixir for learning, the "secret potion" if you will.

Water is one of the most important and most abundant inorganic substances in the body. It makes up eighty percent of our body weight at birth, and seventy percent of an adult's body weight.[1] Lean people have a greater proportion of water to total body weight because fat has very little water, while muscle has a lot. Water comprises more of the brain (with estimates of ninety percent than of any other organ of the body, with muscles next at seventy-five percent, and then kidneys.[2] Under normal conditions, it is recommended a person drink one third of an ounce of water per pound of body weight (about a quart per hundred pounds of body weight) each day with that amount doubled or tripled in times of stress.

Why is water so essential to learning, and to life? To answer that question we need to look at the crucial roles it plays in electrical activity within the body, in the distribution of oxygen, and in nutrition.

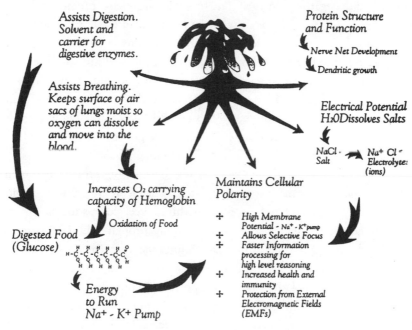

Figure 9.1: Water Assists Learning

WATER AND THE BODY ELECTRIC

Our bodily systems are electrical. Ultimately, it is the electrical transmissions within the nervous system that make us sensing, learning, thinking, acting organisms. Water, the universal solvent, is essential for these electrical transmissions and for maintaining the electrical potential within our bodies.

The membranes of our nerve cells (and of all our cells) are polar (have a charge) due to the interplay between positively and negatively charged atoms called electrolytes. The electrolytes (ions), such as sodium (Na+), potassium (K+), and chlorine (Cl-) come from the salts in our diet. When you put regular table salt into water, it dissolves. Water causes salt to disassociate into the atoms that make it up. In the case of table salt (NaCl), water will cause it to disassociate into two atoms with unequal charges: Na+ and Cl-. These then have the ability to transmit electrical current.

A living cell is positively charged on the outside and negatively charged on the inside thanks to a molecular process occurring at the cell membrane, which is called the sodium-potassium pump. This pump actively transports sodium ions (positively charged atoms) to the outside of the cell leaving large, nondiffusible negatively charged ions (organic phosphate, protein and chlorine) trapped inside.[3] The polarity of the cell is called the resting membrane potential. A resting nerve cell membrane maintains an average voltage of -70 mv (millivolts) inside. This implies a voltage of +70 mv outside.[4] (It is more difficult to measure voltage outside the cell due to dilution within tissue fluids.) This differential between the -70 mv on the inside and the +70 mv outside is the membrane potential. This potential is commonly indicated by referring only to the inside charge: -70 mv. The greater the differential (for example -80 mv / +80 mv), the higher the membrane polarity.

Optimal nerve and muscle function depend on proper membrane potential (polarity). The water/electrolyte balance is so critical to the living system that if the membrane potential within the cells drops to -30 mv and remains there, death will ensue. This can occur through radical dehydration or malnutrition. Even under normal circumstances, the polarity across the membrane can decrease just from inadequate levels of water in the body.[5]

High cellular polarity (membrane potential) raises the threshold of sensitivity at the cell membrane, effectively increasing the integrity of the cell membrane by lowering its sensitivity to outside stimuli. Surrounded as we are by a world of stimuli, high membrane polarity gives us a choice. It takes more of a stimulus to activate a nerve impulse, so we can choose what stimuli we wish to focus our attention on and not be distracted by irrelevant stimuli. As we will see, this enhances selective focus for increased learning, strengthens immunity and health, and protects against the effects of external electromagnetic fields.

The sodium-potassium pump uses ATP (adenosine triphosphate), as its energy source to actively transport the positively charged atoms to the outside of the cell. ATP is formed as the food we eat (mainly carbohydrates) is broken down by oxygen (oxidation) to release energy. The released energy is trapped in the ATP molecule and carried to the sodium-potassium pump as its energy source.[6]

A CLOSER LOOK AT A NERVE IMPULSE

At the microscopic, cellular level all the activities by which we define and know ourselves depend on tiny electrical impulses that occur through the movement of electrolytes in and out of the cell. Though minute and executed in a flash, they profoundly affect our ability to learn, remember, feel, think and physically act in our lives.[7] How do they work?

Figure 9.2: Membrane Polarity and Neuron Impulse Transmission

In its polarized state, the nerve cell has an action potential, the means to respond to a stimulus. When a strong enough stimulus activates an area on the nerve cell membrane, the sodium-potassium pump shuts down at that spot, allowing sodium to rush from the outside to the inside. With basically equal amounts of positive and negative ions on the inside, the membrane is no longer polar: it is depolarized. The sodium-potassium pump next to this spot is deactivated, and a wave of depolarization moves, like falling dominos, down the entire length of the nerve cell as an action potential. Action potentials measure about 100 millivolts in amplitude, are one millisecond in duration and can be generated at 200 per second.[8]

Depolarization waves move at 100 meters per second, sending a message from sensory organs to the brain or from the brain to muscles and glands. This is similar to the alternating (+ to -) current found in electrical circuits. But at 100 meters per second, the nerve transmits messages at less than 1 millionth the speed at which electrical signals move on a copper wire.[9] Even at that relatively slow rate, your brain takes only a few milliseconds to arrange a specific pattern of millions of signals, which is then instantly dissolved, never to be repeated that same way again. The sodium-potassium pump immediately reestablishes its functioning, thus repolarizing the cell membrane again so it is ready to send the next message.

With the nervous system's ability to process at least one thousand new bits of information every second, examining all that occurs in the body/mind system in this simple example would take volumes, if not a library, to explain.[10]

To put that last paragraph in perspective, I'd like you to do an experiment, and notice how long it takes. "Move your left big toe." The following is a very basic sketch of what is happening in that simple act:

1. Your eyes are moving, picking up the words on the page, "move your left big toe."
2. This activates sensory nerve endings (rods and cones) in the retina at the back of the eye.
3. Waves of depolarization travel down the sensory neurons to the synapses in the Central Nervous System where neurotransmitters bridge the gap and activate the Great Intermediate Net, Command Central.
4. The nerve networks are activated to decipher the command, connecting the visual stimuli with words, memory and sensations in the association areas of the occipital, parietal and temporal lobes of the brain.
5. The brain then discriminates between right and left, and determines "big" compared with "little." It must then pull out a physical memory of "toe."
6. Then it activates nerve impulses to the motor cortex of the right frontal lobe of the brain which connects with the left big toe muscles, the basal ganglion for movement orchestration and the cerebellum for gross motor movement.
7. Through branching neural pathways of association neurons, the appropriate motor neurons are activated sending a wave of depolarization down the myelinated axons of the nerves.

8. At some point, either in the brain or spinal cord, the motor neurons cross to the left side, and travel along nerve pathways in the sciatic nerve.
9. The impulses travel down the left leg to the muscles of the big toe causing them to contract.
10. Another message is instantly sent from proprioceptive sensors in the big toe to the sensory cortex of the parietal lobe of the brain to tell you that you have just moved your left big toe.

And it took you how long? Theoretically you could move your left big toe 200 times a second, because the system has the potential to generate new impulses at that rate.

The smooth functioning of this system is highly dependent on water, oxygen and nutrients with water taking first place as the most necessary ingredient.

COFFEE, TEA OR BRING ON THE CHOCOLATE!

Certain chemicals, called diuretics, dehydrate the body. Indiscriminate use of these chemicals may actually decrease learning potential. These include alcohol and caffeine, found in coffee, tea, some carbonated beverages and chocolate.

The body naturally attempts to maintain a balance between salt and water. Have you ever eaten a whole bag of salty potato chips only to find you are very thirsty? All those fiendishly tasty potato chips drive the salt level in the body way above the water level. To compensate, the thirst centers in the hypothalamus are activated, making you thirsty. If you obey that signal and drink water, the water is absorbed into the blood and carried to the kidneys, which monitor salt/water balance. Certain hormones in the kidney, like Antidiuretic Hormone (ADH), facilitate reabsorption of water back into the blood, so it is not lost as urine. This way the water level increases until the salt and water are in balance again.[11]

Coffee, tea, chocolate and alcohol are all diuretics. They inhibit the reabsorption of water in the kidneys, causing more water to be lost in urine. You may have noticed that you urinate more when drinking these substances. With this loss of water from the system, optimal polarity and membrane potential can't be maintained in the nervous system. As you lose the water, a salt/water imbalance occurs. As available water levels decrease from drinking these dehydrating substances, the thirst centers in the hypothalamus of the brain are stimulated to send out an "I'm thirsty" call. So, we drink another of the same, which dehydrates us more and makes us even more thirsty. Remember that "cotton" mouth feeling the morning after? Bars even supply free salty peanuts and popcorn to intensify the thirst call, and then make their money on the drinks.[12]

These diuretic substances are also implicated in headaches, as they dehydrate the brain by decreasing cerebrospinal fluid production through vasoconstriction of blood vessels to the brain. The cerebrospinal fluid's job is to surround and bathe the brain, keeping it hydrated and protected from abrasion. When the water levels in the body are low, less fluid is available to produce this protective cerebrospinal fluid, and a mere 2% drop in body water can trigger fuzzy short-term memory, low energy, grogginess, trouble with basic math, and difficulty focusing on the computer screen or on a printed page. Proper amounts of water regulate body temperature, carry nutrients to cells, remove waste, keep our skin moist and elastic, cushion joints and protect our organs and tissues.[13]

Interestingly, when people are the most dehydrated, they are not thirsty. The body loses its alertness to dehydration. Your lips may be dry, your tongue may be sticking to the roof of your mouth, but you don't recognize that you are thirsty. That is the result of ignoring the body's thirst message for so long.[14]

Incidentally, fruit juice, soda and milk are high in sugars and salts, which bind up water in the body, depleting the supply available for maintaining electrolyte levels in the nerves. The body treats these as food rather than water sources, and though they eventually supply some metabolic water, initially water is used to form digestive juices to break down these drinks, so they are not an adequate source of usable water.[15]

The most sensible drink is water, and it doesn't have to be bottled water. A study done in Cleveland, Ohio showed that of the fifty-seven bottled water samples tested, only three were as pure as the local tap water.[16] Having water available in handy one-quart bottles makes regular sipping easy and keeps the system hydrated and working at optimal efficiency. An important note: drinking a lot of water all at once, may cause important salts and minerals to be washed out of the digestive system before they can be absorbed, thus decreasing the body's electrolyte balance.[17] It is better to sip water throughout the day. The inside of the mouth is pink because blood vessels lie close to the surface. Water is one of the only fluids that can go directly across the membranes of the inner mouth, into the blood vessels and then traverse the body five times every minute.[18] If this simple, but very healthful habit is new to you, it might take a little getting used to. During the first week of increased water intake, the kidneys will need to adjust, thus more bathroom breaks may be necessary.

WATER, MALNUTRITION, HEALTH AND THE NERVOUS SYSTEM

As we have seen, anything that decreases membrane polarity damages the functioning of the nervous system. Decreasing membrane polarity is, in fact, one of the effects of malnutrition. From the point of view of brain development and learning, it is one of malnutrition's most dangerous and insidious consequences.

Proteins in our diet form albumins which hold water in the blood, preventing it from seeping out just anywhere, and assuring that it will arrive where it is most needed, usually the brain. If protein intake is very low or incomplete (missing any of the ten essential amino acids), there are not enough albumins formed. This causes water to seep into body cavities, like the belly cavity (a process called third-spacing) instead of being distributed adequately to the brain and nervous tissue. We have all seen this sad outcome in pictures of malnourished children with large bellies and thin arms and legs.[19] It is also seen in people with anorexia nervosa and bulimia, or in pregnant women with preeclampsia (toxemia) where edema is very evident. For the developing fetus, it inhibits proper development, resulting in premature and low birth weight babies.[20]

The fluid/electrolyte balance is so delicate that during malnutrition, water intake may be harmful until albumin levels rise. In 1991, I was discussing the importance of water with a group of Russian psychologists when one woman mentioned that medical doctors in Russia were telling pregnant women not to drink much water. I was astounded until a doctor explained that, due to meat rationing (one pound of protein per person per month) many pregnant women suffered from toxemia. If they were to drink lots of water, it would carry other essential nutrients and salts away in their urine, possibly causing death.

People with syndromes such as inappropriate ADH secretion or psychogenic polydipsia (compulsive water drinking) might have to be careful not to drink too much water. However, for the vast majority of people, albumin levels are adequate, and drinking at least five eight ounce glasses of water daily is essential.[21] An important longitudinal study over 28 years showed that drinking five or more glasses of water daily, decreases the risk of fatal heart disease by half.[22] This supports other research that shows drinking five glasses of water a day decreases the risk of colon cancer by 45%, decreases the risk of breast cancer by 79% and decreases bladder cancer by 50%.

OXYGEN

We know that oxygen is as essential for learning as it is for life. It is essential because it breaks down food to release the energy needed for body/mind functioning. The energy that is provided by oxidation of food is so essential to the system that death occurs within only a few minutes after ceasing to breathe.

The brain makes up only one fiftieth of the body's weight and yet it uses an amazing one fifth of the body's oxygen.[23] The first artery coming out of the heart carrying freshly oxygenated blood, the carotid, goes directly to the brain. The whole system tends to take care of the brain's needs first.

Water again enters the picture as a crucial player in assisting oxygen distribution to the brain. It keeps the surface of the air sacs of the lungs moist so oxygen can dissolve and move into the blood. Researchers at the National Institute of Diabetes and Digestive and Kidney Disorder have also discovered that increased water intake increases the capacity of hemoglobin (a large protein that depends on adequate water for its structural integrity) to carry oxygen by one hundred to one thousand times.[24] Hemoglobin is the iron-bearing pigment in red blood cells that carries oxygen. Similarly, water assists digestion of foods in the digestive tract by dissolving them so enzymes can easily break them down producing the end products needed for oxidation.[25]

Once the oxygen has reached the cell, it oxidizes food there, releasing energy for production of ATP:

$$C_6H_{12}O + 6O_2 \longrightarrow 6CO_2 + 6H_2O + ATP \text{ (Used for Na}^+\text{K}^+ \text{ Pump)}$$
(glucose) (oxygen) (carbon dioxide) (water) (energy)

ATP traps energy from food and makes it available to structures within the cell, such as the sodium-potassium pump. Interestingly, a group at the Oregon Health Sciences University have provided evidence that ATP tends to be low in patients with depression and Alzheimer's disease.[26] This ATP deficiency may be due in part to inadequate oxygen uptake and distribution to the cells, caused in turn by low levels of water in the system.

It takes a physically fit body to supply the massive oxygen needs of the brain. Movement is not only essential for nerve net development and learning, but also for adequate heart and lung development to support brain function. The National Association for Sport and Physical Education (NASPE) reminds America that "Physically active, healthy kids learn better!" In order for this to happen, they recommend that elementary school students have a minimum of 60 minutes of moderate and vigorous activity every day, while middle and high school students should have a minimum of 30 minutes every day.[27] However, in 1994, only 36.3% of school children in America had daily physical education classes and that percentage has decreased currently with the push for more academic assessment. Added to that, the American Academy of Pediatrics found that 40% of all children in the United States, between ages five and eight, have at least one risk factor for heart disease. Also, fewer than half of all school children get enough exercise to develop healthy hearts and lungs.[28]

Currently, even in the face of the growing crisis in childhood obesity (up from 4.0% in 1974 for children six to elevan years old, to 15.3% in 2000), type two diabetes and increasing sedentary lifestyles, most states do not live up to the 1996 Surgeon General's report that calls for requiring daily physical education for all students from kindergarten through twelfth grade.[29] Because of concern about obesity, Scotland launched an extensive study that showed children establish a sedentary lifestyle at an early age. The median time of sedentary behavior was 70% at age three years, and 76% at age five years. Median time spent in moderate to vigorous physical activity represented only 2% of monitored hours at age three years and 4% at age five years.[30]

Movement has also greatly decreased in adult populations in the United States. Robert Dustman found that getting inactive men and women in their fifties and sixties, on a four-month brisk walking program increased their performance on mental ability tests by 10%. William Greenough and James Black found that active rats had 20% more blood vessels in their brains than sedentary rats.[31] Movement facilitates the development of increased blood vessels that carry learning-essential water, oxygen and nutrients to the brain.

Clean air is also important. Smoking during pregnancy is implicated in low birth weight babies and a higher percentage of children with learning disabilities, lower standardized test achievement, and less likelihood to go on to college.[32] In a study with 4,399 American children, it was found that even small amounts of secondhand smoke (one parent smoking less than a pack a day) reduced IQ scores by an average of two points.[33] Preschool children whose mothers smoked heavily (ten or more cigarettes daily) during pregnancy scored significantly lower (an average of nine points) on standardized IQ tests than kids whose mothers did not smoke. Smoke-exposed children may not reach their full intellectual potential. Cigarette smoke contains an estimated 2,000 to 4,000 chemicals, some of which could damage new developing nerve cells.[34]

THE EMF CONNECTION

Our bodies produce low frequency electromagnetic fields (EMFs) from the electrolyte action and polarity across each of our cell membranes. Aside from being part of the communication system within our nerves, these low-frequency electromagnetic fields provide the body with a specific rhythm of vibration. We can measure these EMFs in the brain with the EEG (Electro-encephalogram), or across the heart with the EKG (Electrocardiograph). We can even study the body's structure and function by polarizing the body in an electromagnetic field to obtain organ resonance with an MRI (Magnetic Resonance Imaging).[35]

Our EMFs are specific and delicate. Much research has been done in the past ten years about the effects of external EMFs on the human body. The research has mainly focused on possible links with fatal disease like cancer. But some of the more subtle effects may be far more important to our learning potential.

As we look at our present environments, it is very apparent that the external electromagnetic fields we are dealing with today are different from those twenty years ago. Reach back to a memory of your home twenty years ago. What were the electrical appliances and machines you had then compared to now? Today we are dealing with external fields not only from high tension wires, but satellite discs, cable TV, microwave ovens, fluorescent lights, computers, VCRs, all-electric kitchens, laundry rooms, heating, cellular phones, copy machines, analog clocks and clock radios, hair dryers, safety alarm systems, can openers, shavers and electric blankets to name a few. Electricity provides two-thirds of the energy used in residential and commercial buildings and one-third of energy used in industry, and demand is projected to double over the next forty years. There are nearly two million miles of electric lines that reach into almost every building in the nation.[36]

The earth's geomagnetic field at the middle latitudes is a thousand times more intense than the magnetic field generated by appliances in an average American home, but it is static and the human body has evolved in homeostasis with it. We now live in quite a different electromagnetic environment.

The EMFs in our homes are not static but possess alternating current producing a magnetic field that easily passes through the human body. In America, the alternating electric current goes through a complete cycle 60 times per second (60 hertz) and the associated magnetic field changes direction 120 times per second. The standard measurement of magnetic fields is in milligauss (mG) units.[37] The average background level of EMFs in a home, school or office may be 0.5 mG. When a person stands close to wiring or other conduits in the walls or floors, the levels of exposure can be 10 mG. Close to electrical devices or appliances, it can be even higher.[38]

Examples of milligauss readings on some basic appliances at a distance of 10 inches are: refrigerators average 2.6 mG, color TVs 7 mG, computers 7 mG, electric ranges 9 mG, fluorescent lights 10 mG, analog clocks and clock radios 14.8 mG, and microwave ovens 36.9 mG. At 4 inches, can openers can produce 1300-4000 mG, electric shavers produce 14-1600 mG, circular saws 200 to 2100 mG, and vacuum cleaners 230-1300 mG. These fields drop rapidly with distance. A refrigerator's EMFs drop to 1.1 mG at 2 feet and roughly 0.4 mG at 4 feet. Electric shavers drop to 0.8 –90 mg, vacuum cleaners to 20-180 mG and can openers 31-280 mG.[39, 40]

Many studies, like those from the Electric Power Research Institute (EPRI), are being done on the effects on human health of these increased non-static electromagnetic fields.[41] A thorough occupational study done in Canada and France examined more than 4,000 cases of cancer occurring over a twenty year period among some 220,000 male electric utility workers. The workers were carefully monitored for daily EMF exposure. Interestingly, those exposed to the strongest magnetic fields showed no overall increase in cancer risk. But 50% of those exposed to average fields of 1.6 mG or more show a twofold increase in the risk of developing a type of adult leukemia called acute nonlymphoid leukemia.[42]

RX FOR EMFS: PRUDENT AVOIDANCE

My interest lies in the effect of these weak (average) EMFs on our ability to learn. Closer to home, then, it is not high frequency EMFs but the ELFs (extremely low frequency electrical fields) in the previous study and in our appliances that prove most harmful because they are closest to our own EMFs. According to researchers at the Medical College in Milwaukee, Wisconsin and Sci-Con Associates in Flagstaff, Arizona, effects of EMFs appear to relate to a combination of field intensity and frequency, therefore "less is not necessarily better." They suggest "prudent avoidance" of EMFs, especially with children.[43] Experts suggest we: 1) make sure our homes are properly grounded, 2) maintain an arm's length distance from appliances, and 3) move electric alarm clocks as far from beds as practical.[44]

It seems that the technology on which our culture heavily depends gives us a big head start in developing the SOSOH traits we spoke of in the last chapter. Dr. Dee Coulter cites research showing that more newborns in technologically advanced cultures are exhibiting an "excited" state — almost a state of shock at birth. They lack the natural rhythm and coordination that, in previous generations, was established in the womb.[45] The fetus lies in amniotic fluid, a fluid/electrolyte bath that easily transmits external EMFs to the fetus. Outside EMFs may interfere with the fetus' own natural EMFs. If we consider the constant bombardment of EMFs that many pregnant women are exposed to, we can understand why babies are born "excited" and may remain that way throughout life.

The fetus normally learns rhythm and vibration through the mother's heartbeat and breathing as well as from the constant electrical impulses and EMFs being given off by these organs. This is one of the functions of the vestibular system, which fully develops and myelinates by five months in utero. Frequent exposure to external EMFs may interrupt those maternal rhythms, and may affect the baby's learning of rhythmic patterning. Learning this basic rhythmic patterning is essential to understanding patterns in math, language and basically, all learning. Babies born without this sense of internal rhythm cannot calm themselves with self-generated rocking, crooning or sucking. Instead, they just fret and more important, lose their ability to learn as easily.[46]

There is a greater likelihood that these natural rhythms may be disrupted if the mother spends hours a day at a computer, in a highly electrified office with fluorescent lights, near electrical appliances, ironing, blow drying other peoples' hair in a beauty parlor, or sleeping under an electric blanket.

Stanford University chemists noted the ability of weak external EMFs to disrupt lipid membranes such as those that serve as the gatekeepers for chemicals entering or exiting cells (for example, the sodium-potassium pump). This would not only affect cellular function in a developing embryo/fetus, but would also affect that child's later learning skills (all of which are dependent on proper functioning of sodium-potassium pumps in the nervous system).[47] I wonder what are the effects of sonograms and fetal monitors, routinely used, often as early as the fourth or fifth month when the vestibular system is developing?

Awareness and prudent use of electricity in our living and learning environments might achieve a lot. In my own experience in the classroom, I have observed the remarkable effect of just turning off the fluorescent lights. There is often a physical sigh from the students, and the excited energy decreases markedly. Today, schools are often built with no windows and banks of fluorescent lights. As a result, children may have to work extra hard to overcome the unbalanced EMFs from the fluorescent lights, with little energy left over to concentrate and learn.

Natural lighting, and even incandescent lights have a great advantage over fluorescent lights. Sunlight is easier for the eye to process, and does not increase the ambient EMFs in the work or school environment. In Russia, classrooms have a wall of large windows and very few light bulbs. And in

Denmark, it is mandated by law that every school child and working adult be able to see nature from their seat or workspace. Every building in Denmark is full of windows.

When I have spent the day working on my computer, I can definitely sense a major energy drain. If I don't take the time to get out in nature and walk, I have just barely enough energy to drag myself onto the couch to be zapped by more external EMFs from the TV.

Bone and fat (low water content tissues) are less affected by external EMFs than high water content tissues like the brain, muscles and kidneys. Considering that the brain is approximately ninety percent water, external EMFs must have some effect on its efficiency.

The importance of drinking water in order to maintain adequate, balanced electrolyte concentrations for high polarity across all the cellular membranes, cannot be overestimated. Water is an essential ingredient in maintaining the body's natural EMFs against these external fields.

10

⮾

Basics for the Brain: Nutrition

We all know that good, balanced nutrition is important to learning, but what does that mean? It means making sure the raw materials for healthy bodies, and especially the nervous system, are available. These include protein, carbohydrates and fats. It also means being careful not to weaken the body's ability to protect and restore itself by over-eating the unhealthy things, notably sugar.

Proteins and fats provide the major building blocks for the membranes of all the cells in our body. Specifically, they form the structure of the developing nerves and their networks. Proteins also form the structure of the sodium-potassium pump to maintain polarity and assure proper nerve transmission throughout our system. In addition, they are involved in the hemoglobin structure (which enables blood to transport oxygen), in the contractile elements in muscle fibers, and serve as antibodies, hormones and enzymes.

Proteins are made up of long chains of amino acids that are assembled according to our DNA code. As proteins form, they fold on to themselves to create characteristic crystalline structures that facilitate their specific functions. Water plays an essential role in the building of the protein molecule. Proteins trap water as they crystallize, with water accounting for 27% to 77% of the crystal's volume. This allows water to influence and maximize the fine-scale structure and function of the protein.[1, 2]

Our diets must be balanced to include all ten essential amino acids necessary for the synthesis of proteins and the essential fatty acids that produce our hormones and myelin sheaths. These essential amino and fatty acids cannot be synthesized by the human body from molecules present in the body. Chicken eggs and fish provide all the essential amino and fatty acids. Dairy products that have been pre-digested such as yogurt, cottage cheese, kefir, feta cheese and goat cheese are good sources of the essential amino acids. Nuts, fish oils and olive oil are good sources of healthy fatty acids. Vegetarians must be very careful to combine foods in such a way that all essential amino and fatty acids are included in their diets.[3]

Pregnant women should be eating approximately 70 grams of protein and about the same of fatty acids a day to provide the building blocks for the developing fetus. Children especially need extra protein and fats, as they form 90% of the nerve cells and dendritic extensions in their bodies before age five. They also need more proteins and fats to provide the membranes of new growing cells all through their growth years. The diets of children with learning difficulties are often deficient in proteins and fats. Just having a child eat an egg in the morning, instead of cereal, and providing snacks of cheese, yogurt, or nuts, will go far towards giving them the needed building blocks for learning.[4]

Carbohydrates, which consist of long molecular chains of sugars, provide the main energy source for our bodies. They are the primary ingredients of grains, fruits, vegetables and dairy sugar. Each of these sources contains two simple sugars, one of which is a molecule of glucose — the main source of energy for the brain. This is the molecule that is broken down (oxidized) by oxygen to yield energy that is then trapped in ATP. The byproducts of this process are carbon dioxide (CO_2) and water, which are then exhaled and later recycled by plants back into more food. Carbohydrates are essential, but they must be balanced with proteins and fats.

SUGAR AND THE SOSOH PERSON

When I speak at schools, I am often asked what I would do immediately to assist learning. My answer always begins with three items: First, ban TV, computers and video games before the age of eight to give imagination a chance to develop. For older children, keep viewing time to a minimum (less than 1 hour a day) and monitor the programs for violence to cut out a major source of adrenalin producing stress in the learner's life. (I've already discussed TV in Chapter 4, and will again in Chapter 12.) Second, institute a daily integrative movement program for the whole family that is fun. An hour of outdoor unstructured play or inside rough-and-tumble play, walking, swimming, dancing and integrative sports that are cooperative rather than competitive would be best. Brain Gym, Tai Chi, yoga are examples of movement programs for every learner both in classrooms, workspaces and at home. These insure optimal learning readiness and frontal lobe activation. And third, decrease or, better yet, eliminate simple sugars in peoples' diets. If glucose is essential for brain function, why do I make this statement?

This recommendation actually encompasses more than sugar. Sugar is one player in a whole cycle of stress, disease, and immune system factors that contribute to learning problems. The whole cycle probably starts with stress and increased adrenalin, leading to lowered membrane potential and polarity. This in turn leads to food sensitivities (usually milk, wheat and corn) with 6 – 8% of children under age three having allergies[5] and a depressed immune systems, which of course leads to infections, particularly respiratory disorders and ear infections.[6] Persistent, recurring ear infections (discussed in Chapter 11) are seen in 94% to 97% of children with learning disabilities. These chronic infections damage the vestibular system and inhibit maximal stimulation to the reticular activating system. This decreases the brain's ability to stay alert, focus and learn.[7]

Persistent, recurring ear infections also lead to long term, repeated treatments with broad spectrum antibiotics. Antibiotics do nothing for viral infection. Waickman notes that "Sixty percent of illnesses which take children to doctors are viral. Yet, many of these viral illnesses are treated with antibiotics."[8] Broad spectrum antibiotics alter all the natural flora of the body, decreasing the beneficial lactobacillus organisms which produce acid that holds down the growth of yeast and other organisms. Antibiotics can also interfere with the ability of the immune system to limit fungal (yeast) infections by decreasing the ability of white blood cells to destroy (phagocytize) yeast organisms.[9]

Since the yeast (candida albicans) grows back faster than the lactobacillus, yeast flourishes in the system. It then thrives and reproduces on excess

Figure 10.1: The Stress-Infection-Antibiotic-Yeast-Sugar-Toxins Cycle

sugars in the body supplied by diets rich in carbohydrates and sugars. This reproduction causes a yeast overgrowth situation. Yeast utilizes sugars as its main food source, releasing toxins (acetaldehyde and alcohol).[10] These toxins further adversely affect the immune system by decreasing the availability of essential omega-3 and -6 fatty acids. These fatty acids are necessary for the formation of prostaglandins, which stimulate T-lymphocyte function to resist allergies and infections.[11] T-lymphocytes, produced in the thymus gland, are key elements in the immune system.[12] With fewer T-lymphocytes, the body becomes overly sensitive and reacts to other foods (chocolate, cola, citrus, eggs), and to environmental allergens, chemicals and other stimuli.

This oversensitivity to environmental stimuli from the stress-infection-antibiotic-yeast-sugar-toxins cycle often manifests itself in fears and phobias prevalent among dyslexics. Harold Levinson identifies heightened sensitivity to fluorescent lights and photo-phobia as consequences of ear disorders from childhood infections and high sugar diets which result in yeast overgrowth.[13] Children with reduced sensory acuity, poor hearing and balance due to infections, don't fully experience their environments. It seems likely that these children could develop fears and phobias leading to even greater stress.

Greater stress would, again, lead to infections as the cycle continues. With high sugar consumption thrown in, yeast overgrowth and the ensuing toxins could lead to over-sensitivity. External, low frequency electromagnetic fields might also exacerbate this whole cycle as they disrupt and weaken cellular membranes.

The toxins released by yeast overgrowth include alcohol. Dr. Waickman found that 60% of the population has some yeast in the alimentary tract capable of producing some alcohol in the stomach.[14] With diets high in carbohydrates and sugars, the conditions are right for further yeast overgrowth and alcohol production. Alcohol is easily carried directly into the blood from the digestive system, and primarily affects the frontal lobes of the brain. Within the frontal lobes, it inhibits nerve net growth and proper development and function. The symptoms show up as decreased attention span, behavior problems, disruptive conduct, irritability, increased sugar cravings, hyperactivity, depression and autistic behavior.[15, 16] This is dramatically seen in Fetal Alcohol Syndrome.

The effects of alcohol in the system can be far-reaching, particularly in the frontal lobes, because they are responsible for fine motor coordination, high level formal reasoning and inner speech to control one's behavior. If you have had a "bit to drink," what do you notice about your fine motor coordination? How about your high level formal reasoning? And what does alcohol do to your ability to control your behavior in alignment with social norms? These are the same symptoms I have noticed consistently in SOSOH people. Close to one hundred percent of the SOSOH people I've known and worked with have had high dietary sugar and carbohydrate intake.

In the past fifty years, sugar has become more readily accessible to the general public and its use has skyrocketed. Between 1957 and 1977, dairy product consumption declined by 21%, while sugar consumption increased dramatically: soft drink consumption up 80%, cookies pies and desserts up 70%, and snacks up 85%. TV has contributed to this trend, familiarizing children with sugar more than any other kind of food.[17]

One way to stop the yeast overgrowth/alcohol cycle is to cut sugars in the diet. It is important to note that all carbohydrates are simply chains of sugars and that fruits are very high in sugars. Sugar also means brown sugar, honey, molasses, maple syrup, fructose sugar, and corn syrup. So even such an ordinary meal as breakfast cereal with sugar and fruit is a real sugar whammy.

Reading food labels is essential in any sugar reducing effort. Very important is a balanced diet, rich in protein (meat, eggs, nuts, yogurt, cottage cheese, beans), vegetables that supply calcium, magnesium, Vitamin C and the B complex, chromium, zinc and essential fatty acids. I would love to see vending machines in schools that provide nuts, apples, yogurt, cottage cheese or vegetables in place of the usual fare. SOSOH children and adults I have worked with have commented that their sugar cravings have decreased when they drink more water.

The same symptoms of SOSOH occur in Fetal Alcohol Syndrome, which is believed to cause frontal lobe damage in utero that then can affect learning the rest of the child's life.[18] Also a genetic predisposition to alcoholism has been found to be connected with hyperactivity.[19] If you have been around alcoholics, you've probably noticed that they gravitate to sugars when they are "on the wagon." The bottom line is that with stress and high dietary intake of sugars, anyone can produce their own alcohol, which will affect frontal lobe functioning. Even as "teetotalers," these children and adults are producing their own alcohol from the stress/sugar/yeast cycle.

We should be aware of one additional and remarkably adverse characteristic of yeast in our system: they have receptor sites for cortisol, which means that yeast produces cortisol. As we will see in our consideration of stress in Chapter 12, while cortisol serves a valuable purpose for the mind and body on alert for danger, it decreases learning and memory function.[20]

11

The Vestibular System and Learning Disorders

All learning in the first fifteen months of life is centered on vestibular system development. The word vestibule means entryway, and this system is the entry way into the conscious brain. Balance, locomotion, discrimination of speech and language, coordination of vision with movement, all of these fundamental abilities, which we learn early and rely on the rest of our lives depend upon the proper functioning of the vestibular system. Additionally, the vestibular system maintains the all important arousal state (through the reticular activating system RAS) necessary to be conscious, alert and responsive.

HOW THE VESTIBULAR SYSTEM GETS DAMAGED

Disturbance to the vestibular system causes major learning difficulties. Researchers Frank and Harold Levinson found that 94% to 97% of children with dyslexia and learning disabilities showed two or more abnormal neurological or ENG (electronystagmographic) parameters indicating a cerebellar/vestibular system dysfunction.[1,2] All of these children had experienced trauma to the cerebellar/vestibular system in the form of ear infections, allergies, or having been "shaken" as infants. The two major causes of ear infections in the U.S. are: sidestream cigarette smoke from a smoker in the home, and bottle feeding, where the position the baby is held in causes milk to reflux up the Eustachian tubes. In both cases, infection occurs in the Eustachian tubes and moves to the inner ear, affecting normal vestibular development and function.

As we saw in Chapter 10, yeast overgrowth has also been implicated in cerebellar/vestibular system dysfunction.

Damage can occur even before birth. A study of seasonal birth patterns showed that viral infections (influenza, measles) during the second trimester of pregnancy (when the vestibular system and VIIIth cranial nerve, the vestibulo-cochlear are developing) are contributing causes of hyperactivity, language difficulties and mental retardation, as well as of autism and schizophrenia.[3]

LACK OF VESTIBULAR DEVELOPMENT AND LABELED BEHAVIOR

In children identified as ADD (Attention Deficit Disorder), Hyperactive or ADHD (Attention Deficit Hyperactive Disorder), stress and lack of vestibular system development cause low or erratic RAS function. These children may flicker in and out of wakefulness, especially if there is no movement stimulation, which leads to hypo- or hyper-vigilance with difficulty in maintaining attention, concentration or focus.[4] They tend to lose their balance easily and have more playground accidents. They often invade other people's space without knowing it, exhibiting an incomplete understanding of spatial relationships in their environment. They can't stand still, but they can run, since running is more like a propelled fall and doesn't demand as much balance as standing still, standing or hopping on one foot, skipping, jumping or doing the slow, cross-lateral movements that stimulate new cell growth in the hippocampus.[5] They "noodle" in their desks because the back and neck muscles haven't been adequately trained to hold their bodies upright against gravity.[6] If these children are not given full freedom and encouragement to move and practice balance when they are little, there may be too little vestibular activation to assist proper growth and development.

Children truly want to be "good." In order to "stay alert" where there has been inadequate vestibular development, they must move, wiggle and constantly turn their heads. Often this is precisely how they first get tagged with the ADD, Hyperactive or ADHD labels. Teachers become frustrated with their constant movement and tell them to "sit still." Wanting to stay alert, the children's next strategy is to activate their balance centers by tilting their chairs so that only the back two legs of the chair are supporting them. The teacher's response is to demand that they "sit up right and pay attention." But this is a contradiction for these children. If their heads and bodies are still, there will be reduced activation of their brains. These children are also the ones asked to stay in during recess to complete work — when the best thing for them would to go outside and move.

At least one in five U.S. grade-schoolers with average or above-average intelligence encounters severe difficulties in learning to read.[7] Dyslexia has been considered a visual problem because it shows up and by definition is associated with reading difficulties. Interestingly, the central deficit with dyslexia, which is universal in all languages, is related to the metalinguistic ability to decompose words into sounds, link the sounds (phonemes) to symbols and to make these skills automatic.[8] The development of that phonemic understanding is thought to begin in utero, possibly as early as 9 weeks, as the semicircular canals develop and the embryo responds to sound with movement. At that time the Moro reflex develops which allows the embryo/fetus/child to respond to danger with a protective action. If there is much maternal stress, the fetus will often be in the Moro reflex and the other reflexes important for vestibular development, will be delayed. Without this development, the fetus and child will have difficulty hearing the patterns of language, the phonemes, and later linking them to symbols to read. [9, 10, 11, 12]

The primary area of the brain implicated in phoneme deficit is the temporal gyrus that has to do with hearing.[13, 14] Dyslexic individuals, also show a significantly smaller corpus callosum.[15] Incidentally, research shows that the temporal lobes and corpus callosum are larger and more developed in musicians and singers. The primary sensory and motor cortex, premotor cortex, and supplementary motor area (SMA) also show up as undeveloped .[16] All of these areas are developed through movement as the reflexes mature into balanced integrated movement and a well developed vestibular system.

Regarding the eyes, lack of cerebellar/vestibular development shows up in the muscles that control the movement of the eyes (extraocular muscle dysmetria) causing them to overshoot or undershoot their position of optimal effectiveness when reading — again a symptom of an underdeveloped vestibular system. The dyslexic must concentrate so much on moving his eyes that cerebral input for comprehension or retention is limited. Lack of movement and keeping the head still for long periods of time (as with watching TV, or having to sit still and be quiet in school) has also been implicated in acquired dyslexic symptomology.[17, 18] Movement, music and much interactive communication in the child's early environment promotes the development of hearing discrimination whereby the child is able to say the phonemes and actively voice the language, and then associate the sounds with symbols later on, in order to read.[19, 20, 21]

In Denmark, fifty percent of the children spend between ages two and a half and six in Forest Kindergartens where they climb rocks, trees, hills, roll, jump, balance and play at least four hours a day no matter what the weather.[22] These children's vestibular systems are so well developed that learning difficulties and dyslexia are rare. If teachers do notice a child is having learning difficulties, they immediately involve the child in music and/or choir, and set up a movement program with an Occupational or Physical Therapist, which develop the vestibular system and stop the difficulty.[23]

The vesibular system and sound are so important to the whole learning process, specifically language development, and pattern understanding in areas such as mathematics, that I have dedicated two chapters to this subject in *Awakening The Child Heart, Handbook for Global Parenting*.[24] There you will find the research behind possible steps to dyslexia and how to make a difference.

WHY INTEGRATED MOVEMENTS, MUSIC AND PLAY HELP

When children move, damaged tissue to and from the vestibular system can be overridden as new nerve nets develop and myelinate. As we saw in Chapter 3, the benefits of cerebellar vestibular stimulation — movement — on cognitive growth during infancy are well established.[25] Gross motor and cognitive retardation in deaf children can be eliminated by stimulating the semicircular canal system through movement.[26] First graders who engaged in physical exercise periods that emphasized movement requiring maximum cerebellar/vestibular system control, sharply reduced their rates of academic failure.[27] Another study reports that movement and stimulation of balance greatly assist attentional disorders and improve reading.[28]

Figure 11.1: Forest Kindergarten Children Developing Their Sense Of Balance

Integrated cross-lateral activities such as crawling, climbing, rolling, spinning, walking on uneven ground, skipping, jumping, Brain Gyms®, Tai Chi, Yoga, and spontaneous joy-filled play specifically stimulate and develop the cerebellar/vestibular system.[29] Walking on low boards, or climbing a rope ladder, monkey bars, large rocks or trees requires an amazing amount of balance, thus activating the vestibular system and strengthening hand-eye coordination. Spinning, rolling down hills, and balancing on an exercise ball involves the core muscles of the torso, and activates the semi-circular canal system, which activates all muscles and assists vision. Simply placing the hand on the navel, as in Brain Buttons, assists balance and brings attention to the gravitational center of the body.

Sounding one's own voice is a strong stimulator of the vestibular system. Imaging studies show that the frontal lobe areas of the brain connected with the vestibular system, enable proper construction of the syntax of both music and language. Many areas of the brain handle related aspects of language and music. When singing, the tongue ligaments directly stimulate the semicircular canals. The intricate cross-lateral movements required to play a musical instrument or even to dance, directly stimulate the vestibular system, growing and strengthening it.

Brain responses depend on the experience and training of the listener Even a little training can alter the brain reaction. Youngsters, age 4 and 5 years old, who have received greater exposure to music in their homes showed enhanced brain auditory activity, compared to 8 year old children who did not get the music exposure. These youngsters showed greater ease in learning, speaking and reading the language.[30] Students who studied music in the curriculum did far better on Stadardized tests than students without music — and over time, students who took music lessons for four or more years scored the highest on Stadardized tests. In a study of slow readers, just five months of playing a musical instrument (violin, recorder or other instrument where rhythms could be felt against the body or teeth), improved their reading scores by an average of four and a half years.[31, 32, 33, 34, 35] The auditory cortex of musicians is more extensive with a 130% larger volume than non-musicians, making it easier for them to discriminate and respond to sounds and understand the important patterns of language, math, and all cognitive learning.[36]

Simply put, integrated movements, done in a playful, coherent way with music, activate the entire vestibular system, large areas of the motor cortex, and frontal eye field area of the frontal lobes; and produce chemicals, such as dopamine which assist enthusiastic learning and memory. Consistent, frequent activation of the motor cortex and frontal eye field area, promotes nerve-net elaboration, growth and myelination into the rest of the frontal lobe including the pre-motor and superior pre-frontal cortex for high-level thinking and creativity as well as more grace, balance, and control of all our muscles The profound healing that occurred in Amy and Brandy, whose stories I shared in Chapter 1, are directly related to developing the vestibular system.

12

~

Fight or Flight — The Stress Effect on Learning

The highest priority of all living organisms is, simply, to live. From the moment we are born, food, oxygen and water are essential to daily life maintenance. No less critical for survival is the capacity to sense and avoid danger. Nourishment and protection from danger are so essential that a whole range of instinctive drives and automatic processes have evolved in the human body/mind system to insure that these fundamental requirements are satisfied. Of course, hunger and thirst are familiar experiences to everyone. Less evident perhaps are the self-protective instincts that our body/minds trigger whenever we sense threatening circumstances in the environment.

What we have coined "the stress reaction" is actually our survival reaction to perceived threat of death that prepares the individual to mentally and physically take protective action. In times of real danger, these survival instincts are invaluable. They heighten our sensitivity to the environment, making us hypervigilant. They intensify muscle strength, blood flow and oxygen distribution. But the stress/survival response does not make us smart, creative or rational. In fact these instinctive processes are largely carried out in the brain stem and sympathetic nervous system with little activation of the rational areas of the brain.

Unfortunately, we often allow this excellent survival mechanism to take over during the many non-threatening situations in our lives. Living with chronic stress has detrimental, far-reaching consequences. The American Medical Association contends that well over 90% of illness is stress related. In this chapter we will explore the dynamics of stress, its impact on our nervous and immune systems, and its effects on our health and capacity to learn.

WHAT HAPPENS WHEN WE GO ON ALERT

When we are confronted with a threat, one of our body's responses is to send out powerful chemical messengers that put our entire systems on high alert for danger, and provide extra energy for the system to fight or flee. Among the most well known of these substances are adrenalin (norepinephrine) and cortisol.

Though everything that happens in our life is simply an event, the creativity of the mind determines how we perceive things. If we perceive something as a threat, adrenalin and cortisol are secreted to protect us from danger. Threats come in many forms and degrees, depending on our unique perceptions of the world. How do you feel about taking a test, meeting someone new, giving a speech, handling a business deal, being on a plane, being in an airless room with smokers, work or school deadlines, having a party, getting married, dealing with death, or even taking some quiet time alone? The possibilities are endless. As long as we continue to perceive a situation as a threat, we secrete adrenalin into our system.

The survival response is initiated by the heart and amygdala, and orchestrated by the brain stem, with adrenalin being secreted at the nerve endings of the sympathetic nervous system and the adrenal medulla of the adrenal glands. The sympathetic nervous system — a part of the autonomic nervous system — usually operates without conscious control and regulates the activities of smooth muscles, cardiac muscle and certain glands. The sympathetic branch is concerned with processes involving the expenditure of energy, particularly during perceived danger, and sets up the fight or flight response. Adrenalin reinforces the body's primary defenses by increasing blood flow to the heart, lungs and large muscles, especially of the arms and legs, away from the digestive system and the brain. This blood flow insures a greater dispersal of electrolytes to the membranes of these muscles so they can contract — preparing us to fight or flee. That's probably the original reason why we are warned not to swim directly after we eat. If you feel that swimming is dangerous, your fear can cause adrenalin to be released, which in turn moves blood away from the digestive system to the big muscles. This causes stomach cramps. So if you perceive swimming as dangerous, swimming immediately after eating might indeed be dangerous.

This overall bodily dispersal of electrolytes causes cell membrane potential throughout the body to decrease from the normal of -70 mv to -60 mv or lower. It's like turning on all the faucets in an apartment building — everybody gets some water but the pressure is low. Every cell gets some electrolytes, but because of more widespread dispersal, the levels are lower, thus lowering the membrane potential.

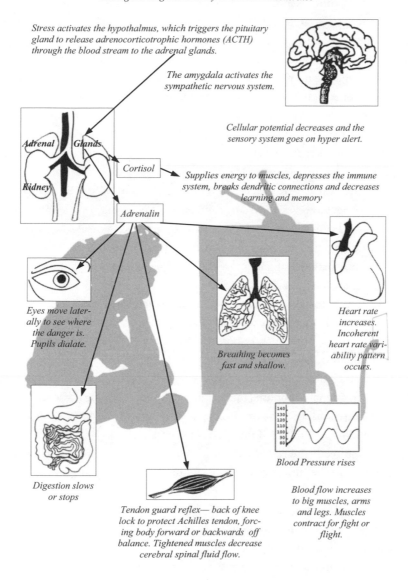

Stress produces upper beta brain waves for reaction. Blood flow decreases to the cerebral cortex especially to the frontal lobes and non-dominant hemisphere causing learning and memory to decrease. Incoherence

Stress activates the hypothalmus, which triggers the pituitary gland to release adrenocorticotrophic hormones (ACTH) through the blood stream to the adrenal glands.

The amygdala activates the sympathetic nervous system.

Adrenal Glands

Kidney

Cellular potential decreases and the sensory system goes on hyper alert.

Cortisol

Supplies energy to muscles, depresses the immune system, breaks dendritic connections and decreases learning and memory

Adrenalin

Eyes move laterally to see where the danger is. Pupils dialate.

Breathing becomes fast and shallow.

Heart rate increases. Incoherent heart rate variability pattern occurs.

Blood Pressure rises

Digestion slows or stops

Tendon guard reflex— back of knee lock to protect Achilles tendon, forcing body forward or backwards off balance. Tightened muscles decrease cerebral spinal fluid flow.

Blood flow increases to big muscles, arms and legs. Muscles contract for fight or flight.

Figure 12.1: Physiological Reaction to Stress

When the membrane potential is lower, it requires less stimuli to activate the defense systems throughout the body. Our sensory apparatus becomes hyper-sensitive, alert to everything that is happening in the environment so we know where danger lies. Even the eyes move peripherally and the pupils dilate to better take in every aspect of our environment that might pose a threat. Meanwhile, as muscles contract in preparation for fight or flight, they generate heat. To protect delicate internal organs from this heat, the body sweats, thus increasing water loss and decreasing cell membrane polarity further by -16 mv or more, from the average of -70 mv to -54 mv, or less.

Blood flow is markedly decreased to the cerebral cortex of the brain, especially the frontal lobes and the non-dominant hemisphere. This decrease in function may act as an efficiency mechanism, allowing the body to react without the need for higher thought processing.[4, 5] Lower membrane potential, while making us more alert to smaller stimuli, disables our capacity to selectively focus and control our sensory input. At such times, learning is very difficult.

Adrenalin release is a graded response dependent on the level of threat to the system. However, once adrenalin is released at the nerve endings and into the blood from the adrenal glands, it takes a while to break it down. The liver must detoxify all the adrenalin before we feel completely calm again. We all know the experience of going to a scary movie, and returning home only to find it takes a while to relax.

During stress, the cortex of the adrenal glands also secretes a group of hormones called the glucocorticoids. Cortisol (hydrocortisone) is the most abundant of these hormones, responsible for about 95% of all glucocorticoid activity. In stress conditions, cortisol causes the release of fat and sugar into the blood stream to provide the needed energy for efficient muscle function. If the circulating fat is not used up in fight or flight it can clog the arteries that feed the heart leading to heart disease, and obesity as the unused fat settles back into body tissues.[6, 7, 8] Obesity has become a real problem world-wide, and may be directly linked to higher stress levels today. Cortisol also constricts blood vessels to the surface of the body, which increases blood pressure to the core of the body and the muscles to protect the surface of the body so it will not lose valuable fluids if wounded.[9] (Cortisone cream, widely used as an anti-inflammatory, causes swelling to go down by constricting blood vessels and reducing fluids to an injured area.)

Cortisol also decreases the uptake of protein by 70% so new cells, both nerve and other body cells, don't have the building blocks necessary to grow and develop, and it causes dendrites and nerve branches to die off, leading to greatly decreased learning and memory.[10, 11, 12, 13] Research at McGill University concluded that increased cortisol correlated with decreased learning and memory as well as attention problems.[14] When we are under stress, we normally remember less than we otherwise would, and this relates directly to increased cortisol in the system. No wonder it is difficult to focus and remember under stress!

When we are on alert, geared up to fight or flee, the entire system is very sensitive to any and all external stimuli — a flash of movement, a pencil dropping, someone whispering, etc. The brain waves become faster (in the higher Beta range), and we react.[15]

Any or all of the stressors mentioned in the chart "What Inhibits Learning" in Chapter 8, can be perceived by a child as a threat rather than a learning experience or healthy challenge. Children in situations they perceive to be dangerous react with scattered attention, "climbing the walls" and fighting. This is a normal response to stress. And yet we label these children "ADD — Attention Deficit Disorder," "ADHD — Attention Deficit Hyperactive Disorder," "Hyperactive" or "emotionally handicapped" rather than seriously addressing the stressful situation so the child can learn.

THE TENDON GUARD REFLEX

Another example of the body/mind's profound and intricate reaction to stress can be found at the muscular level, in the "tendon guard reflex." This reflex, an automatic process triggered by stress, shortens the calf muscles and locks the backs of the knees, thereby preparing the body to stand and fight or run from danger. The tendon guard reflex is a feedback mechanism that protects tendons and associated muscles from excessive tension. It causes the muscles associated with the Achilles tendon (gastrocnemius) to contract while antagonistic muscles (tibialis) relax, thus shifting movement to the toes.[16]

When the back of the knees lock and the body moves forward onto the toes during stress, the rest of the body must align to maintain balance. The muscles of the lower back and neck contract to keep us straight and balanced. The tendon guard reflex is meant to occur only for a short time as we prepare to fight or run. But with such high levels of stress in our society today, many people end up with their knees, lower backs and necks almost perpetually locked. This immobility of the spine also decreases natural cerebral spinal fluid flow around the brain. And back muscles can be pulled so tight that people end up with lower back problems or herniated discs between the vertebrae. In the U.S., eighty percent of the population is hobbled with lower back pain during their lives, sixty-four percent with pathologies, most probably due to stress.[17]

Shortened calf muscles, as evidenced by "toe walking" often show up in autistic and speech-impaired people. These people may be exhibiting an exaggerated tendon guard reflex in response to intense stress. From the work I've done with autistic and speech-impaired children, I believe there may be a link between shortened calf (gastrocnemius) muscles and the inability to speak. In a perpetual state of stress, the calf muscles naturally tend to shorten, and at the same time speech is inhibited. It is difficult to talk when you are running or fighting for your life!

The potential significance of the link between the tendon guard reflex and speech was first suggested to me by my experience with an autistic eight-year old boy who had never spoken. He was placed in the hearing-impaired class at his elementary school, where he would sit in the corner and rock all day. His teacher, a specialist for the hearing-impaired, used Brain Gym® activities she had learned from me at a Hawaii State Teachers Association conference. Some calf relaxing activities were among the Brain Gym® activities she used three to four times a day.[18] After about two weeks he began participating in some of the activities in a limited way. Two weeks later he uttered his first words which grew into sentences within that week. The teacher contacted me to talk to the excited and joyful parents.

In my subsequent personal work with autistic and speech-impaired children, I have continued to use activities that consciously bring neural attention away from the survival response, and relax the calf muscles and the whole back of the body. The results have included dramatic success with speech development. All the autistic children I have worked with who had never spoken before were able to speak within weeks after doing these activities. This link with relaxed calf muscles and speech is profound and should be more closely investigated.

Parents can assist their child in relaxing the tendon guard reflex. The child sits or lays down on her back on the floor and the parents place both hands on the bottoms of her feet, gently pushing the ball of each foot (the rounded broad part between the toes and arch) forward so that the calf muscles relax. Many children love to push simultaneously with their feet against the parent's applied pressure, especially when goaded to "push me away," "push me really hard." The contraction during the push allows the calf to further relax. This relaxation has an interesting link to verbal skills, and I've found it to greatly facilitate communication in speech-impaired and autistic children.

CHRONIC STRESS

In a tight spot, the survival response is more compelling than formal reasoning. We can afford to give up some focus and rationality once in a while to get out of a jam fast. But the cost quickly mounts when stress is pervasive.

Perpetually responding to a stressful world with survival oriented (SOSOH) behavior takes its toll on the nervous system. Because the nerve net development and myelination is focused in the survival areas, nerve net development into the limbic system and neocortex is limited. People who live with a great deal of stress may inadequately develop the neural pathways that form the foundations for new learning, reasoning and creativity.

When a person is attentively learning, their dopamine levels are high and their adrenalin and cortisol levels are low. If confronted with a threat, the dopamine levels drop, adrenalin levels rise sharply and cortisol rises, but not as high as adrenalin. In this state, the person subconsciously believes they can successfully run or fight to save themselves.[19]

Chronically stressed out survival oriented people are often unaware of how stressed they are, because for them it has become a way of life. Hans Selye calls that unawareness the General Adaptive Syndrome (GAS), a complex physiological mechanism designed to permit the body to adapt continually to stress. If this mechanism is functioning normally, the body and mind are able to adapt to a wide range of stresses and assaults.[20] Adaptation, however, does not include higher thinking skills or creative functioning.

Often in our Western society, this state of adaptation becomes one of hopelessness and turns into depression. In the depressed state, cortisol is high, adrenalin is not quite as high and dopamine is very low. Dopamine provides that emotional spark of enthusiasm in the brain that motivates us to live fully, so when it is low, the person lacks motivation and can become depressed. In 1999, 2.5% of children and up to 8.3% of adolescents in the U.S. suffered from depression.[21, 22] The onset of depression in children is occurring earlier and earlier.[23] Depression in children and adolescents is associated with an increased risk of suicidal behaviors. Suicide was the third leading cause of death in 1997 in people aged ten to twenty-four years old. As many as seven percent of young adults who develop major depression as adolescents may commit suicide.[24, 25, 26]

Consider some of the seemingly ever-present stressors in our technological society that might lead to depression and lack of learning and memory: projected fear of violence or death (perpetuated by the news media and by TV programming with an average of twelve acts of violence every hour), insecurity about the future with unstable home, school and work situations; mandated testing and assessment programs; competition in schools or the job market and; the fast pace of life. Without effective stress management, we limit our ability to be creative, productive, joyfully learning individuals throughout life.

COMMUNICATING STRESS TO CHILDREN

Our stress response may start early in life, even as early as the womb. Fetuses can be affected by their mothers' adrenalin levels. Pregnant women, when they feel stressed, often notice a difference in their babies' in-utero movements compared to times when they feel peaceful and relaxed. Because the mother's stress causes her heart rate variability to be incoherent, the child may later have difficulties with organizing patterns of information to easily learn language or math, for instance.[27] Babies who have experienced high stress in utero exhibit sleep and feeding disorders, reduced resistance to disease, and can have as much as a sixty percent delay in their normal development. Since the womb is such a profound place of learning, awareness of stress and how to manage it should be a priority during pregnancy.

Infants are highly sensitive to the emotions of their caregivers (parents, family and friends). They can immediately sense the fears and tensions around them, and become stressed themselves. This is often apparent in first babies, especially boys.[28] Because boy babies are developmentally about two to three weeks behind girl babies at birth, their digestive systems aren't as well developed as girls'. They need to eat more often, urinate more often, thus they sleep less and cry more. If the parents become overly tired or concerned, their fears and anxieties can be perceived by the child, whose primary focus is survival; and he may become colicky. Aside from teething, parental anxiety is possibly the main cause of fussiness in healthy babies whose basic needs have been met.

Twenty percent of mothers suffer from pre or postpartum depression.[29] They tend to be anxious and feel their lives are out of control. Their babies are more likely to be small (low birth weight), also more likely to be drowsy as infants, cry a lot, and show tension by squirming and arching their backs. As toddlers, they tend to be especially emotional and later on exhibit a variety of behavior problems, many of which last into adolescence.[30, 31]

SOSOH AND THE FAMILY

The family is where all the important first modeling of behavior occurs. Coherent, peaceful and safe home environments help to shield children from many of the factors that lead to SOSOH. Alternatively, if parents and other caregivers live highly stressful, disruptive lives, their children may imprint that training onto their own nervous systems.

Many home-based factors can promote SOSOH behavior. Poorly performing students are often from low socioeconomic families. They may have experienced poor nutrition, lack of early sensory enrichment and high family stress, even violence.[32] We are also seeing a higher percentage of "abandoned children" from wealthy families, children abandoned to TV, computers and videogames with a lack of human connection. When children are heavily stressed in dysfunctional homes, they suffer. They may not get support and attention. The essence of who they are may never surface. In their efforts to be OK in the face of their models, the SOSOH pattern develops. The symptoms develop from the instinct for survival and the need to be accepted, not from conscious understanding. With survival as their primary goal, the higher centers of thought and regulation may just not develop, though the full potential is there.

Sharon Wegschneider Cruise's portrait of the "Mascot" survival role fits a majority of SOSOH people. According to Cruise, Mascots tend to play the clown, vying for either positive or negative attention. This serves two purposes: to be recognized, and to siphon off family or social tension by their actions. They are caught in a painful contradiction: what they experience in their lives is chaos, but they are told everything is fine. Because they trust what is being said to them, Mascots become unable to trust their own intuition and may have the illusion of being crazy. They feel fragile, insecure and anxious, thus exhibiting a lack of confidence and self-esteem. Their actions are geared to gain attention at any cost. Sometimes, if they push, they get this attention in the form of physical abuse, but at least it provides the basic human need for touch.[33, 34]

Scientific findings show that children are more highly susceptible to their environment than was previously believed. Such stressful experiences as witnessing domestic violence and undergoing abuse activate the survival hormones that impair normal cerebral development, and can lead to intellectual and behavioral problems in adulthood.[35] Early trauma can so change brain functioning that a lifelong pattern of brain activity producing an exaggerated response to stress becomes established, leaving the body at a loss to adapt appropriately.[36]

As a counselor, working with variously labeled SOSOH children in grades K-8, I found about 95% of them assuming the Mascot survival role. Realizing that survival is the priority of each of these children, it is incongruous to ask them to do high level deductive reasoning and to control their behavior rationally without first giving them tools to manage the stress..

The importance of caregiver modeling cannot be overstated. Putting more attention on coherent, supportive early family relationships may reap more benefits with SOSOH people than anything else. There was a noticeable absence of SOSOH people in the African and Balinese villages I visited where every adult is an important caregiver, and every child is valued as a unique and integral part of the clan.

Training adult caregivers to manage stress effectively and control their own behavior, and then teaching their children these techniques, is at least as effective, if not superior to Ritalin. Good learning and good problem solving require active involvement and persistence by the model caregivers.[37]

Children must also learn to take responsibility for their actions. If caregivers play the Family Hero or Enabler role, always doing everything for their children, the youngsters will not learn and gain confidence in their ability to take responsibility and be in control of their lives.[38, 39] Caregivers can assist children in developing responsibility, starting before the age of two, by modeling and then allowing and encouraging them to take care of their toys, pets and other people. I highly recommend the Love and Logic work begun by Jim Fay,[40] and the Loving Guidance work of Becky Baily [41] in assisting with coherent caregiving.

STRESS AND VULNERABILITY TO DISEASE

Stress has enormous health consequences as well. We are most vulnerable to disease in times of increased stress because adrenalin and other stress-induced neurotransmitters lower cell membrane polarity thus putting the very health of the cell at risk. The bacteria and viruses (pathogens) that prey on cells are essentially scavengers, searching for the vulnerable cells in an organism. They mostly attack cells with lowered membrane polarity and systems with lowered DHEA (dehydroepiandrosterone).

George W. Crile graphically demonstrated this connection with membrane polarity in an experiment in which two electrodes with the same charge (either positive or negative, but not both) were placed approximately four inches apart on a person's forearm. A charge was generated for a short time, and then the area on the forearm was carefully studied. Within a day, a lesion had formed on the site. Cultures were then taken from both forearms to assess the extent of bacterial and fungal growth. The lesion showed no greater concentration of bacteria and fungi than the untreated forearm. Within days, however, the lesion became densely populated with disease-causing organisms. These ever-present organisms on the skin did no damage until the integrity of the skin cells was destroyed by lowering the membrane polarity. The lowered membrane polarity left the cells vulnerable and open to pathogenic attack.[42]

Also, dehydroepiandrosterone (DHEA), a transmitter substance extremely

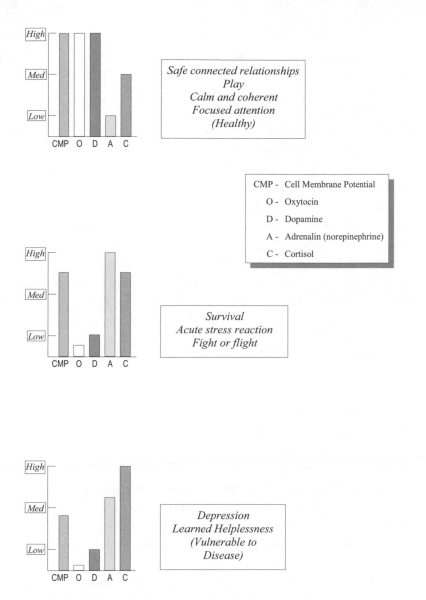

Figure 12.2: Cell membrane potential and chemical information response

important in bolstering the body's immune system has the same precursor substances (progesterone and pregnenolone) as cortisol. Under chronic stress more cortisol is manufactured from the precursors, so the production of DHEA goes down as does our immunity. Cortisol has been considered the most violent immunodepressent known to man. It is implicated in AIDS, MS, diabetes, coronary artery disease, cancer, and Alzheimer's disease. [43, 44]

The opportunity for illness is always present. We are constantly breathing in pathogens and some (such as viruses) live in our body for long periods of time. When stress levels rise, disease organisms can finally enter cells and cause sickness.

With all the stressors in our world today, it is little wonder that infants exhibit elevated adrenalin levels and are more vulnerable to chronic ear infections. Harold Levinson discovered that over 90% of children with learning difficulties had ear infections as infants.[45] Nature apparently intended the stress response to be short lived, getting the body out of danger in a life-threatening situation and then going back to normal. To maintain high stress levels for long periods of time leaves the body open to disease and chronic ear infections in children.

The way we choose to perceive and process our experiences determines whether we handle them calmly or allow them to trigger the stress response. The human mind is very active and can create stress-inducing future scenarios that cause us to worry and live in fear. This fear takes a definite toll on our health. We can choose to see any situation as a learning opportunity or as a threat. It truly is our choice and our children will follow our lead.

EMOTIONS AND HEALTH

The immune system is regulated by the limbic system, the area of the brain that processes emotions. In the 1980's, researchers at the National Institute of Mental Health discovered receptor sites for limbic system neuropeptides and neurotransmitters on cells of the immune system, particularly monocytes. Monocytes, a type of white blood cell, are key players in the immune system that migrate to areas of infection and destroy the pathogenic organisms of disease. Damage or lesions to the hypothalamus (part of the limbic system) will cause changes in monocyte and other white blood cell activity, and therefore in the immune system.[46, 47]

The close association of neuropeptides and neurotransmitters with both the emotions and the immune system suggest that emotions and health are deeply interdependent. If being happy, sad, thoughtful, and excited triggers the production of neuropeptides and neurotransmitters in our limbic system, then the immune cells must also be affected when we are happy, sad, thoughtful and excited.[48, 49]

With the nervous and immune systems linked chemically, our emotions naturally affect the whole body. The heart, traditionally designated as the seat of emotions and love, has been downgraded in that role in favor of other organs. And yet, the heart is chemically linked directly to emotions. The atrium area of the heart produces a hormone (Atrial Natriuretic Factor - ANF) that dramatically affects every major organ of the body including the regions of the brain that regulate our emotional state (amygdala) and influence our learning and memory. ANF operates in response to environmental factors and a strong emotion from the limbic system, whether that be anger or love. It impacts the thalamus and its dynamic with the pituitary, the master endocrine gland for body regulation. It also influences the hypothalamus and pineal gland, regulating the production and action of melatonin, which affects circadian rhythm and mood swings. Thus the heart via ANF, plays a key role in our emotional state, immune system function, memory and learning.[50, 51]

Our growing awareness of the emotion/immune system link underscores the importance of responsibly expressing our emotions. The responsible expression of emotion requires an integration of all parts of the body/mind system at the time the emotions are felt. This facilitates the linking of insight and reasoning with emotion. Learning this process begins with limbic brain development around fifteen months of age. If the emotions that are expressed by the child are listened to seriously, in a safe, supportive environment, the child will learn to express them responsibly. By the age of five, the child is able to connect reason (from the neocortex) with the emotions; and by age eight, adds insight (from the frontal lobes) to refine the emotions. Over time the responsible expression of emotion becomes a valuable tool, absolutely essential to a healthy person — and a healthy society.[52]

When strong emotions (fear, anger or sadness at an injustice) cannot be, or are not expressed, they remain unresolved. These unresolved emotions end up being relegated to the sympathetic nervous system, where they can build over time into fear and may eventually explode as anger and violence, or manifest internally as disease. In either case, the stress response is stimulated, leaving the system vulnerable to disease and inhibiting the learning process. Research has found a connection with people and personality types who are unable to express their emotions and the increased chance of cancer and heart disease.[53]

It has been determined that sexually abused people, who have been unable to express their emotions about the abuse, produce high levels of adrenalin and endorphins and exhibit weakened immune systems. Frank Putnam of the National Institute of Mental Health and Martin Teicher of Harvard Medical School found that chronically high adrenalin levels can kill neurons in brain areas crucial for thinking and memory. They found that sexual abuse arrested growth of the left hemisphere, hampering development of language and logic, and increased levels of an antibody that significantly weakened the immune system.[54] The link between sexual abuse and emotions is dramatically shown in research conducted by Dr. Lenore C. Terr. She found that sexually abused people showed an indifference to pain, a lack of empathy, an inability to define or acknowledge feelings, and an abhorrence of emotional intimacy.[55]

In contrast to the stress reaction, when we are able to responsibly express and resolve our emotions, or feel positive, exhilarated, excited, getting the "Ah-Ha"s of learning, we actually boost our immune system. When we are relaxed, genuinely happy, elated, joyful, there is an increase in interferons and interleukins, which are secreted at the cellular level and dopamine production in the brain. Interferons and interleukins increase membrane polarity, making cells invulnerable to pathogenic organisms. Dopamine assists nerve health and growth as well as learning. Adrenalin, interferons and interleukins are all life-protecting chemicals: adrenalin for acute survival, and interferons and interleukins for health and longevity.[56]

WHY TOUGHING IT OUT MAY MAKE YOU WEAKER

Men die earlier in our society than women, the main natural cause of death being cardiovascular disease. It now appears, contrary to the old Hollywood stereotype, that a stout heart is not one that is indifferent to emotion, and a "broken heart" may be more than a metaphor for what happens when love is not expressed, or the emotional needs for love and connection are not met. And yet, despite all the evidence that disease is stress-related and that it is healthy to express emotions, thereby releasing stress, society continues to promote a non-emotional model to our youth, especially males.

Research demonstrates intriguing correlations between the ways males and females conduct relationships, their sense of self-esteem, and ultimately their health. In a study of people ages 14-28, females turned out to have a very different basis for their self-esteem than males did. Girls with high self-esteem tend to be cheerful, assertive, emotionally open, warm and able to work well with others. Boys with high self-esteem tend to be stern, humorless, unemotional and lacking in social skills. This study asserts that relating to others well fosters self-esteem in females, whereas managing one's anxiety with an unemotional attitude significantly aids male self-esteem. Not surprisingly, males in this study showed higher stress levels and hyperactive ratios than females.[57] Similar studies have shown that women handle stress more effectively than men, due to their intimacy with close female friends and willingness to seek social support.[58, 59]

Where do notions of male or femaleness come from? We have only to look as far as the TV sitcoms and our mass media in general to find them. Our boys and men are truly at a disadvantage in this culture with learning how to effectively and humanely express their true emotional nature. Fortunately, these natural emotional needs are now being addressed in excellent books written to assist boys in their emotional development, thus assisting them to live longer, more passionate lives.[60, 61, 62]

Adequate expression and resolution of emotions helps to mitigate stressful situations. How we experience and express our emotions, particularly negative ones, largely determines whether we secrete adrenalin or other neuropeptides. When such intense negative emotions as anger and grief are responsibly and humanely expressed rather than suppressed, adrenalin is released in minimal amounts, or not at all. Expressing the emotion prevents the stress associated with it from becoming chronic. When we can truly express grief, we can also deeply express joy. Then life becomes a rich, alive, passionate adventure of learning and health.[63]

TV, THE NOT SO HIDDEN STRESSOR

There is a growing realization that the stress of excessive TV watching and TV violence may be linked to learning difficulties. By 1977 more than one hundred published papers representing fifty laboratory and field studies and other experiments involving ten thousand children and adolescents from every conceivable background all showed that TV violence affects viewers. Current research confirms what these early studies demonstrated, that TV is linked to learning difficulties and that TV violence makes children more willing to harm others, more aggressive in their play and more likely to select aggression as the preferred response to conflict situations.[64, 65]

Currently, pediatricians almost universally agree that children's use of media negatively affects children in many different areas including school performance, eating habits and risk of obesity, lowered physical activity levels and children's aggressive high-risk behaviors. The American Academy of Pediatrics recommended: 1) discouraging TV viewing among children ages two and younger, 2) limiting children's viewing time, and 3) encouraging alternative entertainment for children.[66]

In the face of these recommendations, consider some of the disturbing trends in our society's viewing habits: In October, 2003, the Henry J. Kaiser Family Foundation released the results of a survey of 1,065 parents with children ages six months to six years. It was found that 43% of the children age two and younger watched an average of two hours of TV per day and that 26% of these young children had a TV in their bedroom.[67] American pre-school children ages three years of age watched an average of 3.6 hours per day and over 28 hours per week.[68, 69] Approximately one half of American parents have given up setting limits on what children watch.[70] And it's not just the children, one quarter of American adults cannot conceive of a large enough amount of money to persuade them to stop watching TV.[71]

Commercial television for children is 50-60 times more violent than prime-time programs for adults, with some cartoons averaging more than 80 violent acts per hour. Cartoon violence is carefully and deliberately used to lure the child to watch, and to attract the largest possible audience for the purpose of selling products. The primary purpose of commercial television is not to entertain or to educate but to sell products. Violent cartoons have been found to be the easiest means of attracting the entire two to eleven year age group. The most serious and widespread effect of this marketing scheme is desensitization and the development of thick-skinned, detached, cynical human beings living in a climate of fear, who learn that violence is the acceptable solution to conflict.[72] By age thirteen, children will have seen well over 18,000 simulated murders and 200,000 acts of violence on TV.[73] Children as young as fourteen months model behaviors they see on TV. An extensive, fifteen year longitudinal study in the United States, Canada and South Africa, showed long-term childhood exposure to TV as a causal factor behind approximately one half of the homicides, rapes and assaults committed in these countries.[74]

HOW TV CAUSES STRESS

Dr. Byron Reeves of Stanford University conducted studies of TV viewers' brain activity. Their brains responded to movements on the TV as if they were actually real, causing the nervous system to prepare for a physical response.[75] Our brains are very sensitive to quick movements, sudden noises, and especially light changes that might signal danger, so we prepare for fight or flight to protect ourselves. TV programmers know and use this to keep us watching, even when we may not want to. In order to get a sense of how programmers increase light changes, you can count all the lighting changes and flickers that occur during a TV show and commercials. These same flickers occur on a computer screen and can be seen if the screen is videotaped.

These light flickers can produce abnormal brain-wave patterns, such as what happened in 1997 in Japan when a five-second sequence of light flashes in a Pokemon cartoon sent 618 children to the hospital with seizures. Similar reactions can regularly affect one in 4,000 viewers.[76] Because there is a natural physical reaction to danger when there is a light change in the environment, and there is no outlet for the reaction when watching TV, the watcher may develop hyperactivity, frustration or irritability that can affect other areas of his life.[77, 78, 79, 80]

My daughter, as a preschool teacher working in an affluent preschool, noted how desperately these young children (left in preschool from 7:00am until 5:00pm) clung to her everyday. She and I decided it was because of the amount of TV and computer time, and lack of parental involvement in the home. When children watch TV, they elicit the survival response, their body feels fear, so these children, in this irritable state, cling to the parents (their natural source of safety) and fight with siblings for that parental attention and security. And when it is not addressed, they remain in this state of hyper-vigilance (hyperactivity), irritability and fear and then cling to any adult that provides safety.

Parents who have taken the TV out of the home find that, after the initial resistance, the children are much calmer, less fearful, more curious and imaginative; and over a short period of time learn to play and create again. These parents report they have more productive time to themselves because the children are not needing their constant attention.

Besides safety, the brain is geared to insure the care and longevity of humans so the whole species will survive. During limbic system development, we begin to learn about relationships, emotion and bonding for species survival. When young children see people being harmed or killed on TV, it triggers their innate concern for species survival. Anything that goes against species survival during those first four years could precipitate the stress reaction.

At the same time, children have an instinctive desire to imitate observed behavior without reasoning whether it ought to be imitated or not. Infants, as young as fourteen months of age, observe and incorporate behavior they see on TV.[81, 82] They mimic anything, including destructive and anti-social behavior.[83]

Up through age four, children cannot distinguish between truth and fiction when they view TV. For preschoolers, TV is a source of entirely factual information about how the world works. TV violence, through stimulating the survival response, can become a commonplace, daily thing. It seems that the innate species survival sense can be dulled, and replaced by an impression of the power and allure of violence. In later years, under severe stress, adolescents and adults revert to their earliest impression of what violence is and its role in society. Much of this impression could have come from TV.[84] This shows up dramatically in a study of male felons imprisoned for committing violent crimes (homicide, rape and assault). 22% to 34% admit to consciously imitating crime techniques learned from TV, usually successfully.[85] In studies of violent, antisocial men and young murderers, it was found that normal play behavior was virtually absent throughout their lives.[86]

TV viewing has been linked to shortened attention span and the development of Attention Deficit Hyperactive Disorder (ADHD).[87] Hyperactivity is exhibited in boys eight times more often than in girls.[88] Boys are given very vivid models through male violence on TV. They are given strong messages to be tough and "play it cool" in the face of violence. With no acceptable way to release or express the stress they feel, adrenalin pumped into their muscles may lead to a hyperactive state where excess energy causes them to constantly move or fidget. The next step is a SOSOH label — Hyperactive, ADHD, ADD, or Emotionally Handicapped.

THE MORPHINES IN OUR HEAD

There are other neuropeptides secreted in response to high levels of stress and pain. These neuropeptides, the body's natural painkillers, are called enkephalins and endorphins and are located in the thalamus, hypothalamus and parts of the limbic system. First discovered in 1974 by Candace Pert and Solomon Snyder at John Hopkins University, these natural opiates (morphines) assist pleasure at very low levels, but at higher levels they are a throwback to the time when immediate pain relief meant that animals could flee from an attacker without delay.[89]

The marathon runner offers a good example of how these painkillers operate. There is a point at which the balanced exercise of running starts to become painful, and the body sends messages to the brain that it's time to stop before major tissue damage occurs. Runners refer to this as "The Wall." If the runner ignores the body's message and continues to run, the brain receives the message that this is a life-threatening situation and that it is essential to keep moving. At that point, the brain over-secretes endorphins to block the pain sensation to the brain so that the runner can get his body out of danger.

The runner experiences a sense of euphoria because the pain has stopped. But by not listening and responding to the body's message to stop, and masking the body's distress with chemical signals that the body is still in imminent danger, runners end up with unnecessary injuries. With the competitive push today, I wonder if we haven't developed a society of endorphin addicts that are getting high on their own morphine. This may be an attempt to block out the pain in their over-stressed lives.

I have also seen a decreased dopamine and increased endorphin response in children who "space out" at school, leaving the pain of their world behind. That pain may include trauma and abuse at home, a highly painful experience in school, or in many cases, both. Again the system is all too quick to label these children Hyperactive, Emotionally Handicapped, and ADD.

Balanced aerobic activity, where we don't go beyond our bodies' messages and over-secrete endorphins or diminish dopamine, increases oxygen intake so important to learning. Aerobic exercises such as swimming, walking, running and cycling that use the large muscles of the body, mainly legs, are healthful activities that keep the heart rate up. The President's Council on Physical Fitness and Sports recommends a minimum of half an hour per day for physical and intellectual health.[90] Doctors and psychotherapists dealing with stress in patients are now recommending exercise, particularly walking (the Cross Crawl), as a highly effective stress-management therapy.[91]

Non-competitive, co-operative physical education programs that encourage student input are fun for everyone. They decrease the stress and, therefore, increase learning power. Taking the unnecessary competition out of our lives will render life less painful and decrease the need for endorphins.

In addition to acting as pain blockers, endorphins affect our health in another critical way: when produced in response to emotional stress, they suppress the activity of T-Cells, thus lowering our resistance to pathogens, cancer and autoimmune disease. T-Cells, also called T-lymphocytes, are white blood cells from the thymus gland that are especially effective in destroying bacteria, viruses, fungi, and cancer cells. The disease AIDS greatly decreases T-lymphocytes in the blood. Though many people have the AIDS virus, the ones that manifest the disease may be dealing with emotional stressors that increase endorphin levels in the system.[92]

CONNECTION, CALM, FOCUS AND LEARNING

Because stress has become a way of life in our culture, we have put our focus there. It is now time to focus attention on the body chemistry that provides for connection with others, motivates us to be curious and explore our world for the fun and learning, and allows us to selectively focus our attention.

Oxytocin, the birthing and bonding chemical produced in the hypothalamus, is the first we'll look at. It is transported to the posterior lobe of the pituitary gland, and released into the blood to activate the parasympathetic nervous system and cells all over the body. The important bonding and closeness that women depend on for safety during stress elicits the production of this very powerful and calming hormone. Oxytocin is produced in similar quantities in both men and women, but our society has a more generous view of women being close to, touching and calming other women as compared to men doing the same, even if it would increase their health and longevity.

Aside from being produced during the birthing process, oxytocin production is stimulated through touch, smell and physical closeness. Just being rhythmically stroked on the face, hands, back or shoulders raises oxytocin and makes a person less sensitive to pain, less fearful, more curious, optimistic, creative and available to explore unfamiliar surroundings and social interactions. This nurturing allows the person to open up and express emotions in a way that assists, rather than hinders the immune system. It also sets up the safe, secure environment necessary for optimal learning to occur.

The release of oxytocin increases parasympathetic function, resulting in effective digestion, storage of nutrients, decreased cortisol, decreased blood pressure, decreased heart rate, healing, and cell division and growth. Oxytocin secretion is stimulated by dopamine, serotonin, glutamate, noradrenalin and oxytocin itself. Endorphins, Cortisol and GABA decrease oxytocin secretion. Importantly, a rise in oxytocin is characterized by a feeling of peacefulness, relaxation, contentment and more nurturing behavior towards others.[93]

Unfortunately, in our Western Culture today there is increasing independence and preoccupation with TVs and computers that alter the natural patterns of close contact with others, either physically or psychologically. We rarely have the time or energy to just be close to each other, holding a hand or being touched in a nurturing fashion. With less contact there is less touch and less oxytocin. It is time to honor the close ties and friendships that used to be inherent in our culture, for their profound effects upon reducing stress, allowing for emotional expression, and setting the stage for learning and creativity.

Next comes dopamine and it's important effect on motivation, curiosity, learning and memory.[94, 95] Dopamine is produced in cells in the limbic system which have branches to the frontal lobe, olfactory area, amygdala, hippocampus, prefrontal cortex, and other areas associated with organization of movement, motivation, sensory-seeking and goal directed behavior and integrated learning.

Dopamine provides the spark to explore new things in our lives and is very important in "stamping-in" memory that attaches motivational importance to otherwise neutral environmental stimuli such as school lessons. The pleasure a person experiences from success at a sport, academics, human relationships or any other endeavor, comes from increased dopamine, and that pleasure sets up the motivation for more actions (goals) that are pleasurable and reward infused. Dopamine seems to stamp in the feelings of pleasure that go with discovery and success, the stimulus-reward associations that are essential for controlled behavior learned from all our past experiences.[96] Likewise, when a person constantly fails, believes they "can't do it", is frequently punished or neglected, the dopamine levels drop markedly, goal-seeking decreases, motivated behavior stops, and the person is more susceptible to depression — the act of giving up.

Dopamine is important to cognitive processing because it activates the amygdala around emotions having to do with new, exciting, novel experiences and the internal reward necessary in learning and memory.[97] During play, as children and adults are actively enjoying, being curious about and exploring a new situation, taking risks, being fully present and coherent, dopamine levels rise significantly and learning takes place naturally as the person is highly motivated to discover and learn. Dopamine is the chemical that motivates us to be creative, learning, growing individuals.[98]

To maintain focus in order to reason and remember new information it is essential for the brain to block out non-important stimuli. The third neuropeptide is GABA (gamma-aminobutyric acid) which blocks out unimportant stimuli by hyperpolarizing the membranes of post-synaptic neurons, increasing the membrane's polarity (to more than -70 mv inside) to the point that it will respond only to specific chosen stimuli.[99, 100] We activate neurons that secrete GABA when, for example, we are reading a highly absorbing book. We choose to become unaware of our environment and the passage of time, so the brain is not distracted as it maintains complete focus. We also intentionally secrete GABA at night in order to block out light, sounds and the feel of the bed on our bodies so we can go to sleep. With GABA, the system can choose its focus rather than react, as it does with adrenalin, to all the stimuli around it.

We consciously choose which membranes to hyperpolarize with GABA. For example, when I was a new mother, I could block out the DC-10's that flew over our house at night, but if my daughter made the slightest whimper, I was awake immediately. My daughter's welfare was my conscious intention. So while raising the threshold of awareness to aircraft noise, I lowered the threshold in areas of the nervous system associated with awareness of my daughter's well being. Similarly, during a learning session, we use GABA to block out irrelevant stimuli such as the sounds of a pencil dropping, kids giggling, or street noises. This gives us the ability to focus our attention.

GABA gives us the control to be fully present, mentally and emotionally, thus overriding the adrenalin reaction. We learn to secrete it through practice, in an environment with good models, where quiet, focused time is encouraged. People who have not acquired this highly important body/mind skill, are among those likely to be labeled "hyperactive." They tend to take in and react to all the stimuli around them, but cannot selectively choose when it is appropriate to ignore certain stimuli. They haven't fully developed the ability to calm and focus their own system. Again, I have found that integrative, coherent movement can be very helpful to these people. The areas of the brain that house the neurons that secrete GABA are associated with movement, particularly fine, coordinated movements. It would seem, therefore, that doing fine coordinated movements like Brain Gym, Tai Chi or Yoga, would increase the stimulation and proliferation of dendrites from those neurons, thus increasing the availability of GABA in the system to bring about focused attention.

Managing stress means using the whole body/mind system in a more efficient and healthful way. It requires consciously moving the focus and nervous energy of the body/mind system away from the survival centers, and bringing coherence to all areas of the system. We can't expect ourselves, or our children to learn optimally under the shadow of stress. The ability to manage stress in every part of our lives opens the door for all meaningful learning and joy-filled living.

13

Mis-Education and The Labeling Game

Because of the infinite variation in the way individuals are assembled, it must be assumed that the sentient properties of any one person, like his or her fingerprints, could never be identical with those of another. It is probable, therefore, that there does not exist or ever will exist one person exactly like another. If uniqueness were an indispensable requirement for an evolving society, every person would be indispensable.

— *Paul MacLean*[1]

Competition is so pervasive in our society that even school children are afflicted by the omnipresent pressures that lead to stress. School itself is a big source of stress, even more so for those children whose academic performance is poor. Inevitably, school is a defining experience for nearly everyone. Self-esteem, choice of career, expectations in life are greatly influenced by the grades and rewards we receive in school. Poor performance in school brings out a lot of negative emotions, which lead to fear and perceptions of threat. That is stress. As we have seen, stress further disables the learner, setting off a vicious cycle that sends grades spiraling downward.

It does not have to be this way. If instead each student felt valued and supported, a great deal of stress could be eliminated from learning situations. A lot of poor schoolwork is attributable to educational practices, particularly in schools that do not accommodate for learning differences. People learn differently, yet school is set up to favor certain styles of learning and schoolwork focuses on certain kinds of tasks.

On the whole, school teaches, tests and values logic brain tasks. Logic, sequence, computation, categorization, verbal skills are all highly prized abilities in school. Intuition, emotion, vision, humor, rhythmic movement, image formation, and other gestalt brain capacities are not practiced, tested or particularly valued at school. It is only in the real world, outside of the classroom, where success depends upon entrepreneurship, imagination and insight that we begin to appreciate the importance of the gestalt brain. School is very lopsided, and many students suffer and end up exhibiting SOSOH behavior because of this bias.

OUR INNATE LEARNING STYLES & DOMINANCE PROFILES

We are all uniquely wired. Our specific life experiences shape our perceptions, the way we learn and in essence, who we are. Some of our neuronal wiring, (our nerve networks), however, are determined by innate factors. For instance, we all show a preference or lead function for one hand over the other, one eye over the other, even one ear over the other. We also exhibit a preference for one brain hemisphere over the other, which may be directly connected to our survival.

Under stress, a PET (Positron Emission Tomography) Scan or EEG (Electro-encephalogram) will show decreased blood flow across the whole neo-cortex, but especially to the non-dominant hemisphere of the brain.[2] This homolateral pattern may allow the dominant hemisphere to more efficiently direct the survival reaction without having to consult with the other hemisphere across the corpus callosum. Under stress the brain also exhibits a fast Beta brain wave pattern that facilitates reaction and movement, while alpha and theta waves for thinking and learning decrease.[3] From my research, I strongly suspect that we develop this homolaterality at about nine weeks in utero when the Moro Reflex for survival develops. Lead functions allow us to react fast without having to think which leg to move forward, or which arm to throw a punch with. This dominant brain wiring is also used during new learning experiences, perhaps because it was laid down so early in our development and is the most familiar. It constitutes our unique learning style and determines our perception and how we approach learning with specific preferences for how to accomplish a task.

In recent years, several systems for analyzing and identifying learning styles have been developed by educators and psychologists. Very useful in my work is a simple method to gauge and characterize individual learning styles originally taught to me by Colleen Gardner, a kinesiologist. This approach identifies the basal dominance of eyes, ears, and hands in relation to the dominant brain hemisphere and gives important information as to how we most easily take in and process new learning.

When we are under stress, we rely most on our dominant senses and our preferred ways of processing. In less stressful situations, our dominance profiles can fluctuate. As we meet changing situations that require new learning and adjustments throughout our lives, we depart from our basal dominance profile, assuming adaptive or compensatory dominance profiles. These adaptive profiles reflect self-designed learning strategies that work for us. However, under stress we react by immediately returning to our basal profile. Under stress, only one hemisphere, either the gestalt or logic brain is efficiently functioning, and we only have access to the senses that feed into or are expressed through that dominant hemisphere.

When we are confronted with a new learning situation, we will access information most easily through our dominant senses (eyes or ears), and express (either verbally, with gestures or in writing) with our dominant hand. Because of our innate neural circuitry, the left hemisphere controls movement and receives sensory information from the right side of the body. The right hemisphere controls movement and receives sensory information from the left side of the body.

Figure 13.1: Domi-Know from The Dominance Factor

Figure 13.1 presents the Domi-Know a schematic drawing that will help you to visualize the dominance profiles. A darkened area of the Domi-Know, indicates dominance in that hemisphere, hand, eye or ear.

The efficiency of sensing depends upon whether or not the dominant eye, ear or hand is on the side opposite the dominant brain hemisphere. For example, visual input is most efficient when the dominant eye is opposite the dominant brain hemisphere. If the left brain and right eye are dominant, then vision is facilitated. The left brain controls the muscular movements of the right eye, thus optimizing the efficiency of three dimensional and two dimensional focus, tracking and peripheral vision. The same would be true for the right brain/left eye dominance.

Fig. 13.2: Visual Learner

If however, both the left eye and left brain are dominant (homolateral), then vision is less effective because the dominant brain is not controlling the muscular movements of the dominant eye. Also, since much of the non-dominant brain shuts down during stress, visual information coming in from the eye opposite the non-dominant brain is limited. Homolateral refers to the dominant eye, ear, or hand being on the same side as the dominant brain, decreasing

Fig. 13.3: Visually Limited Learner

efficiency, especially under stress when the functioning of the non-dominant hemisphere is limited. I will refer to homolateral profiles as limited.

The eyes facilitate seeing and visual interpretation of our world. The ears facilitate hearing, listening and memory. The hands facilitate communication: oral, written and gestural. The left hemisphere initiates language (both verbal and written) expression in the right hand. The right hemisphere initiates expressive movement and physical manipulation in the left hand. When both the left hemisphere and left hand are dominant, communication becomes limited. The same is true if the right hemisphere and right hand are dominant. These are simplistic explanations that only touch on the high degree of complexity these profiles represent.

The following is a chart of basal profiles, giving an idea of how the hemispheres, eyes, ears and hands work together. Some people have cross-lateral profiles for specific senses, and some have homolateral profiles for specific senses. These can also be mixed in any combination, for example, a person may be cross-lateral for eyes and homolateral for ears.

CROSS-LATERAL PROFILES

Dominant Sense	Dominant Hemisphere	Preferred Learning Style
Right eye	Left	Visual
Left eye	Right	Visual
Right ear	Left	Auditory
Left ear	Right	Auditory
Right hand	Left	Verbal
Left hand	Right	Kinesthetic

HOMOLATERAL PROFILES

Dominant Sense	Dominant Hemisphere	Learner Style
Right eye	Right	Visually limited
Left eye	Left	Visually limited

Visually limited learners prefer to learn through their other senses. They may close their eyes or look away to concentrate on information they really want to learn or express.

Right ear	Right	Auditorially limited
Left ear	Left	Auditorially limited

Auditorially limited learners may not hear what is being said and may tune out when people talk too much, as in lectures. They also have more difficulties with learning languages and auditory memory.

PET scans of subjects verbalizing show that under stress only primary areas in the left hemisphere known as Wernekes and Broca's area and an area in the parietal lobe that connects them are functional.[4] This connecting area (Geschwind's territory) is thought be important for acquisition of language in childhood. It is also the last area in the brain to mature, coinciding with the full development of reading and writing skills.[5] Further, when you look at the diagram for speaking (communication) Figure 5.3, and match it with the brain map, Figure 3.4, you will notice that the primary speaking area is connected with the hand, and secondarily with the mouth. Thus, people who are left brained and right handed are verbal learners, needing to talk to learn or talking to clarify, in a linear way, a stressful situation.

Right hand	Right	Communication limited
Left hand	Left	Communication and Kinesthetically limited

On the other hand, communication limited learners can't speak easily under stress. If they are right brain dominant they won't make linear, logical sense when they speak, and their communication will be full of emotions and rather kinesthetic. If they are left brain dominant and left handed, they will have a hard time speaking and communicating their thoughts.

Girls learn linguistics faster than boys, with girls exhibiting much greater cell packing density in Wernekes area than boys. Structural and functional MRI's done when students were reading rhyming words, show that males process more on the right frontal lobes of the brain, while females use the left side incorporating the frontal, temporal and parietal areas more with more processing across the corpus callosum. The parietal operculum for language and attention are on the right side of the brain and more easily accessed in girls.[6, 7]

Our society tends to believe that people who are good at language and can read are intelligent, thus we tend to push our children ever younger to speak and read. Boys often don't speak well until they get to school or later, and thus are already at a disadvantage, which shows up with more boys in special ed than girls.

Between 65-70% of the population is clearly right handed. However, it was discovered that Einstein was left-handed, and that left handers show representation of language centers in both hemispheres of the brain with much larger corpus callosums than right-handed people. Forced right-handedness that occurs often in our society, though it might assist verbalization is also associated with stuttering.[8] Perhaps it is better to simply honor innate handedness.

Dominance profiles became a valued addition to my counseling work with Special Education and Emotionally Handicapped students. Used in Individualized Educational Programs (IEP's), the profiles informed and supported each child's understanding of his or her unique way of learning. (IEP's are usually yearlong educational goals, set up for each individual child and agreed upon by the teacher, counselor and parent of the child.) The dominance profile also gave the parents and teachers an understanding of how to approach and honor each child's learning style. Some teachers even began using it in regular classrooms as part of student self-understanding and self-esteem programs.

DOMINANCE PROFILES AND EDUCATIONAL LABELING

After using this dominance profile assessment in many schools with many students, I began to see certain patterns emerge. I noticed, for example that many of the students who were gestalt brain dominant and/or sensory limited were also the ones who had been labeled as having learning difficulties. In 1990 I undertook a more formal study to compare dominance profile types with schools' systems of labeling students.[9]

Using the basal dominance profiles, I collected data from a random sample of 218 students attending Denver, Colorado and Kona, Hawaii schools. The dominance assessment was done using muscle response checking, a diagnostic method used by doctors, kinesiologists, chiropractors, and other health professionals, while bringing the subject's attention to each arm, each eye, each ear, and each hemisphere of the brain.[10, 11] The students were also identified by the following labels as established by assessment criteria in these schools:

GT = Gifted and Talented (children chosen for this program excelled academically and had high SAT scores, thus succeeded at language and math skills)

N = Normal (children doing OK in the regular classroom)

R = Remedial (children with specific reading difficulties)

X = Special Education/Emotionally Handicapped (children labeled with learning disabilities and Attention Deficit Hyperactive Disorder - ADHD).

HSR = High School Redirection (an alternative high school for students who had previously dropped out of other schools)

The following graph shows my findings with percentages of each group checked. (The columns representing logic and gestalt for each group total 100%.)

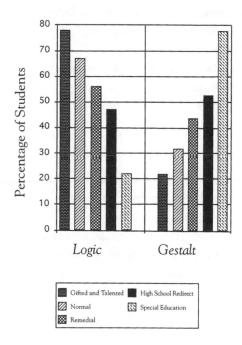

Figure 13.4: Hemisphere Dominance in a Random Sample of 218 Students Attending Denver, Colorado and Kona, Hawaii Schools

In the past 14 years, I have continued the dominance profile research, and consistently found the same patterns.

In 2000 and 2002, school principal Brother John Wu, SBD and Amy Choi, obtained dominance information in two high schools in Hong Kong, one with 180 students in Lam Woo Secondary School consisting of the academically top 20% of students, and one with 123 students in Ng Siu Mui Technical School consisting of the bottom 10% of students. [12]

Here is their comparison:

Function	Lam Woo Secondary	NgSiu Mui Technical
Gestalt (left) Brain Dominant	57%	33%
Verbal learner (left Brain, right Hand)	27%	11%
Instructor Follower (left brain, right Foot)	28%	15%
Visual Learner (opposite brain and eye)	47%	63%
Auditory Learner (opposite brain and ear)	48%	34%

Figure 13.5: Hemisphere Dominance in a Sample of 303 Students Attending two Hong Kong Schools

This data is similar to my findings and shows the vast difference in successful students and those with less success, even in a culture that prizes its children and works very hard at assuring their success.

HOW RIGHT BRAINERS ARE WRONGED

In my research, the first thing that struck me profoundly was the contrast between the label applied to 78% of the logic dominant students and the label assigned to 78% of the gestalt dominant students. In the schools I studied, students with high verbal abilities and logic brain processing were more often labeled gifted and talented. Those with gestalt processing and low linear verbal skills were more frequently labeled as learning disabled/Special Education.

As is well known (and as I explained in Chapter 5), logic dominant processors, usually called left brained, focus on the details: specifically, in language, on the words, syntax, and sentence structure. In math they are more able to use linear detailed processing in problem solving. They are also more adept at learning the details of technique in art, music, dance and sports. In music, they tend to do well with note reading, timing and specific technique in holding or playing the instrument. Since music is generally taught in a linear fashion, starting with notes, timing and technique, left brain processing is useful at the beginning. But if logic brained music students do not adequately develop gestalt brained capacities, they may have difficulty accessing the image, passion, rhythm and flow necessary to make their music come alive.

As the chart shows, students with logic brained talents are more often positively reinforced with the Gifted and Talented label by the educational system. They are more likely to have high self-esteem and experience less stress, because school work is geared toward their competencies. This allows them the confidence to explore gestalt avenues of learning. (But only if they are not overly stressed by competition and the pursuit of ever higher grades). With less stress in the long run, they have a better chance of obtaining more integrative learning strategies, nerve-net development and myelination across the corpus callosum.

Gestalt processors, usually called right brained, are able to take in the big image, feel the emotional connections, access intuitive understanding, are very spontaneous and need to learn kinesthetically through movement. In art, music, dance, drama and sports they access the passion, movement and big picture — all elements crucial to creativity. They prefer to approach music as a whole, exploring, playing and singing what they hear and feel.

If they are not adequately using their left brains (in times of stress for instance) they will have difficulty managing details and linear processing. Gestalt learners more than logic learners are affected by the early push, between ages 5 and 7, to learn linear functions both in language and math. These children begin to judge themselves as "dumb" and develop "learned helplessness."

A study comparing brain wave activity in "learning disabled" and "normal" children discovered a major difference. "Learning disabled" children, exhibited 1) less overall left-hemisphere activation, even with verbal tasks, and 2) significantly fewer shifts from one hemisphere to the other when tasks required different processing strategies.[13] I believe this directly relates to stress in these children. Due to stress in the learning environment, they end up depending only on their dominant hemisphere (gestalt), the brain stem and sympathetic nervous system. They become unable to explore and adequately access their logic hemisphere. Thus they are trapped in a vicious cycle. The stress of schooling heightens their inability to learn in a logical way, diminishing nerve cell growth and myelination and easy access between both hemispheres. Gestalt learners in our society have been strongly discriminated against!

Gestalt learners have to struggle to make it through our educational system. Albert Einstein, besides being left handed, was also a gestalt learner. His early academic failures are legendary, and he frequently referred in later life to his reliance on visual imagery rather than linear logic. "The words of the language," he said, "as they are written and spoken, do not seem to play any role in my mechanisms of thought. The psychical entities which seem to serve as elements in thought are certain signs and more or less clear images which can be voluntarily reproduced or combined."[14] Fortunately, he sought out holistic learning situations that fed his curiosity and lust for understanding and passionately played the violin, which assisted his brain integration. As a world we have been blessed with his incredible insights, all of which were more intimately bound to his internal images and feelings than to strictly linear processing.[15]

Our educational system does little to encourage holistic, intuitive, image-based (as opposed to verbal-based) thinking. But where would we be without these capacities? Gestalt learners have talents that are too frequently undervalued in school. If as a result, gestalt learners undervalue themselves we run the risk that they stop contributing in significant ways. We must strive to understand and facilitate the learning process of gestalt learners so we do not lose this valuable resource.

HOW THE EDUCATIONAL SYSTEM FAVORS FULL SENSORY ACCESS

Our educational system favors students that can process linearly, take in information auditorially and visually, look at the teacher, and restate pieces of information in a logical, linear fashion. In my study these students are listed as "full sensory access" (in general they are left brained, right eyed, right eared and right handed). They make up, on average, only 15% of the test population. Those labeled "gifted and talented" are the largest segment of this full sensory access group.

Fig. 13.6: Full Sensory Access Learner

These students usually do well on the verbal and mathematical skills tests commonly given in our schools, including the Scholastic Assessment Tests (SAT's), which despite their limited scope, are considered in the United States to be reliable assessments of intelligence. You will notice that this profile is highly dependent on logic brain functioning. But if these learners are not encouraged to use gestalt brain processing, they may not adequately develop some very important abilities like: seeing the big picture, relating empathically with others, feeling the emotional implications of ideas or spontaneously generating new ideas. Yet the whole system is geared to teaching predominantly logic processing skills.

Let's examine some of the other implications of this study. In Figure 13.8, note the column marked auditorially limited. When the dominant ear

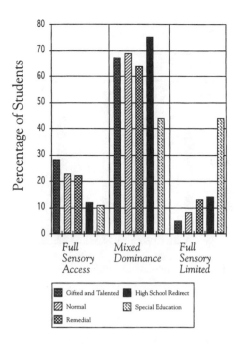

Figure 13.7: Sensory Access Patterns in the Same Sample of 218 Colorado and Hawaii Students

is on the same side of the body as the dominant hemisphere, auditory functioning is less effective and the person might not easily hear what is being said. In my study, the auditorially limited profile represents an average of approximately 52% of the population. Yet lecturing is our primary way of teaching. A typical lecture, then, is likely to be missed by over half of the audience. Thinking Caps and The Energy Yawn (discussed in Chapter 7) are excellent at tuning up listening capacities when done prior to a lecture.

Also notice that a high percentage of both the Gifted and Talented and the Special Education students were auditorially limited. Here is an interesting and seemingly paradoxical commonality that can be explained when you consider that the vast majority of "gifted and talented" students are logic dominant and therefore verbal. So even though they are auditorially limited and may not hear what is being said, they talk — and so are believed to be more intelligent. The opposite is true for the Special Education students, mainly gestalt dominant, who are not verbal. Our society equates verbal skills with intelligence, and therefore labels those who speak well as Gifted and Talented. Less verbal students are more likely to be labeled Special Education.

Figure 13.8 Ear/Hemisphere Dominance Patterns in the Same Sample of 218 Colorado and Hawaii Students

In this same study, among the students with cross lateral profiles for hands and hemispheres, 22% of the Gifted and Talented group were kinesthetic and not verbal compared to 89% of the Special Education group. We highly value linguistic ability in our traditional educational system and in our society. Our SAT tests reflect this by testing the linguistic and logical/mathematical intelligences. As Howard Gardner has observed, this bias ignores at least five other intelligences, including the kinesthetic, visual/spatial, musical, interpersonal and intrapersonal.[16, 17] The typical school curriculum offers very few if any kinesthetic learning techniques even in light of the research on the importance of movement to the learning process, showing that drama, music and art increase SAT scores for both linguistic and mathematical assessment.[18]

WHEN LOOKING AT THE TEACHER MEANS NOT PAYING ATTENTION

We also tend to believe that people are learning only if they are looking at us when we are teaching. Being a teacher for so long, I know it does feel good to have people looking at me when I talk. But, notice in Figure 13.9 the column marked visually limited. This represents any profile where the dominant eye is on the same side as the dominant hemisphere and constitutes approximately half of the population. With only 27.8% of the Gifted and Talented group

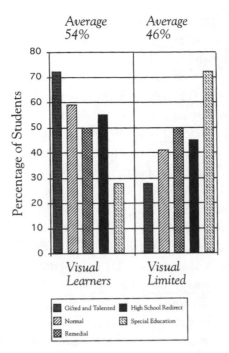

Average
54%

Average
46%

Figure 13.9: Eye/Hemisphere Dominance Patterns in the Same Sample of
218 Colorado and Hawaii Students

compared to 72.2% of the special education group being visually limited, there might be an overemphasis on visual learning in the classroom. If concepts are new and difficult to understand, visually limited people may need to look away or shut their eyes in order to take in the information more easily through their dominant senses. Unfortunately, this is often construed as inattentiveness.

A fifteen year old girl was sent to me because she was failing math. She was left brained, right handed, right eared and left eyed, therefore her basal profile showed visually limited, logic dominance with full auditory and communication access. Auditory learners with logic brain dominance usually do well at math. So I decided to sit in on the class. The teacher had put her in the front of the room, directly in front of him. Every time he verbally stated or wrote a math problem on the board she would close her eyes and turn her right ear toward him. She was doing her best to optimize her preferred sense (hearing) in what had become a stressful situation for her. He immediately said "look at me, look at the board!" As soon as she

Fig. 13.10: Logic
dominant, visually
limited, full auditory
and communication
access

had to look at the teacher or the board, she lost her auditory concentration and her optimal ability to learn.

All three of us learned a lot from this observation. As a result, the teacher put her in the third row on the left side of the room facing the teacher. She had full right ear access. He was no longer disturbed by her seeming lack of attention when she closed her eyes. Meanwhile, she began doing Brain Gym® daily to enhance her preferred auditory sense and get her vision activated. Within a month she was getting straight A's on her math work.

I had a similar case in an Anatomy and Physiology class I taught at the University. A woman came back to school after 25 years of practical nursing to get her bachelors degree in nursing. She sat in the back of the room and knitted during the whole class. She never took a note and very seldom looked at me. She got one of the highest grades in the course and knitted nine sweaters that semester! She was an auditory learner and did not need to look at me or the board to learn. And by using both hands in knitting, she was accessing both hemispheres and keeping them equally activated. In European schools, children knit as part of their skills training. This is an excellent activity for facilitating development of fine motor coordination, frontal lobe functioning and hemispheric integration for ease of learning.[19]

The visually limited profile also affects ease of reading, especially in stressful circumstances. Under stress, the eyes will react by moving peripherally (to see where the danger is), and if asked to read, the person uses their non-dominant eye because their dominant eye is looking out for danger — survival being the primary function. The dominant eye muscles will not receive full motor function from the non-dominant brain because it is partially shut down. This makes foveal focus and tracking across a page of reading difficult. Integrated sensory input will also be minimized. Lazy 8's for Eyes (discussed in Chapter 7) help the eyes work together for maximal visual intake of information.

ARE LEFT EYED READERS BETTER OFF IN ISRAEL?

The left eye dominant trait also sheds an interesting light on learning. We are not truly binocular. The large protuberance (our nose) between our eyes interferes with complete binocular vision. So, we have one main tracking eye with the other eye following. The right eye naturally tracks from left to right while the left eye naturally tracks from right to left.[20]

The learner with a left eye dominant pattern will want to look at the right side of the page first and then move to the left. In languages that are read from right to left (Hebrew or Chinese), left eyed students would have the edge. Perhaps they would be the Gifted and Talented students, reading easily and therefore gaining acclaim. In Israel, the students having the greatest difficulty with reading were right eye dominant.

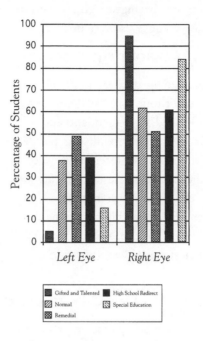

Figure 13.11: Eye Dominance in the Same Sample of 218 Colorado and Hawaii Students

Notice that in my study, the remedial students have the highest percentage of left eye dominance. Eighty-one percent of these students were also left eyed/right handed. Since the eye naturally wants to track from the right to the left, it will also guide the hand from the right to the left which may cause writing difficulties or letter reversals. This would also indicate a connection with hand-eye coordination and difficulty with writing. These are the children in remediation programs who reverse letters and numbers and have difficulty with beginning reading. They simply need some work in eye teaming to facilitate ease of tracking in the opposite direction. Exercising the eyes by moving them in all directions, looking far away after looking at things up close and tromboning (tracking a finger that moves toward and away from the nose) strengthens the eyes muscles and their teaming abilities. The vision training, taught by Paul and Gail Dennison, strengthens eye function by activating tracking in all directions while holding specific acupressure points. Brain Gym® activities for eyes, especially the Lazy 8's, facilitate tracking and foveal focus to assist with both reading and writing. Juggling balls or scarves is also highly effective in hand-eye coordination. And because the vestibular system orchestrates eye movements, having students sit or move on an exercise ball, or balance board while reading is also very helpful.

HOW ABOUT THE TEACHERS?

My study also profiled the teachers in the subject schools. Fully three out of four, 75% of them, were logic dominant, right handed, right eyed, and auditorially limited. Under stress, people with this profile tend to talk about the details, not listen, and expect students to look at them. Of course teachers are as stressed out as anyone else, maybe even more so. With crowded classrooms and SOSOH children acting out in class, teachers may revert to their own basal dominance profiles. Stress creates a circle of frustration for everyone concerned.

Fig. 13.12: Logic dominant, visual and communication access, auditorially limited

THE PROFILE OF A DISADVANTAGED GROUP

The most disadvantaged group of learners are those who are full sensory limited, especially when they are gestalt brain dominant. Figure 13.4 presents a comparative graphing of this group in the column marked full sensory limited. Only 5% of the Gifted and Talented students are fully limited compared to 44% of the Special Education group. People that are fully gestalt limited (right brained, right eyed, right eared, right handed) have difficulty taking in sensory input during times of stress. They withdraw and process through internal images, movement and emotions, unable to explain themselves verbally.

It is important for them to have quiet time alone to process the situation. Again, in our very verbal society, we want people to articulate their thoughts and feelings. The gestalt fully limited learner, may see the big picture but have difficulty expressing it in language. In their frustration at not being able to verbalize, they may strike out emotionally. They may end up in fights or become emotionally volatile in the classroom, thus earning the label of emotionally handicapped.

Gestalt fully limited people can be assisted when several factors are included in the learning environment. These include: (1) moving to learn, (2) getting the whole picture first, then tieing in the details later, (3) starting linear processing at age 7-8, not before, (4) feeling secure in their emotions and relationships, and (5) taking quiet time out to process new learning in an intrapersonal way. With highly traditional crowded classrooms, mostly logic brained teachers, and curricula based on detail first, these limited learners spend a lot of time in survival mode. This can lead to "learned helplessness", depression, violence and the astoundingly large

Fig. 13.13: Gestalt, Full Sensory Limited

numbers of gestalt learners (between 3 and 4 million) in our expensive special education and emotionally handicapped programs.

MEMORIES OF A GESTALT LEARNER

My personal profile is the gestalt fully limited dominance pattern. I believe that is why Brain Gym® and the successes from it have been personally important to me. I see myself in the children I have worked with. I know the system is stacked against them.

Personally, I had a great deal of difficulty with cognitive skills in school. I didn't read until age 10. It was only after a tutor honored my developmental pace and learning style that reading finally clicked for me. Then I became a voracious reader. The weekly spelling tests left me numb from fear and it didn't take me long to believe I was "dumb." By the fifth grade, my self-esteem plummeted when I had to memorize times tables. Later I grew to hate math as I failed algebra two years in a row. It was frustrating, I could come up with the answers, but I didn't know how to go through the linear steps to demonstrate them. The more I struggled, the less I understood. A most humiliating day occurred when the teacher made me take the test in a separate room because she believed that my answers came by cheating. I simply had a learning style that didn't fit the system. If I were in grade school today, I would undoubtedly be in a special education class with a learning disabled label. I was fortunate that in my grade school in the 1950's they hadn't yet heard of special education.

In my grade school, there was a strong physical education program. Movement, art and music were daily integral parts of the curriculum. These subjects brought me enough excitement and success in school to keep me coming back each day, even with all my self-doubt and "retarded" cognitive skills. I also had the freedom to spend quiet time alone in nature with my imagination, and a curiosity that stimulated my life-long interest in biology. I am a successful educator, biologist, neurophysiologist and international lecturer in spite of it all, though at times those little voices of self-doubt from my school struggles creep back in.

I recognized this same frustration in my daughter as her joy of learning diminished with each advancing year of school. Though she struggled with the traditional system, she soared the six months she attended a Montessori school at age 7 and later at High School Redirection (an alternative school in the Denver Public School System) that accommodated her unique learning style. She is currently a top student in graduate school majoring in International Social Work.

As I worked with the wonderful children in the special ed and emotionally handicapped programs at various schools, I could see through their frustration to the unheralded intelligence inside each of them. I've found them to be spontaneous and to excel in kinesthetic, musical, visual/spatial and interpersonal intelligence. By honoring the arts, movement and interpersonal relationships more in our schools and society, these students may one day become our leaders.

RIGHT BRAIN PROBLEM SOLVING

Though our educational system espouses and rewards left hemisphere problem solving, the role of the right hemisphere in problem solving is gaining recognition. One researcher, Grayson Wheatley, has addressed an aspect of right brain problem solving that I recognize as my own specific way of processing math, particularly algebra.

According to Wheatley, the right hemisphere excels in tasks that are non-verbal, spatial and less familiar.[21] It grasps the whole and solves the problems at once. The left hemisphere processes the stimulus information so the stimulus can be described in language. In problem solving, it is important not to force children to use language as the vehicle for thought when imaging is more appropriate. Children can know without being able to state the thoughts in words. Bob Samples elaborates this thinking by noting that problem solving requires restructuring of elements, not just following rules.[22]

We are still leaning too heavily on algorithmic (linear, mathematical, rule oriented) learning, still expecting students to learn primarily through rote memorization, all the way up through college. Why? Memory and linear skills are easy to test and quantify. These kinds of tests give objective comparisons.

But what do they measure? Facts and linear skills are useful acquisitions, but are they the most important part of a person's education? Shouldn't we be more concerned about thinking, creativity, application of knowledge to real life situations. The emphasis on low level skills and memory testing fosters an emphasis on low level thought processing — teaching to tests. Consequently, practice in high level thinking can be and often is shortchanged. As Herman Epstein has observed, "More than half the population in the United States never reach the Piaget stage of formal reasoning. We have knowers but few thinkers!"[23]

The stress of constant testing diminishes the ability to see problem solving in a larger context. It turns education into a numbers game where competition, rather than cooperation, is encouraged and information is not moved to applicability or creative thought. If we can advance to an education that balances memory and thinking, and honors each person's learning processes, agile learners with valuable thinking tools can emerge. Or, to put it more cerebrally, as Bob Samples does: "We discovered that if the right hemisphere functions are celebrated, the development of left hemisphere qualities becomes inevitable."

TEACHING TO THE WHOLE BRAIN

I've been in classrooms where math is being taught only from story problems. Students access images when they solve story problems and work from a three-dimensional, real life perspective. The students themselves are encouraged to devise the story problems, making them emotionally relevant as well as accessing deeper imaginative thought. The problems are then solved in cooperative learning groups of three to four students. Though all the answers in the classroom may be identical, the way each group arrives at the answer may be unique. The groups then share their problem solving methods, and each student gains insight into the overall problem solving process.

In a university setting (for example, an economics course of three hundred students), it makes much more sense to use a cooperative learning model than to simply lecture, which is bound to miss a large proportion of the students. (In my study 52% of students were auditorially limited.) Divide students into groups, give them guidelines and let them discuss, write, diagram, learn and anchor in personal experience with the information presented. The movement of putting their thoughts into language, writing or pictures, and gaining insights from each other will expand high level formal reasoning and move us toward being a nation of thinkers.

McKim goes one step further in contending that flexibility is the key to productive thinking. He believes it advisable to stop thinking consciously about a problem, relax, take a walk or sleep on it, allowing the thinking to proceed unconsciously without stress.[24] Dr. Czikszentmihalyi calls this state of being present without consciously thinking "Flow" out of which all truly creative thought and action progresses.[25] When children and adults are truly at play, they are in a state of "flow" and learning occurs naturally and abundantly. In school we must allow movement and integration time to insure high level problem solving.

Awareness of learning style differences has motivated teachers and whole school systems to be more innovative in their curricula. Programs such as those based on Howard Gardner's Multiple Intelligences, Bernice McCarthy's 4-MAT system derived from David Kolb's work, and Rita Dunn's work facilitate learning style differences and are gaining acceptance.[26, 27, 28] Gardner's rethinking of the definition of intelligence has contributed a great deal to reshaping educational theory and practice. In Gardner's view, intelligence: 1) is the ability to respond quickly to a new situation; 2) is of importance to a specific culture — it helps and supports that culture; 3) has its own developmental patterns; and 4) is of equal potential in everyone.[29] In a situation of catastrophe, the person that does well on SAT and IQ tests may not be the most intelligent to assist others to survive. These tests mainly reflect a person's social and emotional preparation for solving test problems, which are saturated with cultural assumptions, and have unfortunately set the criteria for intelligence in our society.

As long as we hold inflexible beliefs about what makes someone valuable, or intelligent or right, we promote the labeling and petty competition that can destroy our human diversity and potential. This is seen graphically in a study of African villagers living on the shores of Kenya's Lake Victoria. The higher the school-aged children scored on a test of practical knowledge about herbal medicines used in their families, the lower they scored on academic intelligence and achievement tests. Children whose parents emphasized academics got the best grades in school and the highest IQ scores, but lacked a grasp of practical knowledge.[30] Under Howard Gardner's criteria, which children would be considered the most intelligent?

Heather Goodmanson, a third grade teacher in Hawaii, had her students figure out their own dominance profiles at the beginning of the school year. She then had them organize themselves according to their easiest sensory access: visual learners in front; auditory learners in the next row with right ear dominants on the left side of the room and left ear dominants on the right side of the room; and the gestalt fully limited in the back of the room with clay or wax to manipulate kinesthetically during class. This facilitated understanding and honoring of all the students resulting in high self-esteem for all. Though eight year olds can be very judgmental of other students, in this classroom they would notice a classmate having a bad day, look at their profile and address them, using their dominant strengths, with compassion and empathy.

Each day the students did Brain Gym® activities for five minutes at the beginning of the day, after recess and after lunch. At the end of six weeks, students were allowed to change seats, which they did with a deeper understanding of their preferential patterns and learning strengths. The stress levels in the classroom had become minimal and classroom management became a co-creative process for everyone. In the end, each student gained the highest academic success they had yet achieved in their schooling. This was a simple, commonsense way to honor each learner.

HONORING ALL STUDENTS

A majority of teachers continue to believe that learning only occurs when a child is quiet, still, listening and handing in all their homework. Competition is so keen in the learning arena that parents don't trust their own insight that play (especially parent and child play) and learning social skills is more important for their child than pushing cognitive skills on them much too early. If their child is not performing at the same level or higher than the child down the block, parents worry and take them for evaluation and diagnosis of "learning disabilities" even before they turn a year old. How can we judge a unique child who has his or her own pace of development and who is just becoming?

Parental expectations seem to heighten as the child enters school and much pressure is put on teachers to make sure the child succeeds academically. Honor students are even touted on bumper stickers: "Proud parent of an honor student." If we truly "honor" our learners, we will be sensitive to their developmental and learning style needs and realize that every person is an "honor student." Tools like the dominance profile assist that process and help to bring understanding and compassion while eliminating the need for competition. Dominance profiles can also bring understanding to couples in conflict, during parent/child conflicts, or with conflicts in the work or play setting. More information on profiles and how to determine them are in my book, *The Dominance Factor, How Knowing Your Dominant Eye, Ear, Brain, Hand & Foot Can Improve Your Learning.*[31]

The health of our educational system depends on our nurturing and promoting the learning of all our citizens. We must relinquish judgments that lead to stress-provoking labels and competition. An appropriate thinking curriculum must be established that synthesizes whole body/mind processing through regular art, music and movement in conjunction with cognitive skills. We must give learners body/mind integrative tools that allow them to stop the stress cycle and activate full sensory/hemisphere access. Perhaps then we can fully realize the unique human potential that Paul MacLean invokes, in an evolving society where all people succeed at learning.

People learn instinctively, but what we learn and how we view ourselves as learners very often depends on how we are treated by instructors and other role models in our life. The following paragraphs are excerpted from a letter written by an Australian Aboriginal mother to her child's teacher. With very few words this eloquent woman expresses a universal parental yearning: honor my child.

Dear Sir/Madam

Before you take charge, of the classroom that contains my child, please ask yourself what you are going to teach Aboriginal children ...

You will be well advised to remember that our children are skillful interpreters of the silent language, the subtle, unspoken communication of facial expressions, gestures, body movement and the use of personal space. They will know your feelings and attitudes with unerring precision, no matter how carefully you arrange your smile or modulate your voice.

They will learn in your classroom, because children learn involuntarily. What they will learn will depend on you. Will you help my child to learn to read, or will you teach him that he has a reading problem? Will you help him to develop problem solving skills, or will you teach him that school is where you try to guess what answers the teacher wants? Will he learn that his sense of his own value and dignity is valid, or will he learn that he must forever be apologetic and "try harder" because he isn't white?

Can you help him acquire the intellectual skills he needs without at the same time imposing your values on top of those he already has?

Respect my child. He is a person. He has a right to be himself.

Yours very sincerely
(An Aboriginal Parent)[32]

14

Drugs and Hyperactivity

Man is so made, that whenever anything fires his soul ...
impossibilities vanish.

— *La Fontaine*

Our society has long had strong, but mixed feelings about relying on wonder drugs for the troubles that afflict us. Trust and dependence on magic bullet type cures alternate with suspicions about exaggerated claims of success and concerns about unintended, and unadvertised, side effects. In the treatment of behavior that adversely affects learning, the pendulum is now definitely swinging in the direction of recognizing the need for non-invasive, natural and common sense alternatives to drugs.

The drugs we use to treat hyperactivity are a good place to start. There are compelling reasons to question the continued practice of treating hyperactivity and attention deficit disorders with Ritalin and other such drugs.

First, ADHD (Attention Deficit Hyperactive Disorder) is currently understood primarily as a behavorial label with no proven genetic or pathological background. The causal agents are most certainly environmental factors already delineated in the chart on What Inhibits Learning in Chapter 8. These complex environmental factors are headed up by lack of adult attention and non-stimulating learning environments. Peter and Ginger Breggin point out that when faced with an ADHD labeled child, adults have two divergent choices: transform themselves and then the education system, or suppress the child. Too often drug therapy seems the easier route. Children are naturally curious, active and dependent on parental attention for their learning. When children have something interesting to do, or when they are given a reasonable amount of quality attention, ADHD often disappears.[1]

Second, non-intrusive, child-centered, common sense methods work better in the long run. Suitably applied, these methods will allow children to be in charge of their emotions and physical energy, and give them tools to use throughout their lives.

And third, the risks of drug use usually outweigh the benefits. Drugs interact with the brain and the body in intricate, often undesirable ways. Valium, one of the most commonly used tranquilizers in our society ten years ago, gives us a warning. Valium competes with the neuropeptides responsible for causing feelings of anxiety (octadecaneuropeptides). The drug's calming effect confuses the nervous system as a whole, at the same time preempting emotional release. Valium also acts on the monocytes (white blood cells that destroy disease organisms), thus directly affecting the immune system. The behavior of monocytes is delicate and vulnerable. Adding mood-modifying chemicals to the already complex chemical structure of the body and immune system seems very risky at a time when the incidence of life threatening diseases (cancer, AIDS, and heart disease) is rising.[2]

Candace Pert, one of the great science researchers of our time, reminds us that the Anglo Saxon root of the word, Mind, means "to pay attention to", and that what we pay attention to is what we learn. There is no learning without the motivation of attention and anticipation of pleasure. With this attention and anticipation, our natural chemicals, such as dopamine, endorphins and serotonin, are produced in very subtle doses that connect to receptor sites on cells throughout our body, where they immediately stimulate specific cellular function and are then destroyed. This allows the body to constantly be open and flexible to new experiences. Learning occurs everyplace there is a receptor site, and there is no learning without emotion —anticipation, attention, motivation. Emotions originate in the body with our natural chemicals and these molecules of emotion guide all movement, thought and learning.[3]

Dopamine is a neurotransmitter that plays a major role in learning control of movements and motivation. Nerve cell bodies containing Dopamine project axons widely into the prefrontal area of the frontal lobe as well as to subcortical structures including the basal ganglion.[4] These areas have to do with regulation and control of normal fine motor movements and our motivation to explore and act in our environment in a way that optimizes all learning. Such medical conditions as Parkinson's disease administer dopamine to control shaking and erratic movements.

PET scans of children who were labeled ADD and ADHD showed substantially lower dopamine levels and smaller brain volumes than normal children, particularly in the gray matter in the right frontal area having to do with movement and integration of ideas.[5] Also, two regions at the front of the corpus callosum were found to be smaller in these children: one region connects to the part of the brain involved in suppressing the impulse to fidget; the other activates proper production of dopamine.[6,7]

RITALIN, AMPHETAMINES AND THE BRAIN

Drugs, such as Ritalin (methylphenidate), Dexedrine (dextroamphetamine) Cyleit (pemoline), Adderall (amphetamine) and sometimes the tricyclic anti-depressants (Tofranil and Norpramine) used in the treatment of hyperactivity, all modify the levels of the natural neurotransmitters in the brain. Simply taking Ritalin for several days damages dopamine-rich cells in the brain area called the caudate and habenula nucleus in the frontal lobes. The habenula maintains the connection to cells that produce serotonin and helps regulate dopamine transmission to the brain by slowing its release elsewhere.[8] Ritalin use causes dopamine to go elsewhere and serotonin to decrease: thus the body slows down for a time and the person can focus. [9]

That focus is not a natural process, it comes about because these drugs bind to the dopamine transporter proteins in the brain and thus affect dopamine action on multiple brain systems. These drugs flood the dopamine receptors so the natural endorphins, dopamine, serotonin, etc. can't stimulate the receptors.[10] They must then be detoxified before the receptor sites are free to function again, and this break down takes a long time. Thus, drugs like Ritalin and those mentioned above decrease and/or inhibit our natural, self-produced chemicals; and last a long time in our bodies before they are broken down by the liver.[11]

Most affected are the frontal lobes, basal ganglion and corpus striatum — the brain areas responsible for increased motor control, motivation, integrative thought and sense of time.[12,13] The frontal lobes control our ability to shift from a free association, open state to a detailed, focused state of awareness. This ability to shift from a broader, diffuse state to sharper, narrow focus is important for human thinking and problem solving. This is the way high level formal reasoning occurs as we easily move back and forth between the big picture (broad input) and the details. Ritalin, though it allows for attention to repetitive schoolwork, detail and rote memory, inhibits the ability to shift focus between open and focused consciousness.[14]

Also the motivational drive that makes us creative, unique, happy, curious individuals decreases. The same occurs with other stimulant drug use, television, and video games, reducing our need to acquire stimulation through our own actions.[15] Ritalin and other psycho-stimulants can decrease sensory-seeking behavior that motivates us to actively explore our world and learn.[16] Among school children taking Ritalin, 43% under the age of ten and 50% between the ages of ten and nineteen are depressed.[17, 18]

Ritalin acts on the brain just like "speed" — neuropharmacologically it has the same effects, side effects and risks as cocaine and amphetamines. The FDA classifies Ritalin in the high addiction category, Schedule II, with amphetamines, cocaine, morphine, opium and barbiturates.[19] And there is *no* evidence that Ritalin improves learning, long term academic achievement, psychological well-being or social behavior.[20, 21, 22]

A study of hyperactive adults who had been treated with Ritalin as children showed that nearly one-quarter failed to finish high school. Only one of the hyperactive boys, compared with eight of the control group, went on to obtain a graduate degree. Far fewer members of the hyperactive group held professional-level jobs compared to the control group. As adults, between one-third and one-half continued to experience ongoing hyperactivity.[23] A study has found brain shrinkage in labeled ADHD adults who have been taking Ritalin for years.[24] A PET Scan study on the effects of Ritalin on adults labeled with ADHD showed a stress connection, and though by the end of the study there was less restlessness and improved attention among subjects, their brain activity still exhibited the stress reaction. From these results, David Shaffer concluded that adult ADHD is caused by unrecognized and untreated stress.[25] Again the SOSOH label is more appropriate.

Danger also lies in the long-lasting changes in brain chemistry that may result from long-term use of drugs. It has been shown that when Ritalin was given continuously to young rats, there was a persistent reduction in the density of dopamine transporters in the brain, even after Ritalin was discontinued.[26] Since Parkinson's disease is related to low dopamine production, children who are medicated for hyperactivity may be more prone to Parkinson's disease in later life.[27] Overall, this is not a great record for Ritalin.

Some of the precautions and adverse reactions stated for Ritalin include: loss of appetite, abdominal pain, weight loss, insomnia, tachycardia (irregular heart beat), nervousness and possible hypersensitivity, anorexia, nausea, dizziness, palpitations, headache, dyskinesia and drowsiness. Regarding stress, there is a very specific statement in the Physicians Desk Reference (PDR): "Ritalin is usually not indicated for symptoms associated with acute stress reactions."[28]

The percentage of children labeled with ADHD who were given prescriptions for Ritalin and similar drugs, jumped from 55% in 1989 to 75% in 1996, and 90% in 1998.[29] The annual production quotas of Ritalin almost tripled between 1992 and 1995, and doubled again between 1995 and 2002. The 2002 quota of 20,967 kg. is sufficient to produce a little over one billion Ritalin pills containing 20 mg. of methylphenidate. The quota of amphetamines also increased sharply during 1996-2002.[30] By the year 2000, 15% of all school age children (8 million) were using Ritalin or a similar drug.[31, 32]

Ethically, we are asking our children to "just say No to drugs" and yet we are giving them the message that they are only OK if they are on this drug. The President's Council on Bioethics, in December 2002, asked the following important questions to consider: "What does use of Ritalin and amphetamines teach drug users and their peers about themselves? What does it lead children to become? Do they fail to learn self-control? Do they learn that self-control isn't necessary? Do they see themselves as weak and afflicted? Do they see themselves as excused for bad behavior or poor performance while off-Ritalin, or excused while on it? Do children who have taken Ritalin for years develop moral autonomy and responsibility? What does the spreading adult use of Ritalin and amphetamine teach young people regarding use of such drugs?"[33]

Tucker Janes, A special education teacher in Massachusetts stated it very clearly: "The use of drugs far exceeds our understanding of those drugs, and our motivation in this treatment is disgracefully oriented more towards control than education."

When the research so strongly shows that integrated movement, supportive touch, music and play grow brain areas necessary for increased focus and learning for a lifetime, without detrimental physical effects, why do we use potentially harmful drugs as a first resort? [34, 35, 36, 37]

ALTERNATIVES TO DRUGS

There are beneficial alternative strategies for helping people labeled hyperactive, ADD and ADHD. Dr. Eberhard Mann, a physician and Director of the Hyperactivity Clinic at Kapiolani Counseling Center in Hawaii, advocates a comprehensive treatment for ADHD. "By comprehensive treatment we mean a treatment program that deals with each problem that inhibits a child's learning potential and positive social interactions. Treatment components include special education, peer group counseling, self-control training, parent and teacher education, motivation and self-esteem building, anger management, and in some cases, 'stimulant' medications like Ritalin."[38]

With research showing that rough and tumble play, especially during early adolescence, reduces hyperactivity and the symptoms of ADHD,[39] and that playing with autistic children just 15 hours a week greatly decreases the symptoms of autism,[40] we might consider play, nurturing touch and movement as a first choice in treatment, and revert to drugs only after that has failed. In a short period of time, "hyperactive" children and adults I've worked with using movement, have been able to slow and coordinate their movements, shift easily between details and the broad picture, and not only focus but have fun with learning.

GOING BEYOND THE SOSOH LABELS

Is there really attention deficit disorder? SOSOH people, or all of us for that matter, are much more easily engaged when the lessons and the learning environment are relevant and valued. If the project they are working on interests them, they are able to focus their attention and even lose track of time. Motivation is a key element in focused attention. As our studies of the brain have shown us, there is a close physiological link in the nervous system between the attention center (RAS) in the brain stem and the limbic system, seat of emotion, motivation and memory.

If learning something is valuable to the learner, the brain will be activated. All people are naturally curious, especially about themselves and the world they exist in. Given motivating and interesting challenges, each person will learn and enthusiastically contribute in his or her own unique way. Albert Galaburda puts it succinctly: "Thte way dyslexics — or anyone else — use their brains is a critical factor in modifying them."[41] Even people with true dyslexia, where there may be deficits in the left hemisphere, do well with right hemisphere skills.[42] It's time to let go of our judgments, expectations and beliefs about what is "smart," and glory in learning and in each unique learner.

If there is any doubt about the efficacy of providing a safe, nurturing, personally valuable learning environment and doing playful, conscious movements with grace and coherence daily, I offer a list of what these "learning disabled" labeled students were able to do in a matter of no more than six weeks to six months:

1) relax and have fun in the classroom, enjoying the learning process
2) carry on intelligent conversations

3) focus their attention on a task for a long enough period to complete it well

4) show care and concern for other learners, teachers and themselves

5) listen quietly and attentively as others shared their ideas

6) work and play well with others (fights decreased dramatically)

7) come to an equitable understanding following a fight

8) stand up for themselves in a confident, positive way when being abused by others

9) confidently express their creativity in a myriad of ways, through music, art, poetry, dance and interpersonal relationships

10) appropriately express anger as well as affection

11) attain fine motor coordination and balance

12) exhibit use of inner speech for deductive reasoning and control of their own behavior

13) experience success and celebrate the success of others

14) implant themselves within my heart as incredibly wondrous human beings and magnificent survivors

Can any drug treatment offer these results? And my experiences are by no means unique.

It is time to see each child and every person as unique learners with their own specific time line and pace of learning. Understanding the stressors that lead to the SOSOH labels gives us a place from which to start in setting up optimal learning situations. Simple, natural drug-free tools like hands-on learning, music, creative play, dance, Brain Gym, Tai Chi, yoga, etc. can assist us as we consciously undertake to eliminate all the SOSOH labels concealing the intelligent learner beneath them.

One boy, a third grader in a self-contained classroom for the emotionally handicapped, (he showed a gestalt, fully limited dominance profile) touched my life so deeply with his intelligence that I wrote this poem about him:

THE GIFT

I felt his sticky warmth as he clutched the back of the chair.
"Lost child, hyperactive, L.D., ADHD, emotionally handicapped"
His bloody nose and caked hair covering the mud stained face
and two white rivulets that coursed from his eyes
to spill with anger on the floor.

Caught in the innate act of survival — the playground fight
a desperate attempt to hold some dignity — some sense of
humanhood against a peer's cutting words.
Imprisoned in labels, chiseled on his delicate memory from birth.
Child of light reduced to a psychological/linguistic profile
carefully maintained and elaborated by each new caretaker.

These same lips that now quivered with frustration, had yesterday
led me through his imaginative richness on a fantasy that left
my reality behind in the wake of its intricate beauty.
And these now bloody hands had drawn a man with 17 arms,
each holding a uniquely carved cane, and walking his
rainbow colored dog with fluorescent eyes.

And these legs, bruised and valiantly locked to hold up the
sagging trunk of his body, knew their way expertly around
a soccer ball and could effortlessly sprint his
bare feet down a grass and lava playground.
This child who knew too few hugs and kisses, this exquisite
child with the future in his heart.

I was this child, many years ago — unable to explain my needs
or voice in a logical way my frustration.
Unable to know that the hole in my soul needed a hug,
or someone to see me clearer than I did
to connect me with me —
Or show me how - a quick course in knowing and loving self,
and believing it in the face of all the labels
and limited, socially imposed images.

This moment and this child are a place to start to heal the wounds.
His eyes, a reflection of the world — all sticky,
bruised and filled with FEAR,
deep and honest they don't allow me to turn away.
He is my gift, my wake-up call — one more
God given opportunity to learn LOVE.

15

~

Looking Outward for Models

It surprises me how our culture can destroy curiosity in the most curious of all animals — human beings.

— Paul MacLean[1]

To get a better sense of what makes learning successful, I believe it's time to look at what works — not only in our culture and educational system, but elsewhere in the world. I often think we misrepresent the truth by calling ourselves and our culture "First World," while labeling African villages high in the Lesotho mountains "Third World." The distinction may be apt only if we are referring to the proliferation of technology or economic affluence. But when it comes to learning, it is time for a major re-evaluation. I'm not suggesting we return to B.T. (before technology), but I do believe we have a lot to learn about learning from the insights and practices of other cultures.

INSIGHTS FROM THE THIRD WORLD

In the villages of Lesotho in Southern Africa, social values and communal practices support early childhood development much more effectively than ours do. The benefits for the children are substantial. An occupational therapist who heads an assessment group in Kwa Zulu, South Africa shared her interesting findings with me. Of the 10,000 children assessed for learning readiness prior to school entry each year in Kwa Zulu, the black rural children have consistently scored far superior to the white urban children on all but three of the fifty assessment tests. On two of these three they tested the same. On the third — which tested their foveal (up close, two dimensional) focus — they did poorly (for reasons I explored earlier in Chapter 6). The black children exhibit a high level of learning proficiency, body/mind integration and a strong motivation to learn.[2]

These cultures have much to teach us about valuing people, early sensory-motor stimulation, encouragement of responsibility, language development, and interpersonal relationships. Children, and especially babies, are considered the treasures of the whole clan. In one tribal culture, a newborn baby spends its first six weeks with just its parents and immediate family to allow close bonding. During that time, the whole tribe is involved in clearing any grievances they have with one another. They wear leather aprons with long fringes. They tie knots in the fringe for each grievance they carry against another member of the community. It is their job to clear all the grievances and untie all the knots before the baby is presented to the tribe at the end of the six week period.

Since there are many babies born to this tribe, there is constant reconciliation. This custom guarantees a high degree of social harmony for the good of the young. Ideally, all children are to be brought into a fully loving, cooperative community that works together for the benefit of each child throughout its growth. Additionally, each adult in the tribe becomes responsible for the upbringing of every child. This is another socially cohesive practice that endows children with concern for the collective good, knowledge of the rules and boundaries, and entitlement to security and love.

Upon learning about this system, I realized why I have often felt overwhelmed as a single parent. I have tried to do for my daughter what is naturally handled by at least a hundred other people in a family clan.

In the clan structure, the first year of the baby's life is full of sensory-motor stimulation. This includes the constant touch and attention from everyone in the community, the baby's place in the family bed at night, the rich natural smells of home, family and friends, and continuous physical contact with the mother, even when she works. At work, a mother will firmly attach the baby to her back by a towel or blanket so the baby's ear is next to her heart. From this place, the baby rocks and sways to the mother's graceful dancing movements and feels the vibrations and rhythm of her song as she goes about her work. Babies are lovingly fed on demand. By meeting the basic survival needs for hunger, shelter, warmth, and stimulation, a pattern of safety and security is established. From this secure foundation babies feel free to confidently explore their new environment.

From its position on her back the baby is free to turn its head, strengthening its neck muscles in order to see and hear the vibrant life going on around it from a binocular and binaural perspective. The infant's vestibular and muscular development is rapid, giving the baby even more command over its sensory-motor input.

When the mother is not working, she stretches out the blanket so the child may explore its environment from its belly or back. Core postural muscles strengthen as the baby wiggles, explores its appendages and finally learns to roll over, push up, crawl and sit. Its eyes gain acuity and recognition in a sensory-rich environment. The baby sees constantly moving shades of green as the leaves overhead catch a breeze, the brilliant blue African sky with its ever changing cloud patterns, a plethora of brightly colored birds full of song, and the bobbing, laughing faces of children and adults bringing creatively designed toys made from plants, stones, cardboard, and even plastic shopping bags. These babies are lifted, cuddled, tickled and hugged.

As they start to scooch and crawl, they are given full access to their environment. Their playground is the dirt floor of the rondovelle at night in the midst of dance, song and stories, or the dusty, rocky or rich fields during the day as the mother works. Core muscle movement, gravitational understanding and full shoulder/pelvic girdle function develop naturally before the child takes its first step.

Once walking, the child learns quickly to run to keep up with the other children who, in their bare feet, can traverse any terrain with grace. I vividly remember one little boy who could not have been walking long, who started running with the other children after our truck as we left his village. His sister grabbed his shirt to stop him but he pulled away from her, leaving her standing there, and followed us for a good mile, smiling and laughing at the chase as his little legs and bare feet pumped across the rocky dirt road.

Children are a part of the whole family/clan structure, often being cared for by grandparents after they are weaned. As the children grow older they take care of younger children, and by the age of six are responsible for gathering firewood or looking after a cow, sheep or horse. They are encouraged in carving, weaving, singing, dancing, storytelling, painting and creative, imaginative play.

At night the families in a compound eat together amid animated talk of the day's adventures. You can hear them calling to each other across the valley and over the sound of drums as they close their workday. Then, instead of TV, there are the stories from family or clan members who have come to visit and who speak another dialect or language. Children are multilingual, knowing two or three languages by the time they go to school. There is always song as the night closes softly over the final drum beats and the last strains of multipart harmony to fade and fill the African night with silence and a billion stars.

The strong tribal traditions I experienced have as their core the idea of *ubuntu*, which means: "Because I am, we are; and because we are, I am." The clan structure is based on consensus government. The chief calls the clan together when communal decisions must be made. It may take days or even weeks to decide the outcome, all clan members having the right to state their opinion. The consensus decision is then embraced and upheld by every clan member. Respect for the elders of the clan, and anyone older than oneself is learned early.

What struck me the most was the children's curiosity, and strong desire to learn. They walked long distances to attend school, and did it with utmost willingness. Learning and wisdom are highly prized by all clan members.

A FIRST WORLD LEARNING PLAN FROM AFRICA

Through these African communities, I gained an understanding of the crucial developmental factors necessary for the elaboration of full learning potential. Having observed and been privileged to share their life, I offer this summary as my idea of a "First World" plan to support learning and brain development:

- A rich sensory environment full of natural sound, touch, smell and visual stimuli.
- Lots of movement, play and the ability to freely explore one's own body in space.
- Security and basic needs gratification that fosters full exploration of the physical environment.
- Parents or other adults available as listeners, consultants and interactive participants in each child's growth.
- Plenty of time and practice for pattern recognition — of sensory-motor patterns, language patterns, rhythm and music patterns and human relationship patterns.
- The establishment of responsibilities, boundaries, and respect for self and others.
- Encouragement of imagination, art, music, communication and interactive play.

EFFECTIVE FORMAL LEARNING PROGRAMS

The learning process is supported and nurtured when these factors are present in the home and community during the earliest years of childhood. Equally important in these formative years is how the learning process is regarded in the child's formal education. I have also been fortunate in witnessing and experiencing formal education programs that truly honor the learner, are student centered and democratic, and, more important, have a history of effectiveness. Through community encouragement, these programs are being implemented in schools across America with varying degrees of success. They are certainly raising the consciousness of their communities and allowing them to shed practices that are too often ineffectual.

Some schools in the United States have gone out of their way to accommodate individualized learning. Arney Langburg developed one such program in the High School Redirection Program, an alternative school within the Denver Public School system that gave "last chance kids" another chance. The school was fashioned after a school Arney developed and ran in Evergreen, Colorado to accommodate his own children during their high school years.[3]

There were fourteen criteria each student had to meet for graduation. These included: knowledge of inner resources; caring for self and others; sense of justice; ethics and integrity; risk-taking, self-challenge; ability to change; appreciation for richness of cultural diversity; persistence, commitment; long-term employability; entrepreneurship; basic cognitive skills. Upon entrance, each student did a self-assessment of the fourteen graduation expectations, thus determining where to concentrate with further in-depth work. School policy encouraged all students to set their personal, academic and social goals. With the assistance of a mentor, each learner set up a specific learning program that included apprenticeships in fields of interest.

High School Redirection, with over 300 students in 1992, claimed the lowest absentee rate in the Denver Public Schools. They did a wonderful job, successfully graduating self-directed students with personal integrity, marketable skills, and a solid base for life-long learning success. Unfortunately, rather than becoming the prototype program that would have assisted the whole school system, the funding was cut because money was needed for special education programs, and High School Redirections was dropped.

THE DANISH PUBLIC SCHOOL SYSTEM

A larger scale model of excellent public education is the Danish system. Schools in Denmark are organized around wise, learner-centered educational policies. Learning proceeds at a more brain-friendly pace than in American schools, the curriculum more closely aligned with hallmarks of natural brain development. Students participate in curriculum planning, enhancing their motivation to learn. The schoolwork emphasizes thinking and integration of knowledge. There is less emphasis on quantification of progress, hence less competition.

The education program begins in the first one to two years of life, with one parent given full pay to stay home during this important developmental time so the child feels secure, which allows him to optimally explore and learn. Then a pre-school or forest kindergarten is available to the children where they learn from other children, the environment and much *unstructured* play. These programs foster imagination, curiosity, risk-taking and the development of important social and physical skills that fully develop the learning mechanism and ensure life-long learning. To ensure safety in the learning process, students stay with the same teacher and student family until they reach age twelve. Because the teacher works personally with each student, they know when students are having difficulties and can assist them in effective ways without the need for constant assessments.[4, 5]

Danish public school students don't begin school until age seven and are not tested until approximately age fourteen. These first tests measure only linguistic, scientific, technical and mathematical skills. These are considered basic skills with information processing and creative thought receiving the principal emphasis of the curriculum, rather than the other way around. The final exam, given at age seventeen or eighteen, is not at all like the final exams you might remember from high school. The Danish final demands much more integrative formal reasoning.

Students choose when they will take their final exam. Each is given a piece of art and a piece of literature, poetry or prose (usually one of the classics). They have a period of time to write the exam, usually a couple of weeks to a month. They are expected to prepare an integrated dissertation tieing their assigned pieces to history, biology, physics, chemistry, language, mathematics, art and social sciences. This final exam is written in two languages and then presented to a committee that interviews the student to determine eligibility for graduation.[6]

An impressive level of problem solving and reasoning was evident in all the Danish classrooms I visited, in students ranging from age seven through college. The lack of disciplinary problems was striking, though many classrooms contained thirty-five to forty-five students due to a recent influx of immigrants into Denmark. Students were honored for their thinking skills and imagination and were encouraged to work in groups to develop communication skills.

The curriculum was developed at the beginning of each nine-week period in a democratic process to accommodate the specific interests of the students and teacher. Teachers asked their students which topics they were interested in studying. The selected topics were then explored, setting the curriculum for the core learning sessions for the next nine weeks. Students took responsibility for gathering resources, developing projects in cooperative groups, and sharing their study and information with the rest of the class. Teachers and students learned together. Age appropriate skills were taught and directly connected to the student-determined curriculum to enhance and anchor it.[7]

Each class lesson in the Danish Folkskole was replete with art, music, movement and cooperative group work. Cooperative learning in the Danish schools encouraged students to interact, share their learning preferences, and listen to and learn from one another. Social interaction occurring in the course of all these educational activities honored individual differences and gifts, thus eliminating the labels and limitations to individual initiative and creativity.[8]

A study of selected secondary schools in the United Kingdom, the Netherlands, Germany and Denmark during the 1992-1993 academic year came up with some interesting findings on how these educational systems vary, particularly in the ways they prepare young people for their role as citizens. In Denmark, national law stipulates that the primary function of the Folkskole is to prepare students to be citizens in a democracy. Participation in decision-making at the classroom level begins in the first grade and continues throughout the students' schooling.

The quantitative findings of this study showed that Danish students more confidently communicated and listened to ideas. They showed the highest levels of political efficacy. They also believed their actions could make a difference in their world. The Danish classroom climate was perceived as most open with the greatest opportunity to explore diverse sides of issues. Teachers encouraged students to form and comfortably express their own opinions on issues, even when they disagreed with the teacher's or other students' opinions. Danish students indicated the highest level of support for women in government and for free speech for all people, no matter what their viewpoint.[9]

The ITI (Integrated Thematic Instruction) program, developed by Susan Kovalik, comes as close to the elegant Danish system as I've seen in the U.S. To ensure safety in the learning situation, children are met at the door with a hug or handshake each morning. The first couple of weeks are spent in developing solid caring/sharing relationships and a homey atmosphere in the room with plants, standing lights (instead of fluorescent), couches and a greatly enriched environment.

Children are encouraged to explore and first gain a context through hands-on experience, in order to formulate the questions that lead to understanding at a greater depth. Subjects are carefully selected to be of greatest long-term interest with real-life contexts for the children, and cross subject lines in a highly integrated way. I was impressed by the student enthusiasm and interest I experienced in the ITI classrooms I visited. Fortunately, this program is being instituted in thousands of classrooms nationwide.[10]

RETHINKING EDUCATIONAL GOALS

"In the over-eager embrace of the rational, scientific and technological," David Kolb observes, "we lost touch with our own experience as the source of personal learning and development. The learning process must be reimbued with the texture and feeling of human experiences shared and interpreted through dialogue with one another."[11] Our connection with others and the safety it affords becomes the gateway of possibilities. The research profoundly shows how important the heart is for brain function, and now it is time to lead with our hearts, releasing the competitive thrust that comes with disembodied standardized testing at ever-earlier ages. It is time for cooperative learning where everyone, including the teacher is constantly open to new possibilities. The workplace has changed, the explosion of information in our technological society places, and will continue to place, new demands on every worker. Our schools need to turn out more appropriately educated citizens, what the National Learning Foundation (NLF) calls, Agile Learners. The Agile Learner model empowers people to learn for a lifetime, without fear of change or ambiguity, as enthusiastic explorers of their own lives and environments, and supportive co-creators with others.

The Agile Learner is not a passive sponge of information, but the master of information, capable of reflection, choice, and altruism. According to the NLF, the agile learner will display significantly different attributes and skills from those rewarded today in our school systems. These include:

> *PERSONAL:* Flexible, Creative, Introspective, Curious, Imaginative, Adaptable, Aesthetically aware, Ambiguity tolerant, Acting from integrity

> *INTERPERSONAL:* Celebrates diversity, Altruistically motivated, Effectively interdependent, Collaborator, Team player

> *ESSENTIAL:* Literacy/numeracy, Mastery of technology, Communicaton, Negotiation

> *PERFORMANCE:* Systems thinking, Pattern detecting, Synthesizing, Analyzing, Experimenting, Problem solving, Decision making, Reflecting

The indicators of success with such an education would be: love of learning, high self-esteem, body/mind congruity, self-rescription and community/world consciousness.[12] These are the very qualities I saw in the Danish Folkskoles, so I know this is a practical and feasible goal, especially since we have workable proven models to follow.

Slow integrative, coherent movements experienced in creative dance, playing a musical instrument, Brain Gym®, Tai Chi and yoga act as a bridge between the current educational system and the educational systems emerging worldwide to ensure the development of the agile learner. Integrated movement accommodates all learning styles, enhances myelination between the two hemispheres and balances the electrical energy and integrative processing across the whole brain. These movements support the learner's maximum potential by activating full brain function, decreasing environmental stressors and fully accommodating individual learning styles and pace.

Learning itself is part of a totally fulfilling life, and should continue to occupy a central role from infancy to old age. So the attitudes and practices that favor learning should themselves be studied and cultivated. This is a lesson that is taught by many individuals in many cultures.

Integrative movements, done in a playful context, are an effective, profound, common sense, non-drug option that greatly facilitates lifelong learning. Once we begin using all the capacity of the body/mind system, the learning process becomes immeasurably more effective, rekindling the excitement and joy that come with discovering our world, our relationship to it and our infinite creative possibilities.

Movement, a natural process of life, is now understood to be essential to learning, creative thought, high level formal reasoning, and our ability to understand and act altruistically towards all those that share our world. It is time to consciously bring integrative movement back into every aspect of our lives and realize, as I have, that something this simple and natural can be the source of miracles.

Notes

༄

2: NEURAL NETWORKS

[1] Merzenich, Taub and Greenough. *Neural Plasticity.* **Harvard Brain**, 1999 (vol. 16), pp. 16-20.

[2] Schwartz, Jeffrey M. and Sharon Begley. **Neuroplasticity and the Power of Mental Force**. NY: Harper Collins, 2002.

[3] Kempermann, Gerd and Fred H. Gage. *New Nerve Cells For the Adult Brain.* **Scientific American**, May 1999, pp. 48-53.

[4] Alvarez-Buylla, Arturo & Jose M. Garcia-Verdugo. *Neurogenesis in Adult Subventricular Zone. Journal of Neuroscience*, February 1, 2002 (vol. 22:3), pp. 629-634.

[5] Eriksson, Peter S., et. al. *Neurogenesis in the Adult Human Hippocampus.* **Nature Medicine,** November 1998 (vol. 4:11), pp. 1313-1317.

[6] Gage, Fred H. *Brain, Repair Yourself.* **Scientific American,** September 2003, pp. 47-51.

[7] Eriksson, P. S., et al. *Neurogenesis in the hippocampus of the human brain.* **Natural Medicine**, 1998 (vol. 4), pp. 1313-1317.

[8] Merzenich, Taub and Greenough. **Neural Plasticity**. 1999

[9] Van Praag, Henriette, Gerd Kempermann, & Fred Gage. *Running Increases Cell Proliferation and Neurogenesis in the Adult Mouse Dentate Gyrus.* **Nature Neuroscience,** March 1999 (vol. 2:3), pp. 266-270.

[10] Gould, Elizabeth, et. al. *Learning Enhances Adult Neurogenesis In the Hippocampal Formation.* **Nature Neuroscience,** March 1999 (vol. 2:3), pp. 260-265.

[11] Greenough, William T. et. al. *New Neurons in Old Brains: Learning to Survive?* **Nature Neuroscience,** March 1991 (vol. 2:3), pp. 203-205.

[12] Verghese, Joe, et. al. 2003. *Leisure Activities and the Risk of Dementia in the Elderly.* **New England Journal of Medicine**, 2003 (vol. 348:25), pp. 2508-2515.

[13] Churchill, James, et. al. *Exercise, Experience and the Aging Brain.* **Neurobiology of Aging**, 2002 (vol. 23:5), pp. 941-955.

[14] Panksepp, J., et al. *Modeling ADHD-type Arousal with Unilateral Frontal Cortex Damage In Rats and Beneficial Effects of Play Therapy.* **Brain and Cognition**, June, 2003 (vol 52:1), pp. 97-105.

[15] Stevens, Charles F. *The Neuron.* **Scientific American,** September 1979, p. 1.

[16] Tortora, Gerard J. & Nicholas P. Anagnostakos. **Principles of Anatomy and Physiology. Sixth Edition**. NY: Harper, 1990. pp. 426-445.

[17] Nauta, Walle J.H. & Michael Feirtag. *The Organization of the Brain.* **The Brain, A**

Scientific American Book. San Francisco: W.H. Freeman, 1979. p. 40.

[18] Tortora & Anagnostakos. *Principles . . .* p. 238.

[19] Nauta, Walle J.H. & Michael Feirtag. p. 49.

[20] Posthuma, Danielle and Michelle Luciano. *Scientists Search For the Biology of Smarts.* **Science News**, February 8, 2003 (vol. 163), pp. 92-93.

[21] Tortora & Anagnostakos. pp. 336-337.

[22] Pert, Candice. **Molecules Of Emotion, Why You Feel The Way You Feel.** NY. Scribner, 1997. pp. 135-148.

[23] Tortora & Anagnostakos. pp. 345-348.

[24] Chopra, Deepak. **Quantum Healing, Exploring The Frontiers Of Mind/Body Medicine.** NY: Bantam Books, 1989. pp. 26, 50.

[25] Snyder, Solomon H. *The Molecular Basis of Communication Between Cells.* **Scientific American,** October 1985, p. 33.

[26] Diamond, Marian. **Enriching Heredity, The Impact of the Environment on the Anatomy of the Brain.** NY: Free Press, 1988. pp. 67-77.

[27] Lichtman, Jeff W., Rita J. Balice-Gordon & Lawrence Katz, et. al. *Seeing Synapses: New Ways to Study Ne*rves. **American Association for the Advancement of Science, Annual Meeting in San Francisco,** February 1994.

[28] Stevens, Charles F. *The Neuron.* pp. 1-2.

[29] Holloway, Marguerite. *The Mutable Brain.* **Scientific American,** September 2003, pp. 79-85

[30] Chopra, Deepak. **Quantum Healing.** p. 50.

[31] Masland, Richard H. *The Functional Architecture of the Retina.* **Scientific American,** December, 1986, pp. 131-147.

[32] Merzenich, Michael. *Brain Plasticity Origins of Human Abilities and Disabilities.* **Sixth Symposium, Decade of the Brain Series.** NIMH and the Library of Congress. Washington, DC, Feb. 7, 1995.

[33] Chopra, Deepak. **Quantum Healing.** p. 26.

[34] Levin, Harvey S. & Jordan Grafman (Ed.). **Cortical Reorganization of Function After Brain Damage.** NY: Oxford University Press, 2000.

[35] Roberts, Debra. *ABC News 20/20, Brandy Binder Story.* Documentary Editor, Debra Roberts. October 3, 1997.

[36] Golden, Daniel. *Building A Better Brain — Brain Calisthenics.* **Life Magazine,** July 1994, pp. 63-72.

[37] Schrof, Joannie M. *Brain Power.* **U.S. News & World Report,** November 28, 1994, p. 94.

3: SENSORY EXPERIENCE

[1] Rivlin, Robert & Karen Gravelle. **Deciphering The Senses: The Expanding World of Human Perception.** NY: Simon & Schuster, 1984, p. 11

[2] Niuhuis, J. B. (Ed.) *Fetal Behavior — Developmental and Perinatal Aspects.* **Niuhuis,** New York, Oxford University Press. 1992, p. 133.

[3] Damasio, Antonio R. **Descartes' Error: Emotion, Reason, and the Human Brain.** NY: Putnam, 1994. pp. 112-113.

[4] MacLean, Paul D. *A Mind of Three Minds: Educating the Triune Brain.* **Seventy-Sev-**

enth Yearbook of the National Society for the Study of Education. Chicago, 1978.

[5] Pearce, Joseph Chilton. *Evolution's End, Claiming the Potential of Our Intelligence*. San Francisco: Harper & Row, 1992.

[6] Schiefelbein, Susan. *Beginning the Journey*. *The Incredible Machine*. Washington, DC: National Geographic Society, 1986. p. 36.

[7] Tortora, Gerard J. & Nicholas P. Anagnostakos. *Principles of Anatomy and Physiology*. *Sixth Edition*. NY: Harper, 1990. p. 488.

[8] Ayres, A. Jean. *Sensory Integration and Learning Disorders*. Los Angeles: Western Psychological Services, 1972. p. 58.

[9] Tortora, Gerard J. & Nicholas P. Anagnostakos. *Principles ...* pp. 392, 483-490.

[10] Hendrickson, Homer. *The Vision Development Process*. Santa Ana, CA: Optometric Extension Program, 1969. p. 4.

[11] Schwartz, Eugene. *Seeing, Hearing, Learning: The Interplay of Eye and Ear in Waldorf Education*. Excerpts from Camp Glenbrook Conference of the Association for a Healing Education, June 14-16, 1988. 1990.

[12] Klivington, Kenneth. *The Science of Mind*. Cambridge, MA: MIT Press, 1989. p. 149.

[13] Ayres, A. Jean. *Sensory Integration and Learning Disorders*. p. 70.

[14] Hernandez-Peon, R. *Neurophysiology of Attention*. P.J. Vinkin & G.W. Bruyn (eds.), *Handbook of Clinical Neurology*. Amsterdam: North Holland Pub., 1969.

[15] Friedrich, Patrick. Wald Kindergarten, Zartenerstr. 7, 79199 Kirchzarten, Germany. Communication with originator of school in Kirszarten, Germany.

[16] Minstry of Education and Research, International Relations Division. *Characteristic Features of Danish Education*. Copenhagen, Denmark. 1992. pp. 1-39.

[17] Tomatis, Alfred A. *The Conscious Ear, My Life of Transformation through Listening*. Barrytown, NY: Station Hill Press, 1991. pp. 208-215.

[18] Campbell, Don G. *The Roar of Silence*. Wheaton, IL: Quest Books, 1989.

[19] Schiefelbein, Susan. *Beginning the Journey*. *The Incredible Machine*. pp. 36-39.

[20] Goddard, Sally. *A Teacher's Window into the Child's Mind*. Eugene, Oregon: Fern Ridge Press, 1996, p. 44.

[21] Tomatis, A.A. *Education and Dyslexia*. Fribourg, Switzerland: Association Internationale d'Audio-Psycho-Phonologie, 1978.

[22] Lonsbury-Martin, Brenda. *Using the Sounds of Hearing*. (February 1993 meeting of the AAAS.) *Science News*, February 27, 1993, (vol. 143), p. 141.

[23] Berard, Guy. *Hearing Equals Behavior*. New Caanan, CT: Keats Pub., 1993, pp. 15-37.

[24] Naselmento, Cristane and Sam Ward. *Noise is Major Cause of Hearing Loss*. Ear Foundation and Plantronics. *U.S.A Today*, June 2003.

[25] Stiller, Angelika, & Renate Wennekes. *Sensory Stimulation Important to Developmental Processes*. Neuenkirchen, Germany: Astrup, 31, 1992, 2846.

[26] Hopson, Janet L. *We May Follow Our Noses More Often Than Is Now Realized*. *Smithsonian Magazine*, March 1979, pp. 78-85.

[27] Tortora, Gerard J. & Nicholas Anagnostakos. *Principles ...* pp. 427-433.

[28] Tortora, Gerard J. & Nicholas P. Anagnostakos. *Principles ...* pp. 336-337.

[29] Restak, Richard M. *The Mind*. NY: Bantam Books, 1988. p. 87.

[30] Levi-Montalcini, Rita. *Developmental Neurobiology and the Natural History of Nerve Growth Factor.* **Annual Review of Neurosciences**, 1982 (5), pp. 341-362.

[31] Ayres, A. Jean. **Sensory Integration and Learning Disorders.**

[32] Levine, S. *Infantile Experience and Resistance to Physiological Stress.* **Science,** 1957 (vol. 126), pp. 405-406.

[33] Meaney M.J. et.al. *Effects of Neonatal Handling on Age-related Impairments Associated with the Hippocampus.* **Science**, 1988 (vol. 239), pp. 776-768,

[34] Pearce, Joseph Chilton. **Evolution's End, Claiming the Potential of Our Intelligence.** p. 113.

[35] Francis. D. and Meaney, M.J. *Maternal Care and the Development of Stress Responses.* **Neurobiology** (Current Opinion), 1999 (vol. 9), pp. 128-134. .

[36] Pearce, Joseph Chilton. *The Magical Child Matures.* NY: Bantam Books, 1986.

[37] Liu, D. et. al. Maternal Care, *Hippocampal Synaptogenesis and Cognitive Development in Rats.* **Nature Neuroscience**, 2000 (vol.3), pp. 799-806.

[38] Panksepp, J. et al. *Modeling ADHD-type Arousal with Unilateral Frontal Cortex Damage in Rats and Beneficial Effects of Play Therapy.* **Brain and Cognition Journal**, June, 2003 (vol. 52:1), pp. 97-105

[39] Otzl. M.S. et. al. *Maternal Deprivation Affects Behaviour From Youth to Senescence; Amplification of Individual Differences In Spatial Learning and Memory in Senescent Brown Norway Rats.* **European Journal of Neuroscience**, 2000 (vol.12), pp. 3771-3780.

[40] Hofer, M.A. *On the Nature and Consequences of Early Loss.* **Psychosomatic Medicine**, 1996 (vol. 58), pp. 570-581,

[41] Penfield, Wilder & H.H. Jasper. **Epilepsy and the Functional Anatomy of the Human Brain.** Boston: Little Brown, 1954. p. 28.

[42] Wilson, Frank R. **The Hand; How It's Use Shapes the Brain, Language and Human Culture.** NY: Pantheon Books, 1998, Introduction.

[43] Connolly, Kevin J. (ed.). *The Psychobiology of the Hand.* Reviewed *in* **New England Journal of Medicine**. October 25, 2001.

[44] Panksepp. Jaak. **Affective Neuroscience, The Foundations of Human and Animal Emotions.** NY: Oxford University Press, 1998, pp. 280-310.

[45] Sacks, Oliver. **The Man Who Mistook His Wife for A Hat, And Other Clinical Tales.** NY: Harper & Row, 1987. p. 43.

[46] Crum, Thomas F. **The Magic of Conflict: Turning A Life of Work into A Work of Art.** NY: Simon & Schuster, 1987. pp. 54-56.

[47] Suplee, Curt. *Neurology: Watching, Imagining and Doing.* **Washington Post**, Science Notebook, Oct. 17, 1994, p. 2. (Summarized from *Nature*, October 13, 1994.)

[48] Hainline, Louise. *The Development of Basic Visual Abilities.* **Perceptual Development, Visual, Auditory and Speech Perception in Infancy.** Ed. Alan Slater. East Sussex, UK: Psychology Press. 1998. pp. 5-42.

[49] Tortora, Gerard J. & Nicholas P. Anagnostakos. **Principles ...** pp. 475-480.

[50] Kohler, Ivo. *Experiments with Goggles.* **Scientific American**, 1962 (206:5), p. 62.

[51] Gregory, Richard. **Eye and Brain, The Psychology of Seeing.** NY: McGraw-Hill, 1966. pp. 204-219.

[52] Grady, Denise. *The Vision Thing: Mainly in the Brain.* **Discover,** June 1993 (vol. 14:6), p. 58.

[53] Escher, M.C. *M.C. Escher, 29 Master Prints*. NY: Abrams, 1981.

[54] Thing, N.E. *Magic Eye: A New Way of Looking at the World*. Kansas City: Andrews and McMeel, 1993.

[55] Tortora, Gerard J. & Nicholas P. Agnostakos. *Principles ...* pp. 476-477.

[56] Wallace, Mark. *Study Provides New Insights About Brain Organization*. **Proceedings of the National Academy of Sciences**, February 2004.

[57] Diamond, Marian & Janet Hopson. *Magic Trees Of The Mind*. NY: Dutton/Penguin Group, 1998 p. 30

[58] Diamond, Marian. *Enriching Heredity, The Impact of the Environment on the Anatomy of the Brain*. NY: Free Press, 1988. pp. 9-62.

[59] Thomas, Alexander & Stella Chess. *Temperament and Development.* NY: Brunner/Mazel, 1977. pp. 18-26, 93-107, 183-190.

[60] Thomas, Alexander & Stella Chess. *Genesis and Evolution of Behavioral Disorders: From Infancy to Early Adult Life*. **American Journal of Psychiatry**, 141(1), pp. 1-9.

[61] Russell, Peter. *The Consciousness Revolution. A Transtlantic Dialogue with Stan Groff and Ervin Laszlo*. London: Element Books. 1999.

4: THE ROLE OF EMOTIONS

[1] Damasio, Antonio R. *Descartes' Error and the Future of Human Life.* **Scientific American**, October, 1994, p. 144.

[2] Gelernter, David. *The Muse in the Machine, Computerizing the Poetry of Human Thought*. NY: Free Press, 1994. pp. 46-47.

[3] Gelernter, David. *The Muse in the Machine*. p. 35.

[4] Damasio, Antonio R. *Descartes' Error: Emotion, Reason, and the Human Brain*. NY, Putnam, 1994. pp. 205-223.

[5] Damasio, Antonio R. *The Feeling of What Happens; Body and Emotion In the Making of Consciousness*. NY, Harcourt Brace. 1999.

[6] Damasio, Antonio R. *Descartes' Error: Emotion, Reason, and the Human Brain*. NY, Putnam, 1994. pp. 205-223.

[7] Damasio, Antonio R. *Descartes' Error*. p. 199.

[8] Damasio, Antonio R. *Descartes' Error*. pp. 170-173.

[9] Damasio, Antonio R. *Descartes' Error*. p. 200.

[10] Coulter, Dee Joy. *The Triune Brain*. Longmont, CO: Coulter Pub., 1985. Sound Cassette.

[11] Pert, Candace. *Neuropeptides: The Emotions and Bodymind*. **Noetic Sciences Review and Advances**, Number 2, Spring 1987.

[12] Damasio, Antonio, et. al. *Brain Faces Up to Fear, Social Signs*. *Nature*, December 15, 1994. **Science News**, December 17, 1944 (vol. 146), p. 406.

[13] Buzsaki, Gyorgy. *Sleepy Brains Make Memorable Waves*. **Proceedings of the National Academy of Sciences,** February 8, 2003.

[14] Tortora, Gerard J., & Nicholas P. Anagnostakos. *Principles of Anatomy and Physiology. Sixth Edition*. pp. 400-401.

[15] Middleton, Frank A. & Peter L. Strick. *Brain Gets Thoughtful Reappraisal*. *Science*, October 21, 1994. **Science News**, October 19, 1994 (vol. 146), p. 284.

[16] Pert, Candace. *Molecules of Emotion, Why You Feel the Way You Feel.* NY: Scribner, 1997. pp. 135-148.

[17] Merzenich, Michael, et. al. *Neural Plasticity.* **Harvard Brain**, 1999 (vol.16), pp. 16-20.

[18] Meaney, Michael J., et. al. *Memory Loss Tied to Stress.* **Science News**, November 20, 1993 (vol. 144), p. 332.

[19] Chopra, Deepak. **Quantum Healing, Exploring the Frontiers of Mind/Body Medicine.** Conference in Honolulu, Hawaii, February, 1991.

[20] Tyler, Rachelle, et. al *Maternal Psychopathology and Attachment In Toddlers of Heavy Cocaine-using Mothers.* **Infant Mental Health Journal**, May/June 2001 (vol. 22:3), pp. 316-334.

[21] deBeauport, Elizabeth. **Tarrytown Newsletter.** 1983.

[22] Francis. D. D. and Meaney, M.J. *Maternal Care and the Development of Stress Responses.* **Neurobiology** *(current opinion).* 1999 *(vol. 9),* pp. 128-134.

[23] Oitzl. N.W. et. al. *Maternal Deprivation Affects Behavior from Youth to Senescence: Amplification of Individual Differences in Spatial Learning and Memory in Senescent Brown Norway Rats.* **European J. of Neuroscience**, 2000 (vol.12), pp. 3771-3780.

[24] Goddard, Sally. **A Teachers Window To The Child's Mind, and Papers from the Institute of Neuro-Physiological Psychology.** Eugene, OR: Fern Ridge Press, 1996.

[25] Prescott, James. **Discovering the Intelligence of Play.** 1997. Video through Touch The Future, www.TTFuture.org.

[26] Russek, L.B. and G. E. Schwartz. *Interpersonal Heart-Brain Registration and the Perception of Parental Love: A 42 year follow-up of the Harvard Mastery of Stress Study.* **Subtle Energies** , 1994 (vol. 5:3), pp. 195-208.

[27] Gorski, Peter A. *Contemporary Pediatric Practice; In Support of Infant Mental Health.* **Infant Mental Health Journal.**, Jan-April 2001 (vol. 22:1), p. 188-203.

[28] Amaral, David. *Regions Involving Memory and Emotion Large in Children With Autism.* **Journal of Neuroscience**, July 14, 2004.

[29] Kluger, Jeffrey. *The Quest for a Superkid.* **Time Magazine**, April 30, 2001, p. 53.

[30] Chaloner, Barry, and Ken Wesson. *Brain Research Sheds New Light on Student Learning; Teaching Strategies and Disabilities.* **CEC Today Newsletter,** (vol 10:3) Sept. 26, 2003. Council for Exceptional Children. www.cec.sped.org or email: khorner@uniserve.com

[31] van Praag, Henrietta, Gerd Kempermann & Fred H. Gage. *Neural Consequences of Environmental Enrichment.* **Nature Reviews Neuroscience**, December 2000 (vol. 1:3), pp. 191-198.

[32] Weinberger, Norman M. *Music and the Brain.* **Scientific American**, November 2004, pp. 94-95.

[33] Justin, Patrik & John A. Sloboda. **Music and Emotion, Theory and Research.** Oxford U. Press, 2001.

[34] Ramachandran, V. S. *Mirror Neurons:* 2000. www.edge.org/documents/archive/edge69.html.

[35] Meltzoff, Andrew N. *Infants Emerge as Picky Imitators.* **NeuroReport**, February 2002. AND Gyorgy Gergely, **Nature Neuroscience**, February 14, 2002.

[36] Restak, Richard. **The Mind.** NY: Bantam Books, 1988. p. 319.

[37] Grunberg, Neil E. & Jerome E. Singer. *Attempting To Explain Why the Good Die Young*. **Psychological Inquiry**, 1991 (vol. 2:3), pp. 247-250.

[38] Russek, L. B. and G. E. Schwartz. *Interpersonal Heart-Brain Registration and the Perception of Parental Love: A 42 year follow-up of the Harvard Mastery of Stress Study*. **Subtle Energies**, 1994 (vol. 5:3), pp. 195-208.

[39] Lazarus, Richard S. & Bernice N. Lazarus. **Passion and Reason, Making Sense of Our Emotions**. NY: Oxford University Press, 1994. pp. 203-208, 290-297.

[40] Coulter, Dee Joy. **Children at Risk: The Development of Drop-outs**. Longmont, CO: Coulter Pub., 1986. Sound Cassette.

[41] Pearce, Joseph Chilton. **Evolution's End, Claiming the Potential of Our Intelligence**. San Francisco: Harper, 1992. pp. 44-51.

[42] Coulter, Dee Joy. **Enter the Child's World**. Longmont, CO: Coulter Pub., 1986. Sound Cassette.

[43] Coulter, Dee Joy. **Enter the Child's World**.

[44] Pert, Candace. 1997. pp. 135-148.

[45] Damasio, Antonio. **The Feeling of What Happens: Body and Emotion in the Making of Consciousness**. NY: Harcourt Brace, 1999.

[46] Tulving, Endel, et. al. *Hemispheric Encoding/Retrieval Asymmetry in Episodic Memory: Positron Emission Tomography Findings*. **Proceedings of The National Academy of Sciences**, March 15, 1994, pp. 2016-2020. See also: *Brain Scans Show Two-Sided Memory Flow*. **Science News**, March 26, 1994 (vol. 145), p. 199.

[47] Clifford, Erin. *Neural Plasticity: Merzenich, Taub and Greenough*. **Harvard Brain**, 1999 (vol. 16), pp. 16-20.

[48] Kandel, Eric R. **The Principles of Neuroscience**. Third edition. NY: Elsevier Press, 1991. pp. 1024-1025.

[49] Pearce, Joseph Chilton. **Evolution's End**. p. 141.

[50] Singer, Dorothy and Jerome. **The House of Make Believe, Children's Play and the Developing Imagination**. Cambridge, MA: Harvard Univ. Press, 1990

[51] MacLean, Paul D. **The Triune Brain In Evolution, Role in Paleocerebral Functions**. NY: Plenum Press, 1990. pp. 559-560.

[52] Sylvester, Robert. *Unconscious Emotions, Conscious Feelings and Curricular Challenges*. **Educational Leadership Journal**, November 2000.

[53] Panksepp, J. et. al. *ADHD Deficits and the Effect of Play*. **Brain and Cognition Journal**. 2003 (vol. 52:1), pp. 97-105.

[54] Panksepp, Jaak. **Affective Neuroscience, The Foundations of Human and Animal Emotions**. NY: Oxford University Press. 1998, pp. 281-291.

[55] MacLean, Paul D. **The Triune Brain in Evolution**. pp. 559-575.

[56] Hannaford, Carla. **Awakening the Child Heart, Handbook for Global Parenting**. Captain Cook, HI: Jamilla Nur Publishing. 2002

[57] Loschert, Kristen. Curtain Call. **NEA (National Education Association) Today**, November 2004, pp. 20-29.

[58] Moberg, Kerstin Uvnas. **The Oxytocin Factor**. Cambridge, MA: Perseus Books Groups. 2003.

[59] Siviy, Stephen. *Play*. Psychologist at Gettysburg College, PA.

[60] Byrd, Robert S. *M.I.N.D. Institute Study Confirms Autism Iincrease*. M.I.N.D.

Institute of UC Davis, California Department of Developmental Services. 1999.

[61] Solomon, Rick. Personal communication. Dr. Solomon's work in this area is in preparation for publication. Current research is available at www.aacenter.org and www.playproject.org/research/index/htm. See also: Greenspan, Stanley, Serena Wieder, and Roben Simon. *The Child with Special Needs; Encouraging Intellectual and Emotional Growth*. Cambridge, MA: Perseus Books, 1998.

[62] Trowbridge, Anthony. *Ecology of Knowledge Network*. Paper given at the *Science and Vision Conference*, Human Sciences Research Center, Pretoria, South Africa. January, 1992.

[63] Pearce, Joseph Chilton. *Evolution's End*. pp. 164-171.

[64] Healy, Jane M. *Endangered Minds, Why Children Don't Think and What We Can Do About It*. NY: Simon & Schuster, 1990.

[65] Moody, Kate. *Growing Up On Television*. NY: Times Books, 1980. pp. 37, 51, 53.

[66] Kraut, Robert, etc. al. *Internet Paradox, A Social Technology That Reduces Social Involvement and Psychological Well-Being?* *American Psychologist*, 1998, (vol. 53:9), pp. 1017-1031.

[67] Bryant, Dr. Jennings. IN: Jane Healy, *Endangered Minds*. pp. 201-202.

[68] Singer, Mark, et al. *Contributors to Violent Behavior Among Elementary and Middle School Children*. *Pediatrics*, October 1999, (vol. 104:4), pp. 878-884.

[69] Shapiro, Henry and Siobhan McDonough. *Kids In Homes with Heavy TV Use May Have Reading Trouble, Study Says*. *Kaiser Family Foundation and Children's Digital Media Centers*. October 28, 2003.

[70] Wallis, Claudia. *Kindergarten Rage, Does Kindergarten Need Cops?* *Time Magazine*. December 12, 2003

[71] Rosemond, John K. *Parents Ask Questions About School*. *Hemispheres Magazine* (Delta Airlines), April 1994, pp. 105-106.

[72] Wallis, Claudia. *Time Magazine*, 2003

[73] Gachelmann, K.A. *Dream Sleep: A Risk For Heart Patients? Science News*, February 6, 1993 (vol. 143), p. 85.

[74] Somers, Virend K., Mark E. Dyken & Allyn L. Mark. *Sympathetic-Nerve Activity During Sleep in Normal Subjects*. *New England Journal of Medicine*, February 4, 1993, (vol. 328), pp. 303-307.

5:   MAKING CONNECTIONS

[1] Harvey, Arthur. *The Numbered Brain*. Louisville: Center for Music and Medicine, University of Louisville, School of Medicine, 1985. p. 7.

[2] Chopra, Deepak. *Quantum Healing, Exploring the Frontiers of Mind/Body Medicine*. NY: Bantam Books, 1990. p. 50.

[3] Penfield, Wilder. *The Mystery of the Mind, A Critical Study of Consciousness and the Human Brain*. Princeton: Princeton University Press, 1977.

[4] Begley, Sharon, Lynda Wright, Vernon Church and Mary Hager. *Mapping The Brain*. *Newsweek*, April 20, 1992, pp. 66-70.

[5] Haier, Richard J. *Images Of Intellect, Brain Scans May Colorize Intelligence*. *Science News*, Oct. 8, 1994 (vol. 146), pp. 236-237.

[6] Tortora, Gerard J. & Nicholas P. Anagnostakos. *Principles of Anatomy and Physiology. Sixth Edition.* pp. 433-438.

[7] Tortora, Gerard J. & Nicholas P. Anagnostakos. *Principles ...* p. 433.

[8] Tortora, Gerard J. & Nicholas P. Anagnostakos. *Principles ...* p. 438.

[9] Luria, Alexander R. *Language and Cognition.* NY: John Wiley, 1981. pp. 103-113.

[10] Thompson, Paul M. *Scientists Search for the Biology of Smarts. Science News*, February 8, 2003, vol. 163, pp. 92-93.

[11] Tortora, Gerard J. & Nicholas P. Anagnostakos. *Principles ...* p. 403.

[12] Montgomery, Geoffrey. *The Mind In Motion. Discover*, March, 1989, pp. 61-64.

[13] Orrison, William W. *Functional Brain Imaging.* St. Louis: Mosby Pub. 1995, p. 479.

[14] McCrone, John. *The Ape That Spoke, Language and the Evolution of the Human Mind.* NY: William Morrow & Co., 1991. p. 65.

[15] McCraty, Rollin. *Research Overview, Exploring the Role of the Heart in Human Performance.* FROM: HeartMath Research Center. 1997. www.heartmath.org.

[16] Armour, J.A. *Anatomy and Function of the Intrathoracic Neurons Regulating the Mammalian Heart. Reflex Control Of The Circulation.* I.H. Zucker and J.P. Gilmore (eds) Boca Raton, FL: CRC Press, 1991. pp. 1-37.

[17] Russek, L.B. and G. E. Schwartz. *Energy Cardiology: A Dynamical Energy Systems Approach for Integrating Conventional and Alternative Medicine. Advances*, 1996 (vol. 12:4), pp. 4-24.

[18] Pert, Candace. **Molecules of Emotion, Why You Feel the Way You Feel.** NY: Simon & Schuster, 1999.

[19] Cantin, M. & J. Genest. *The Heart As An Endocrine Gland. Scientific American*, 1986 (vol. 254), p. 76.

[20] Armour, J.A. and J. Ardell (eds). *Neurocardiology.* NY: Oxford University Press, 1994.

[21] Rodriquez, Eugenio, et. al. *Perception's Shadow; Long-distance Synchronization of Human Brain Activity. Nature Neuroscience*, February 4, 1999 (vol. 397), pp. 430-433.

[22] Diamond, Marian & Janet Hopson. *Magic Trees of the Mind.* NY: Dutton/Penguin Group, 1998. p. 80.

[23] Sapolsky, Robert. *Why Stress is Bad for Your Brain. Science*, August 9, 1996 (vol. 273) pp. 749-750.

[24] Sapolsky, Robert. *Why Zebras Don't Get Ulcers: An Updated Guide to Stress, Stress-related Diseases, and Coping.* NY: Freeman, 1998.

[25] Kolb, David. *Experiential Learning, Experience As the Source of Learning and Development.* Englewood, NJ: Prentice-Hall, 1984. p. 47.

[26] Kolb, David. *Experiential Learning.* p. 47.

[27] Williams, Linda Verlee. *Teaching for the Two-sided Mind, A Guide to Right Brain/Left Brain Education.* NY: Simon & Schuster, 1983. p. 26.

[28] Edwards, Betty. *Drawing on the Right Side of the Brain.* Los Angeles: Tarcher, 1979. p. 40

[29] Coulter, Dee Joy. *Our Triune Brain.* Longmont, CO: Coulter Pub., 1986. Cassette.

[30] Pearce, Joseph Chilton. *Magical Child*. NY: Bantam Books, 1980. pp. 29-34.

[31] Piaget, Jean. *The Grasp of Consciousness, Action and Concept in the Young Child*. Cambridge, MA: Harvard, 1976. pp. 208, 346-353.

[32] Shaffer, David. *Attention Deficit Hyperactive Disorder in Adults. American Journal of Psychiatry*, May 1994, pp. 633-638.

[33] Harvey, Arthur. *The Numbered Brain*. pp. 7-8.

[34] Edu-K for Kids graphically illustrates this necessary integration for full mind/body functioning. See, for example, Dennison, Dr. Paul E. and Gail E. Dennison. *Edu-K for Kids*. Ventura, CA: Edu-Kinesthetics, Inc., 1985. On Brain Gym exercises, see below, Chapter 7.

[35] Thompson, Paul, Judith Papoport, Jay Giedd, et al. *Time-lapse Imaging Tracks Brain Maturation from Ages 5 to 20. Proceedings of the National Academy of Sciences*, May 17, 2004.

[36] Mulrine, Anna. *Are Boys the Weaker Sex? U.S. News & World Report*, July 30, 2001. pp. 40-47.

[37] Pollack, William. *Real Boys Workbook*. VA: Henry Holt, 1999

[38] Thompson, Michael. *Raising Cain*. NY: Random House, 2000

[39] Newberger, Eli. *The Men They Will Become*. NY: Harper-Collins, 2000.

[40] Gurian, Michael. *Boys and Girls Learn Differently*. NY: Wiley & Sons, 2002.

[41] Coulter, Dee Joy. *The Sympathetic Thinker in a Critical World*. Longmont, CO: Coulter Pub., 1991. Sound Cassette.

[42] Coulter, Dee Joy. *Classroom Clues to Thinking Problems*. Longmont, CO: Coulter Pub., 1986. Sound Cassette.

[43] Ministry of Education and Research, International Relations Division. *Characteristic Features of Danish Education*. Copenhagen, Denmark. 1992.

[44] Henriksen, Spaet, Svend Hesselholdt, Knud Jensen, & Ole B. Larsen. *The Democratization of Education*. Copenhagen, Denmark: Department of Education and Psychology, The Royal Danish School of Educational Studies, 1990, pp. 1-39.

[45] Connolly, Kevin J. *The Psychobiology of the Hand. New England Journal of Medicine*, October 25, 2001

[46] Wilson, Frank R. *The Hand; How It's Use Shapes the Brain, Language and Human Culture*. NY: Pantheon Books, 1998

[47] Seligman, Martin E. *Helplessness: On Depression, Development, and Death*. San Francisco: W.H. Freeman, 1975. pp. 37-44, 134-165.

[48] Donley, Michele & Sheila Gribben, et. al. *The Homework Ate My Family. Time Magazine*, January 25, 1999. pp. 56-61.

[49] Mandaus, George F., et. al. *Tests Flunk, Study Finds. Science News*, Oct. 24, 1992 (vol. 142), p. 277.

[50] Epstein, Herman T. *Growth Spurts During Brain Development: Implications for Educational Policy and Practice*. J. Chall & A.F. Mirsky (eds.), *Education and the Brain*. Chicago: University of Chicago Press, 1979. pp. 343-370.

[51] Piaget, Jean. IN: Campbell, Sarah F. (ed.), *Piaget Sampler, An Introduction to Jean Piaget Through His Own Words*. NY: John Wiley, 1976. pp. 15-16, 71-78.

[52] Coulter, Dee Joy. *Enter the Child's World*. Longmont, CO: Coulter Pub., 1986.

[53] The College Board, *Profile of SAT and Achievement Test Takers, College Entrance Examination Board.* 1992, p. 3

[54] Cutietta, Robert, et.al. *Spin-offs, the Extra-musical Advantages of a Musical Education.* United Instruments, Inc., Future of Music Project. 2000.

[55] Gardner, Howard. **Frames of Mind, The Theory of Multiple Intelligences**. NY: Basic Books, 1983.

[56] Luria, Alexander R. *The Role of Speech in the Formation of Temporary Connections and the Regulation of Behavior in the Normal and Oligophrenic Child.* IN: Simon and Simon, (eds.), **Educational Psychology in the USSR**. Stanford: Stanford University Press, 1968. p. 85.

[57] Goddard, Sally, **A Teacher's Window Into The Child's Mind**. Eugene, OR: Fern Ridge Press, 1996.

[58] Healy, Jane M. **Endangered Minds, Why Children Don't Think and What We Can Do About It**. NY: Simon & Schuster, 1990. p. 101.

[59] Tomatis, Alfred A. **The Conscious Ear, My Life of Transformation through Listening**. Barrytown, NY: Station Hill Press, 1991. pp. 201-218.

[60] Coulter, Dee Joy. *Movement, Meaning and the Mind.* Keynote Address, Seventh Annual Educational Kinesiology Foundation Gathering, Greeley, CO, July, 1993

[61] Coulter, Dee Joy. **Children at Risk: The Development of Drop-Outs**. Longmont, CO: Coulter Pub., 1986. Sound Cassette.

[62] Blakeslee, Sandra. *Brain Yields New Clues on Its Organization for Language.* **New York Times, Science Times**, Sept. 19, 1991. p. C-1.

[63] Tortora, Gerard J. & Nicholas P. Anagnostakos. **Principles ...** p. 403.

[64] Tortora, Gerard J. & Nicholas P. Anagnostakos. **Principles ...** p. 403.

[65] The Talking Fish activity from Vision Gym and the Energy Yawn from Brain Gym increase activation to the communication centers across the TMJ. These release the tension in the jaw and facial muscles, including eye muscles, so that verbalization and expression can occur together easily. See Chapter 7, Dennison, Paul & Gail Dennison, **Brain Gym, Teachers Edition**. Ventura, CA: Edu-Kinesthetics, Inc., 1989. p. 29.

[66] Goldin-Meadow, Susan, Howard Nusbaum, Spencer Kelly and Susan Wagner. *Gesturing While Talking Helps Memory.* **Journal of Psychological Science**. November 20, 2001.

[67] Rankin, Paul T. *The Importance of Listening Ability.* **English Journal**, (college ed.), 2 (Nov. 1981), pp. 623-630

[68] Werner, Elyse K. *A Study in Communication Time. Master Thesis, Unpublished.* College Park, MD: University of Maryland, 1975.

[69] **American's Use of Time Project**. Ann Arbor, MI: Inter-University Consortium for Political and Social Research, 1993.

[70] Healy, Jane M. **Endangered Minds**. pp. 86-104.

[71] Brewer, Chris & Don Campbell. **Rhythms of Learning, Creative Tools for Developing Lifelong Skills**. Tucson: Zephyr Press, 1991. p. 31.

[72] Fuster, Joaquin M. **The Prefrontal Cortex: Anatomy, Physiology and Neuropsychology of the Frontal Lobe**. Second Edition. NY: Raven Press, 1980. p. 255.

[73] McCrone, John. **The Ape That Spoke; Language and the Evolution of the Human Mind**. NY: William Morrow & Co., 1991 pp. 252-253.

[74] MacLean, Paul D. *The Triune Brain in Evolution, Role in Paleocerebral Functions*. NY: Plenum Press, 1990. pp. 559-562.

6: MOVEMENT

[1] Sylvester, Robert. *A Biological Brain In A Cultural Classroom: Applying biological research to classroom management*. Corwin Press. 2000

[2] Sylvester, Robert. *A Biological Brain in a Cultural Classroom*. Presented at the Teaching & Learning With the Brain in Mind Conference, Toronto, Ontario, Canada, August 20, 2001.

[3] Gardner, Howard. *Frames of Mind, The Theory of Multiple Intelligences*. NY: Basic Books, 1985. pp. 207-208.

[4] Gardner, Howard. *Frames of Mind*. p. 210. Roger Sperry is quoted in E. Ewarts, *Brain Mechanism in Movement*, *Scientific American*, 229 (July, 1973), p. 103.

[5] Connolly, Kevin J. *The Psychobiology of the Hand*. *New England Journal of Medicine*, October 25, 2001.

[6] Verghese, Joe, et. al. *Leisure Activities and the Risk of Dementia in the Elderly*. *New England Journal of Medicine*. 2003, vol. 348(25), pp. 2508-2515.

[7] Middleton, Frank A. & Peter L. Strick. *Anatomical Evidence for Cerebellar and Basal Ganglia Involvement in Higher Cognitive Function*. *Science*, October 21, 1994 (vol. 266), pp. 458-461.

[8] Raymond, Jennifer L., S. Lisberger ,M. Mauk and Jim Bower. *The Cerebellum*. *Science Magazine*, May 24, 1996.

[9] Raymond, Jennifer L. Stephen G. Lisberger, Michael D. Mauk. *The Cerebellum; A Neuronal Learning Machine?* *Science*, May 24, 2996, vol. 272, pp. 1126-1131.

[10] Boyden, Edward S., Jennifer L. Raymond. *Cerebellum-dependent Learning: The Role of Multiple Plasticity Mechanisms*. *Annual Review of Neuroscience*, 2004, Vol 27(1) p. 581.

[11] Middleton, F.A. and P.L. Strick. *Anatomical Evidence for Cerebellar and Basal Ganglia Involvement in Higher Cognitive Function*. *Science*, October 21, 1994, vol. 266 (5184): pp. 458-461.

[12] Strick, Peter L. *Basal Ganglia and Cerebellar "Loops" with Cerebral Cortex; Motor and Cognitive Circuits*. *Research Services VA Medical Center*, Syracuse, NY, November 10, 1997.

[13] Sapolsky, R. *Why Zebras Don't Get Ulcers, An Updated Guide to Stress, Stress-related Diseases, and Coping*. NY: Freeman Press, 1998.

[14] Goddard, Sally. *A Teacher's Window Into The Child's Mind*. Eugene, OR: Fern Ridge Press, 1996.

[15] Masgutova, Svetlana. *Integration of Dynamic and Postural Reflexes Into Whole Body Movement Systems*. Ascension Private Educational Institute of Psychological and EduK Assistance, Moscow, Russia, 1998.

[16] Stiller, Angelika, & Renate Wennekes. *The Motoric Development Across the Body Midline*. Neuenkirchen, Germany: Astrup, 31, 1992, 2846.

[17] Sobell, Laura. *Caution, Save Your Baby, Throw Out Your Equipment*. Santa Barbara, CA: Whole Family Press (P.O. Box 188, Newbury Park, CA: 91319-0188), 1994.

[18] Ratey, John J. *A User's Guide to the Brain*. Harvard Medical School Press. 1999.

[19] VanPragg, H., Schinder, A., Christie, B., Toni, N., Palmer, T., & Gage, F. *Functional neurogenesis in the adult hippocampus*. *Nature*, February 28, 2002 (vol. 415), p. 1031.

[20] Kun, Paula Keyes. *New Study Supports Physically Fit Kids Perform Better Academically*. 2001-2002 study by the California Department of Education. http://www.cde.ca.gov/cyfsbranch/lsp/health/pecommunications.htm

[21] Churchill, James, Greenough, William T., Robert Galvez, et. al. *Exercise, Experience and the Aging Brain*. *Neurobiology of Aging*, September 2002, vol. 23(5), pp. 941-956.

[22] Pollack, William. *Real Boys Workbook*. VA: Henry Holt, 1999.

[23] Coulter, Dee Joy. *Children at Risk: The Development of Drop-Outs*.

[24] Britten, Nick. *Routine that Headmaster Found on Internet Sparks Global Interest*. *British Dyslexia Association Journal*, May, 21,2004

[25] Olsen, Eric. *Fit Kids, Smart Kids — New Research Confirms that Exercise Boosts Brainpower*. *Parents Magazine*, October, 1994, pp. 33-35.

[26] Chaloner, Barry. *Brain Research Sheds New Light on Student Learning; Teaching Strategies and Disability*. November 11, 2003. www.cec.sped.org/bk/cectoday/?module=displaystory&story_id=750&format=html

[27] Heiberger, Debra W. and Margot C. Heiniger-White. *S'cool Moves for Learning*. Shasta, CA: Integrated Learner Press, P.O. Box 614, Shasta, CA, 96087. 2002.

[28] Albalas, Moses, quoted in Dennison, Paul E. and Gail E. Dennison. *Edu-Kinesthetics In-Depth, The Seven Dimensions of Intelligence*. Ventura, CA: Educational Kinesiology Foundation, 1990.

[29] Dennison, Gail E. *The Visioncircles Workshop Teacher's Manual*. Ventura, CA: Edu-Kinesthetics, Inc., 1986.

[30] Quackenbush, Thomas. R. *Relearning to See, Improve Your Eyesight Naturally*. Berkeley, CA: North Atlantic Books, 1999.

[31] Schwartz, Eugene. *Seeing, Hearing, Learning: The Interplay of Eye and Ear in Waldorf Education*. (Excerpts from Camp Glenbrook Conference of the Association for a Healing Education, June 14-16, 1988.) 1990. p. 12.

[32] Interviews with Occupational Therapists for KwaZulu schools and consultants with the Sunfield Home School, Verulum, South Africa. March, 1993.

[33] Pisani, T. du, S.J. Plekker, C.F. Dennis, & J.P. Strauss. *Education and Manpower Development, 1990*. Bloemfontein, South Africa: Research Institute for Education Planning, University of the Orange Free State. p. 17.

[34] Coulter, Dee Joy. *Enter the Child's World*. Longmont, CO: Coulter Pub., 1986. Sound Cassette.

[35] Kobata, G. *What Causes Nearsightedness? Science*, 1985, vol.229, pp. 1249-1250.

[36] Quinn, G.E., et. al. *Myopia and Ambient Lighting at Night*. *Nature*, 1999, vol. 399, p. 113.

[37] Brewer, Chris & Don Campbell. *Rhythms of Learning, Creative Tools for Developing Lifelong Skills*. Tucson: Zephyr Press, 1991.

[38] Wallman J. and J. Turkel. *Extreme Myopia Produced by Modest Change In Early Visual Experience*. *Science*, 1978 (vol. 201), pp. 1249-1251.

[39] Rose, V. L. *Near-sightedness and Light Exposure During Sleep.* **American Family Physician**, 1999 (vol. 60), p. 328.

[40] *Study of Myopia and Night Lights in the Dark.* **Review of Optometry**, 1999 (vol. 136), p. 4.

[41] Young, F.A. *Myopia Development.* **American Journal of Ophthalmology**, 1961 (52), p. 799.

[42] Kelley, C.R. *The Psychological Factors In Myopia.* Unpublished Ph.D. dissertation. NY: New School of Social Research, 1958.

[43] Tonks, A. *Children Who Sleep with Light On May Damage Their Sight.* **British Medical Journal**, 1999 (vol. 318), p. 1369.

[44] Coleman, H.M. *Increased Myopia in Schools.* **Journal of American Ophthalmic Association**, (41) 1970, p. 341.

[45] Mendizza, Michael. *Caring from the Heart.* Nevada City, CA: Perspectives - Touch The Future Organization, 2004.

7: MOVES THAT IMPROVE

[1] Coulter, Dee Joy. *Movement, Meaning and the Mind.* Keynote Address, Seventh Annual Educational Kinesiology Foundation Gathering, Greeley, CO. July 1993

[2] McAllen, Audrey E. *The Extra Lesson, Exercises in Movement, Drawing and Painting for Helping Children with Difficulties with Writing, Reading and Arithmetic.* East Sussex, U.K.: Steiner Schools Fellowship Publications, 1985.

[3] Brink, Susan. *Smart Moves, New Research Suggests that Folks from 8 to 80 Can Shape Up Their Brains with Aerobic Exercise.* **U.S. News & World Report**, May 15, 1995, pp. 78-82.

[4] Masgutova, Svetlana. *Psychological Impact on Children of Catastrophe.* **Psychological Problems**, 1990, pp. 86-92. (A copy of this document can be obtained through the Educational Kinesiology Foundation.)

[5] Curlee, Pam. *Switched On Golf.*

[6] Bentley, Ross, and Ron Langford, *Inner Speed Secrets, Race Driving Skills, Techniques, and Strategies.* Osceola, WI: MBI Publishing Co., 2000

[7] I am presenting only the tip of the iceberg with this work. Further information can be obtained from the Educational Kinesiology Foundation, 1575 Spinnaker Dr. #204B, Ventura, CA 93001. www.braingym.org.

[8] Dennison, Paul E. and Gail E. Dennison. *Brain Gym, Teachers Edition, Revised.* Ventura, CA: Edu-Kinesthetics, Inc., 1994. p. 25.

[9] Tortora, Gerard J., & Nicholas P. Anagnostakos. *Principles ...* p. 591.

[10] Fjordbo, Getti Dollerup. *Why We Have to Crawl... On the Development of Human Motor and Communicative Skills, Aberrations and Interconnections.* Copenhagen, MA Thesis on Audiologopedics. 1995

[11] Delcato, Carl H. *The Diagnosis and Treatment of Speech and Reading Problems.* Springfield, IL: Thomas, 1963.

[12] Goldsmith, Marcelle, and Isabel Cohen. *Hands On, How to Use Brain Gym in the Classroom.* Sea Point, South Africa. 2000. handson-books@mweb.co.za.

[13] Wilson-Heiberger, Debra and Margot C. Heiniger-White. *S'cool Moves for Learning, A Program Designed to Enhance Learning Through Body-Mind Integration.* Shasta, CA: Integrated Learner Press. 2000.

[14] Randolph, Shirley L., and Margot C. Heiniger. *Kids Learn From the Inside Out, How to Enhance the Human Matrix.* Boise, ID: Legendary Pub. Co., 1998.

[15] Olsen, Eric. *Fit Kids, Smart Kids. Parents Magazine*, October 1994, p. 33.

[16] Dennison, Paul E. and Gail E. Dennison. *Brain Gym, Teachers Edition, Revised.* p. 29.

[17] *The Yellow Emperor's Classic of Internal Medicine*, Simple questions (Huang Ti Nei Jing Su Wen), People's Health Pub. House, Beijing 1979. First published in 100 B.C.

[18] Dennison, Paul E. and Gail E. Dennison. *Brain Gym, Teachers Edition, Revised.* p. 30.

[19] Epple, Anita. *Connections, The Guild of Infant & Child Massage.* 22 Elder Close, Uttoxeter Staffs, ST14 8UR, UK. www.gicm.org.uk.

[20] Said, Sumiati and Hadi Chua Muhd. The Brainwaves EduK Consultancy, Blk 744, Bedok Reservoir Rd, #01-3041, Singapore 470744. cohadi@pacific.net.sg; sumi_hadi@hotmail.com

8: WHAT GOES WRONG

[1] U. S. Department of Education, Office of Special Education and Rehabilitative Services. *Common Core of Data Survey*, March 2002. Survey done with all school children from 3 to 21 years of age served in federally supported programs in the U.S.

[2] McGuinness, Diane. *Attention Deficit Disorder, the Emperor's Clothes, Animal Pharm, and Other Fiction.* S. Fisher and R. Greenburg (eds.), *The Limits of Biological Treatment for Psychological Distress.* NY: Erlbaum, 1989.

[3] Wang, M.C. *Commentary. Education Week*, May 4, 1988.

[4] Sapolsky, Robert. *Taming Stress. Scientific American*, September 2003, pp.87-91

[5] Zametkin, Alan J., Thomas E. Nordahl, et. al. *Cerebral Glucose Metabolism in Adults with Hyperactivity of Childhood Onset. New England Journal of Medicine*, Nov. 15, 1990 (vol. 323:20), pp. 1365-1366.

[6] Zametkin, Alan J., et. al. pp. 1361-1363.

[7] MacLean, Paul D. *The Triune Brain in Evolution, Role in Paleocerebral Functions.* NY: Plenum Press, 1990. pp. 561-562.

[8] Thatcher, Robert W., M. Hallett, et. al. *Functional Neuroimaging.* NY: Academic Press, 1994. pp. 95-105.

[9] Giedd, Jay N. *Quantitative Morphology of the Corpus Callosum in Attention Deficit Hyperactive Disorder. American Journal of Psychiatry*, 1994 (vol. 151:5), pp. 665-669.

[10] Snyder, Solomon, et. al. *Opiate Receptors and Opioid Peptides. Annual Review of Neuroscience*, 1979, (2:35).

[11] Gage, Fred H. *Brain, Repair Yourself. Scientific American*, September 2003, pp. 47-91

[12] Sapolsky, Robert. *Stress Exacerbates Neuron Loss and Cytoskeletal Pathology in the Hippocampus. Journal of Neuroscience*, September, 1994 (vol. 14:9), pp. 5373-5380.

9: BASICS FOR THE BRAIN: WATER AND OXYGEN

[1] Zanecosky, Althea. *Water Works*. **Scholastic Choices**, September 2004, vol. 20(1), pp. 21-24.

[2] Tortora, Gerard J. & Nicholas P. Anagnostakos. **Principles of Anatomy and Physiology. Sixth Edition**. NY: Harper, 1990 pp. 37-38, 861-866.

[3] Tortora & Anagnostakos. **Principles ....** pp. 339-342.

[4] Fischbach, Gerald D. *Mind and Brain.* **Scientific American**, September 1992, p. 50.

[5] Tortora & Anagnostakos. **Principles ....** pp. 37-40, 861-862.

[6] Tortora & Anagnostakos. **Principles ....** pp. 788-789.

[7] Tortora & Anagnostakos. **Principles ....** pp. 37-38, 861-866.

[8] Koester, John. *Current Flow in Neurons.* **Principles of Neuroscience. Third Edition**. NY: Elsevier Press, 1991. pp. 1033-1040.

[9] Fischbach, Gerald D. *Mind and Brain.* p. 50.

[10] Harvey, Arthur. **The Numbered Brain**. Louisville: Center for Music and Medicine, University of Louisville, School of Medicine, 1985.

[11] Goodman and Gilman. **The Pharmacological Basis of Therapeutics. Eighth Edition**. NY: Pergamon Press, 1990. p. 622.

[12] Wiggins, Phillippa M. **A Mechanism Of ATP-Driven Cation Pumps. Biophysics Of Water**. NY: John Wiley, 1982. pp. 266-269.

[13] Askew, Wayne. *Drink This Much Water Daily*. Presented at the Experimental Biology Meeting, San Diego, California. July, 2003.

[14] Batmanghelidj, F. **Your Body's Many Cries for Water**. Falls Church, VA: Global Health Solutions, 1993.

[15] Tortora & Anagnostakos. **Principles ....** pp. 837-845.

[16] Zanecosky, Althea, 2004.

[17] Zanecosky, Althea. 2004.

[18] Tortora & Anagnostakos. **Principles....** pp. 736 – 739.

[19] Ferris, Thomas F. *Pregnancy, Preeclampsia and the Endothelial Cell.* **New England Journal of Medicine**, November 14, 1991 (vol. 325:20), pp. 1439-1440.

[20] Tortora & Anagnostakos. **Principles ....** p. 852.

[21] Harrrison, Tinsley Randolph. **Harrison's Principles of Internal Medicine. Twelfth edition**. NY: McGraw Hill, 1991. pp. 281-297

[22] Chan J, S. F.Knutsen, G.G. Blix, J.W. Lee and G.E. Fraser. *Water, other fluids, and fatal coronary heart disease: the Adventist Health Study.* **American Journal of Epidemiology**, May 1, 2002. vol. 155(9), pp. 827-833.

[23] McCrone, John. **The Ape That Spoke, Language and the Evolution of the Human Mind**. NY: William Morrow & Co., 1991. p. 17.

[24] Colombo, Marcio F.; Donald C. Rau & V. Adrian Parsegian. *Protein Solvation in Allosteric Regulation: A Water Effect on Hemoglobin.* **Science**, May 1, 1992 (vol. 256), pp. 655-659.

[25] Tortora & Anagnostakos. **Principles ....** p. 38.

[26] Hollowell, Marguerite. *Unlikely Messengers: How Do Nerve Cells Communicate?* **Scientific American**, December 1992, pp. 52-56.

[27] *Shape of the Nation Report, Conducted by National Association for Sport and Physical Education, 2001*, Executive Summary. p. 6

[28] Olsen, Eric. *Fit Kids, Smart Kids: New Research Confirms That Exercise Boosts Brainpower.* **Parents Magazine**, October-November, 1994, pp. 33-35.

[29] *Shape of the Nation Report*, pp.1-6

[30] Reilly, J.J., et. al. *Total energy expenditure and physical activity in young Scottish children: mixed longitudinal study.* **Lancet**, January 17, 2004 (vol. 363), pp. 182 and 211-212.

[31] Olsen, Eric. *Fit Kids, Smart Kids.*

[32] Hack, Maureen, et. al. *Outcomes in young adults for very-low birth-weight infants.* **New England Journal of Medicine**. January 17, 2002 (vol. 346:3), pp.149-157.

[33] Yolton, Kimberly. *Passive Smoking Dents Children's IQ.* **New Scientists.com.news service**. May 7, 2002.

[34] Olds, David L., & Charles R. Henderson. *Prevention of Intellectual Impairment in Children of Women Who Smoke Cigarettes During Pregnancy.* **Pediatrics**, February 1994 (vol 93:2), pp. 228-233. See also: Fackelmann, K.A. *Mother's Smoking Linked to Child's IQ Drop.* **Science News**, February 12, 1994 (vol. 145), p. 101.

[35] Stuchly, Maria A. *Electromagnetic Fields And Health.* **IEEE Potentials Journal**, April 1993, p. 38.

[36] Society. *Electromagnetic Fields and Health Risks.* **Society**; Nov/Dec. 1998, vol.36 (1), pp. 5-8.

[37] Taubes, Gary. *Electromagnetic Fields.* **Consumer Reports**, May, 1994, pp. 354-355.

[38] Stuchly, Maria A. *Electromagnetic Fields And Health.* p. 35.

[39] Gauger, Jr. *Household appliance magnetic field survey,* **IEEE transactions on power apparatus and systems** PA-104, September 1985.

[40] Associated Press. *Energy fields pervasive throughout environment.* **Consumer Reports**, May 1994, pp. 358-359.

[41] Raloff, Janet. *EMFs Run Aground.* **Science News**, August 21, 1993 (vol. 144), pp. 125-126.

[42] Taubes, Gary. *Electromagnetic Fields.* pp. 355-356.

[43] Hendee, William & John C. Beteler. *Another Way EMFs Might Harm Tissue.* **Science News**, February 19, 1994, p. 127.

[44] Society. Electromagnetic Fields and Health Risks

[45] Coulter, Dr. Dee Joy. *Movement, Meaning and the Mind.* Keynote Address, Seventh Annual Educational Kinesiology Foundation Gathering, Greeley, CO, July, 1993.

[46] Coulter, Dr. Dee Joy. *Movement, Meaning and the Mind.*

[47] Lee, K.Y.C., Jürgen Klinger, & Harden McConnell. *Electric Field-Induced Concentration Gradients in Lipid Monolayers.* **Science**, Feb. 4, 1994 (vol. 263), pp. 655-658.

10: BASICS FOR THE BRAIN: NUTRITION

[1] Wilmanns, Matthias & David Eisenberg. *Three-Dimensional Profiles from Residue-Pair Preferences; Identification of Sequences with Beta/Alpha Barrel Fold.* **Proceedings of the National Academy of Science**, February 15, 1993 (vol. 90), pp. 1379-1383.

[2] Luthy, Roland, James U. Bowie & David Eisenberg. *Assessment of Protein Models with 3-Dimensional Profiles.* **Nature**, March 5, 1992 (vol. 356), pp. 83-85.

[3] Tortora & Anagnostakos. **Principles ....** pp. 801-803.

[4] Insel, Paul M. and Walton T. Roth. **Core Concepts in Health.** Mountain View, CA: Mayfield Publishing, 1988. pp. 256-264.

[5] Newsweek, *Allergies in our world.* **Newsweek**, September 22, 2003.

[6] Crook, William G. **The Yeast Connection: A Medical Breakthrough.** NY: Random House, 1985. p. 201.

[7] Levinson, Harold N. *The Cerebellar-Vestibular Basis of Learning Disabilities in Children, Adolescents, and Adults; Hypothesis and Study.* **Perceptual & Motor Skills**, 1988 (vol. 67).

[8] Crook, William G. **The Yeast Connection.** p. 102.

[9] Witkin, Steven S. *Defective Immune Responses in Patients with Recurrent Candidiasis.* **Infections in Medicine**, May-June 1985.

[10] Crook, William G. **The Yeast Connection.** p. 378.

[11] Truss, C. Orian. *Metabolic Abnormalities in Patients with Chronic Candidiasis.* **Journal of Orthomolecular Psychiatry**, 1984 (vol. 13, 2).

[12] Iwata, K., and Y. Yamamoto. *Glycoprotein Toxins Produced by Candida Albicans.* **Proceedings of the Fourth International Conference on the Mycoses.** PAHO Scientific Pub. No. 356, June 1977.

[13] Levinson, Harold N. **Turning Around The Upside-Down Kids, Helping Dyslexic Kids Overcome Their Disorder.** NY: M. Evans, 1992. pp. 145-153.

[14] Crook, William G. **The Yeast Connection.**

[15] Prinz, R.J., W. A. Roberts, & E. Hautman. *Dietary Correlates of Hyperactive Behavior in Children.* **Journal of Consulting Clinical Psychology**, 1988, 48:769.

[16] Horrobin, D.F. *Alcohol — Blessing and Curse of Mankind!* **Executive Health**, June, 1981 (vol. XVII, no. 9).

[17] Mauro, Frank and Roberta Feios. **Kids, Food and Television, The Compelling Case for State Action.** New York State Assembly Publishers, 1977. p. 102.

[18] Burgess, Donna M., and M.P. Streisguth. *Educating Students with Fetal Alcohol Syndrome of Fetal Alcohol Effects.* **Pennsylvania Reporter**, Nov. 1990 (vol. 22:1).

[19] Donovan, Bernard T. **Humors, Hormones and the Mind: An Approach to the Understanding of Behavior.** London: Macmillan, 1988.

[20] Feldman, David, et. al. *Steroid Hormone Systems Found in Yeast.* **Science**, August 31, 1984 (vol. 225), pp. 913-914.

11: THE VESTIBULAR SYSTEM AND LEARNING DISORDERS

[1] Frank J. & Harold N. Levinson. *Dysmetric Dyslexia and Dyspraxia: Hypothesis And Study.* **Journal of American Academy of Child Psychiatry**, 1973 (vol. 12), pp. 690-701.

[2] Levinson, Harold N. **Turning Around the Upside-Down Kids, Helping Dyslexic Kids Overcome Their Disorder.** NY: M. Evans, 1992.

[3] Livingston, Richard. *Season of Birth and Neurodevelopmental Disorders: Summer Birth Is Associated with Dyslexia.* **Journal of the American Academy of Child and**

Adolescent Psychiatry, May 1993 (vol. 32:3), pp. 612-616. See also: *Science News*, May 1, 1993 (vol. 143), p. 278.

[4] Frank J. & H.N. Levinson. *Dysmetric Dyslexia And Dyspraxia: Hypothesis And Study.*

[5] Van Praag, Henriette, Gerd Kempermann and Fred H. Gage. *Neural Consequences of Environmental Enrichment.* **Nature Reviews Neuroscience**, December 2000, (vol. 1: 3), 191.

[6] Coulter, Dee Joy. *Movement, Meaning and the Mind.* Keynote Address, Seventh Annual Educational Kinesiology Foundation Gathering, Greeley, CO. July 1993.

[7] Bower, Bruce. *Words in the Brain: Reading Program Spurs Neural Rewrite in Kids.* **Science News Online**. May 8, 2004, vol.165 (19).

[8] Grigorenko, Elena L. *Developmental Dyslexia: An Update on Genes, Brains, and Environments.* **Journal of Child Psychology and Psychiatry**. 2001, (vol. 42:1), pp 91-125.

[9] Galaburda, A.M, L.M. Schrott, G.D. Rosen, et. al. *Animal Models of Developmental Dyslexia.* IN: C.H. Chase, G.D. Rosen, & G.F. Sherman (eds), **Developmental Dyslexia**, Baltimore, MD: York Press, 1996. pp. 3-14.

[10] Goddard, Sally. **A Teacher's Window Into the Child's Mind**. Eugene, OR: Fern Ridge Press, 1996. p. 24.

[11] Galaburda, Albert M. *Evidence for Abberant Auditory Anatomy in Developmental Dyslexia.* **Proceedings of the Naitonal Academy of Science,** 1994, vol.91, pp.8010-8013.

[12] Molfese, D.L., , V.J. Molfese, & K.A. Espy. *The Predictive Use of Event-related Potentials in Language Development and the Treatment of Language Disorders.* **Developmental Neuropsychology**, 1999, vol. 16. pp.373-377.

[13] Wood, F.B. & D. L. Flowers. *Functional Neuroanatomy of Dyslexic Subtypes: A Survey of 43 Candidate Regions with a Factor Analytic Validation Across 100 Cases.* IN: D.D. Duane (ed.), **Reading and Attention Disorders: Neurobiological Correlates**. Baltimore, MD: York Press, 1999. pp. 129-159.

[14] Tallal, Paul, et. al. *Neurobiological Basis of Speech; A Case for the Pre-eminence of Temporal Processing.* IN: Tallal, Galaburda and Euler (eds); **Temporal Processing in the Nervous System**. NY: The New York Academy of Sciences, 1993

[15] Hynd. G.W., et. al. *Dyslexia and Corpus Callosum Morphology.* **Archives of Neurology**, 1995, (vol. 52), pp.32-38.

[16] Petersen, S.E. et. al. *Positron Emission Tomographic Studies of the Processing of Single Words.* **Journal of Cognitive Neuroscience**, 1989, (vol. 1), pp.153-170.

[17] Frank, J. & Harold N. Levinson. *Dysmetric Dyslexia and Dyspraxia: Synopsis of A Continuing Research Project.* **Academic Therapy**, 1975-1976 (vol. 11), pp. 133-143.

[18] Levinson, Harold N. *The Cerebellar-Vestibular Basis of Learning Disabilities in Children, Adolescents, and Adults: Hypothesis and Study.* **Perceptual and Motor Skills**, 1988 (67), pp. 983-1006.

[19] Fjordbo, Gitte Dollerup. **Why We Have To Crawl... On the Development of Human Motor and Communicative Skills, Aberrations and Interconnections**. Copenhagen. Masters Thesis on Audiologopedics. 1995.

[20] Johansen, Kjeld. *Frequency Specific Left Hemisphere Stimulation with Music and Sounds in Dyslexia Remediation.* 3rd European Music Therapy Conference, June 1995,

Aalborg, Denmark. paedocon@dk-online.dk

[21] Berard, Guy. *Hearing Equals Behavior*. New Canaan, CT: Keats Pub, Inc. 1993. pp. 15-37.

[22] Ministry of Education and Research, International Relations Divison. *Characteristic Features of Danish Education*. Copenhagen, Denmark. 1992. pp 1-39.

[23] Goddard, Sally. 1996.

[24] Hannaford, Carla . *Awakening The Child Heart, Handbook for Global Parenting*. Hawaii: Jamilla Nur Pub., 2002, pp. 89-119.

[25] Korner, A. F. & E.B. Thoman. *The Relative Efficacy of Contact and Vestibular Stimulation on Soothing Neonates*. *Child Development*, 1972 (vol. 43), pp. 443-453.

[26] Kaga, K., R.R. March, & Y. Tanaka. *Influence of Labyrinthine Hypoactivity on Gross Motor Development of Infants*. IN: B. Cohen (ed.), International Meeting of the Barany Society, *Annals of the New York Academy of Sciences*, 1981 (374), pp. 412-420.

[27] Kohen-Raz, R. *Learning Disabilities and Postural Control*. London: Freund, 1988.

[28] Mosse, H.L. *A Complete Handbook of Children's Reading Disorders, A Critical Evaluation of Their Clinical, Educational, and Social Dimensions*. NY: Human Sciences Press, 1982. vols. 1 and 2. .

[29] Singer, Dorothy G and Jerome L. Singer. *Playing with Baby Begins at Birth: A Parent's Guide*. *Journal of Perinatal Education,* 1995, (vol. 4:4), pp.1-10.

[30] Weinberger, Norman M. *Music and the Brain*. *Scientific American*, November 2004, pp. 92-95.

[31] Deasy, Richard J,. Ed. *Critical Links: Learning in the Arts and Student Academic and Social Development*. Washington, DC: National Endowment for the Arts, 2002

[32] Anvari, Sima H, et. al. *Relations among Musical Skills, Phonological Processing and Early Reading Ability in Preschool Children*. *Journal of Experimental Child Psychology*, October 2002 (vol. 83:2), pp. 111-130.

[33] Rauscher, Frances H. *Can Music Instruction Affect Children's Cognitive Development?* Champaign, IL: ERIC Clearinghouse on Elementary and Early Childhood Education, 2003.

[34] Hansen, Dee and Elaine Bernstorf. *Linking Music Learning to Reading Instruction*. *Music Educators Journal*, March 2002, (vol. 88:5), pp. 17-21.

[35] Campbell, Don. *The Mozart Effect, Tapping the Power of Music to Heal the Body, Strengthen the Mind, and Unlock the Creative Spirit*. NY: Avon Books, 1997.

[36] Peretz, Isabella & Robert J. Zatorre. *The Cognitive Neuroscience of Music*. NY: Oxford University Press, 2003.

12:   FIGHT OR FLIGHT — THE STRESS EFFECT ON LEARNING

[1] Pert, Candace. *Molecules of Emotion. Why We Feel the Way We Feel*. NY: Simon & Schuster, 1997.

[2] Tortora & Anagnostakos. *Principles ....* pp. 455-457.

[3] Restak, Richard. *The Mind*. NY: Bantam Books, 1988. p. 39

[4] Reichal, Marcel. *PET Scans of the Brain*. George Washington University. 1990

[5] Marano, Hara Estroff. *Depression: Beyond Serotonin*. **Psychology Today**, March/April 1999, pp. 33-34.

[6] Ebeling P., and V. A. Koivisto. *Physiological Importance of Hydroepiandrosterone*. **Lancet**, 1994 (vol. 343 :8911), pp.1479-81.

[7] Blackburn, George. *U. S. Data on Obesity*. National Association for the Study of Obesity. 1999.

[8] Musselman, Dominique. *Depression: Beyond Serotonin*. **Psychology Today**, March/April 1999,. pp. 73-74.

[9] Tortora & Anagnostakos. **Principles ....** pp. 523, 526, 807.

[10] Diamond, Marian & Janet Hopson. **Magic Trees of the Mind**. NY: Dutton/Penguin Group, 1998. p. 80.

[11] Sapolsky, Robert. *Why Stress Is Bad for Your Brain*. **Science**, 1996, vol. 273:749-750.

[12] Kempermann, Gerd & Fred Gage. *New Nerve Cells for the Adult Brain*. **Scientific American**, May 1999, p. 48

[13] Sapolsky, Robert. *Taming Stress*. **Scientific American**, September 2003, pp. 87-81

[14] Diorio, Diane, Victor Viau & Michael J. Meaney. *The Role of the Medial Prefrontal Cortex (Cingulate Gyrus) in the Regulation of Hypothalamic-Pituitary-Adrenal Responses to Stress*. **Journal of Neuroscience**, November 1993 (13:9), pp. 3839-3847. See also: *Memory Loss Tied to Stress*. **Science News**, November 20, 1993 (vol. 144), p. 332.

[15] McCrone, John. **The Ape That Spoke, Language and the Evolution of the Human Mind**. NY: Avon Books, 1991. pp. 216-217.

[16] Tortora & Anagnostakos. **Principles ....** pp. 365-366.

[17] Jensen, M. C. et al. *Magnetic Resonance Imaging of the Lumbar Spine in People with Backpain*. **New England Journal of Medicine**, July 14, 1994 (vol. 331:2), pp. 69-73.

[18] Dennison, Paul E. & Gail E. Dennison. **Brain Gym, Teachers Edition**. Ventura, CA: Edu-Kinesthetics, Inc., 1989. p. 20.

[19] Sapolsky, Robert. *Taming Stress*. **Scientific American**, September 2003, p.9 4.

[20] Selye, Hans. *General Adaptation Syndrome and Diseases of Adaptation*. **Journal of Clinical Endocrinology and Metabolism**, 1946 (6), pp. 117-230.

[21] Weissman, M.M., Wolk, S., Goldstein, R., et. al. *Depressed Adolescents Grow Up*. **Journal of the American Medical Association**, 1999 (vol. 281), pp. 1701-13.

[22] Birmaher, B, et. al. *Childhood and Adolescent Depression: A Review of the Past 10 Years. Part 1*. **Journal of the American Academy of Child and Adolescent Psychiatry**, 1996, (35:11), pp. 1427-39.

[23] Klerman, G.B., Weissman, MM. *Increasing Rates of Depression*. **Journal of the American Medical Association**, 1989 (261), pp. 229-35.

[24] Shaffer D, Gould M.S., Fisher P, et al. *Psychiatric Diagnosis in Child and Adolescent Suicide*. **Archives of General Psychiatry**, 1996 (53:4), pp. 339-48.

[25] Hoyert D.L., et al. *Deaths: Final Data for 1997, National Vital Statistics Report*. **DHHS Publication No. (PHS) 99-1120**. Hyattsville, MD: National Center for Health Statistics, 1999; 47(19).

[26] Lewinsohn P.M. et al. *Major Depressive Disorder in Older Adolescents; Prevalence,*

Risk Factors, and Clinical Implications. **Clinical Psychology Review**, 1998;(18:7), pp. 765-94.

[27] Frida, E and M. Weinstock, *Prenatal Stress Increases Anxiety Relational Behavior and Alters Cerebral Lateralization of Dopamine Activity.* **Life Science**, 1988 (vol.42), pp.1059-1065.

[28] Freize, Irene, et. al. **Women and Sex Roles, A Social Psychological Perspective.** NY: Norton, 1978.

[29] Beardslee, William R., et. al. *Level of Social-Cognitive Development, Adaptive Functioning, and DSM-III Diagnoses in Adolescent Offspring of Parents with Affective Disorders; Implications of the Development of the Capacity for Mutuality.* **Developmental Psychology**, 1987 (vol. 23:6), pp. 807-815.

[30] Field, T., D. Sandberg, et. al. *Pregnancy Problems, Postpartum Depression and Early Mother-Infant Interaction.* **Developmental Psychology**, 1985 (vol. 21), pp. 1152-1156.

[31] Field, T. *Maternal Depression Effects on Infants and Early Interventions.* **Preventative Medicine**, 1998 , vol.27, pp.200-203

[32] Bower, Bruce. *Growing Up Poor, Poverty Packs Several Punches for Child Development.* **Science News**, July 9, 1994 (vol. 146), pp. 24-25.

[33] Satir, Virginia. **The Satir Model: Family Therapy and Beyond.** Palo Alto, CA: Science and Behavior Books, 1991.

[34] Wegscheider-Cruse, Sharon. **Another Chance, Hope and Health for the Alcoholic Family.** Palo Alto, CA: Science and Behavior Books, 1989. pp. 137-49.

[35] Hamburg, David. *39 Million Poor Americans — If They Don't Know Their Place, They're Learning It.* Carnegie Corporation of New York Report. IN: **The Washington Spectator**, May 15, 1994 (vol. 20:10), pp. 1-2.

[36] McEwen, Bruce, Watanabe, Y, and Stone, E. *Induction and Habituation of c-fos and zif/268 by Acute and Repeated Stressors.* **Neuroreport**. 1994 (vol. 5), pp.1321-1324.

[37] Healy, Jane M. **Endangered Minds, Why Children Don't Think and What We Can Do About It.** NY: Simon & Schuster, 1990. p. 201.

[38] Wegscheider-Cruse, Sharon. **Another Chance, Hope and Health for the Alcoholic Family.** pp. 132-137.

[39] Satir, Virginia. **The Satir Model.**

[40] Fay, Jim, Foster Cline and Bob Sornson. **Meeting the Challenge, Using Love and Logic to Help Children Develop Attention and Behavior Skills.** Golden, CO: The Love and Logic Press Inc, 2000. www.loveandlogic.com

[41] Bailey, Becky. **There's Gotta Be A Better Way; Discipline That Works!** Loving Guidance, Inc, P.O. Box 622407, Oviedo, Florida 32762, 2001..

[42] Crile, George W. **A Bipolar Theory of Living Processes.** NY: Macmillan, 1926. pp. 104-110, 180-184.

[43] DeFoe, P. *Contribution of Cortisol to Glucose Counterregulation in Humans.* **American Journal of Physiology**, 1989, (vol. 257), pp. E35-E42.

[44] McCraty, Rollin, et.al. *The Impact of a New Emotional Self-Management Program on Stress, Emotions, Heart Rate Variability, DHEA and Cortisol.* **Integrative Physiological and Behavioral Science**, 1998 (33:2), pp. 153-154.

[45] Levinson, Harold N. *The Cerebellar-Vestibular Basis of Learning Disabilities in Children, Adolescents, and Adults; Hypothesis and Study.* **Perceptual & Motor Skills**, 1988 (vol. 67).

[46] Ruff, Michael R., Candace B. Pert, Richard J. Weber. *Benzodiazapine Receptor-Mediated Chemotaxis of Human Monocytes.* **Science**, September 20, 1985, (vol. 229), pp. 1281-1283.

[47] Pert, Candace. *Molecules of Emotion, Why We Feel the Way We Feel.* NY: Simon & Schuster, 1997.

[48] Chopra, Deepak. *Quantum Healing, Exploring the Frontiers of Mind/Body Medicine.* NY: Bantam Books, 1990. pp. 66-67.

[49] Pert, Candace. 1997.

[50] Cantin, Marc and Jacques Genest. *The Heart As An Endocrine Gland.* **Scientific American**, February 1986, (vol. 254:2), p. 76.

[51] Armour, J. A. and J. Ardell (EDS). *Neurocardiology.* NY: Oxford University Press, 1994.

[52] Goleman, Daniel. *Emotional Intelligence.* NY: Bantam Books, 1995.

[53] Grunberg, Neil F. and Jerome E. Singer. *Attempting to Explain Why the Good Die Young.* **Psychological Inquiry**, 1991 (vol. 2:3), pp.247-250.

[54] Putnam, Frank & Martin Teicher. Findings presented at American Psychiatric Association Meeting, Philadelphia, Spring 1994.

[55] Terr, Lenore C. *Adult Memories of Child Abuse.* **American Journal of Psychiatry**, January 1991, pp.68-72.

[56] Chopra, Deepak. *Quantum Healing.*

[57] Block, Jack and Richard W. Robins. *Gender Paths Wind Toward Self-Esteem.* **Child Development**, June 1993. See also: *Science News*, vol. 143, p. 308.

[58] Day, Arla, L. and Holly A. Livingstone. *Gender Differences in Perception of Stressors and Utilization of Social Support among University Students.* **Canadian J. of Behavioral Sciences**, April 2003 (vol.35:2), pp. 78-83.

[59] Nash, Brenda Futrell. *Close Female Friendships; Implications for the Well-being, Parenting, Self-efficacy, and Decreased Personal Strain of Married, Employed Women with Young Children.* **Dissertation Abstracts International: Section B, The Sciences and Engineering**, October 1998 (vol. 59:4B), p. 1864.

[60] Thompson, Michael and Dan Kundlion. *Raising Cain, the Emotional Life of Boys.* NY: Ballantine Books, 2000.

[61] Pollach, William. *Real Boys, Rescuing Our Sons from the Myths of Boyhood.* NY: Henry Holt & Co., 1998.

[62] Kraemer, Sebastian. *The Fragile Male.* **British Medical Journal**, Dec. 2000 (321), pp. 1609 – 1612.

[63] Sylwester, Robert. *Unconscious Emotions, Conscious Feelings and Curricular Challenges.* **Educational Leadership**, November 2000 (vol. 58:3).

[64] Moody, Kate. *Growing Up On Television.* NY: Times Books, 1980. p. 81.

[65] Chaffee, Steven H. and Jerome Singer. *Defending the Indefensible.* **Society**. Sept/Oct. 1984, vol.21(6); pp. 30-36.

[66] Gentile, Douglas, et. al. *Well-Child Visits in the Video Age; Pediatricians and the American Academy of Pediatrics Guidelines for Children's Media Use.* **Pediatrics**, November 2004 (vol. 114:5), pp. 1235-1242.

[67] Wallis, Claudia. *Kindergarten Rage, Does Kindergarten Need Cops?* **Time Magazine**, December 12, 2003.

[68] A. C. Nielsen Company. *Nielsen Report on Television 1990*. Northbrook, IL: Nielsen Media Research, 1990.

[69] Christakis, D.A., et. al. *Early Television Exposure and Subsequent Attentional Problems in Children*. **Pediatrics**, September 2004 (vol. 113), pp. 708-713.

[70] Gallup, G., Jr., and F. Newport. *Americans Have Love-Hate Relationship With Their TV Sets*. **Gallup Poll News Service**, 1990 (55:21), 1-9.

[71] Peter D. Hart Research Associates. *Would You Give Up TV for A Million Bucks?* **TV Guide**, 1992 (40: 41), pp. 10-17.

[72] Moody, Kate. **Growing Up On Television**. pp. 83, 90.

[73] Pearce, Joseph Chilton. **Evolution's End, Claiming the Potential of Our Intelligence**. San Francisco: Harper & Row, 1992. pp. 169-170.

[74] Centerwell, B. S. *Exposure to Television As A Cause of Violence*. G. Comstock (editor), **Public Communication and Behavior**. Orlando, FL: Academic Press, 1989. Vol. 2, pp. 1-58.

[75] Healy, Jane M. *Endangered Minds*. p. 200.

[76] Pizzato, Mark. *Addicted to the Tube*. **Journal for the Psychoanalysis of Culture & Society**, Fall, 2003 (vol. 8:2), pp. 338-340.

[77] Liebert R. & J. Sprafkin. **The Early Window**. NY: Pergamon, 1988.

[78] Moody, Kate. **Growing Up on Television**.

[79] Mander, J. **Four Arguments for the Elimination of Television**. NY: Morrow, 1978.

[80] Buzzell, Keith A. **The Children of Cyclops**. Fair Oaks, CA: Association of Waldorf Schools, 1998.

[81] Meltzoff, A. N. *Imitation of Televised Models by Infants*. **Child Development**, 1988 (59), pp. 1221-1229.

[82] Singer, Mark, et al. *Exposure to Violence, Parental Monitoring and Television Viewing as Contributors to Children's Psychological Trauma*. **Journal of Community Psychology**, September 2004, (vol. 32:5), pp. 489-506.

[83] Meltzoff, A. N. *Infant Imitation After A 1-Week Delay: Long-Term Memory for Novel Acts and Multiple Stimuli*. **Developmental Psychology**, 1988 (24), pp. 470-476.

[84] Flavell, J.H. *The Development of Children's Knowledge about the Appearance-Realty Distinction*. **American Psychologist**, 1986 (41), pp. 418-425.

[85] Heller, M. S., and S. Polsky. **Studies in Violence and Television**. NY: American Broadcasting Company, 1976.

[86] Brown, Stewart. *Through the Lens of Play*. **Revision, Touch The Future Journal**, 1995 (vol. 17:4), pp. 4-12.

[87] Christakis, D.A. et al. *Early Television Exposure and Subsequent Attentional Problems in Children*. **Pediatrics,** 2004 (vol. 113), pp. 708-713.

[88] Biederman, J., S. Faraone, K. Keenan, E. Knee, & M. Twuang. *Family Genetic and Psychosocial Risk Factors in DSM-III Attention Deficit Disorder*. **Journal of American Academy of Child and Adolescent Psychiatry**, 1990 (vol. 29).

[89] Tortora & Anagnostakos. **Principles ....** pp. 408-409.

[90] Olsen, Eric. *Fit Kids, Smart Kids — New Research Confirms That Exercise Boosts Brainpower*. **Parents Magazine**, October, 1994, pp. 35.

[91] Burks, Robert and S. Keeley. *Exercise and Diet Therapy: Psychotherapists' Beliefs and*

Practices. **Professional Psychology: Research & Practice**, 1989 (vol. 20), pp. 62-64.

[92] Ackerman, Jennifer Gorham. *The Healer Within*. **The Incredible Machine**. Washington, DC: National Geographic Society, 1986. pp. 217-219.

[93] Moberg, Kerstin Uvnas. **The Oxytocin Factor, Tapping the Hormone of Calm, Love, and Healing**. Cambridge, MA: Da Capo Press, 2003.

[94] Wise, Roy. *Dopamine, Learning and Motivation*. **Nature Reviews Neuroscience**, June 2004, (vol. 5), pp.1-12.

[95] Fried, Itzhak, et. al. *Increased Dopamine Release in the Human Amygdala During Performance of Cognitive Tasks*. **Nature Neuroscience**, February 2001 (vol. 4:2), pp. 201-207.

[96] Wise, Roy.

[97] Fried, Itzahk, et. al.

[98] Panksepp, Jaak. **Affective Neuroscience, The Foundations of Human and Animal Emotions**. NY: Oxford University Press, 1998.

[99] Restak, Richard M. **The Mind**. p. 40.

[100] Tortora & Anagnostakos. **Principles ....** pp. 349, 407, 409, 531.

13: MIS-EDUCATION AND THE LABELING GAME

[1] MacLean, Paul D. **The Triune Brain in Evolution, Role in Paleocerebral Functions**. NY: Plenum Press, 1990. p. 575.

[2] Reichal, Marcel. PET (Positron Emission Tomography) Scans. George Washington University. 1990.

[3] Hannaford, Carla. **Awakening The Child Heart, Handbook for Global Parenting**. Captain Cook, HI: Jamilla Nur Pub., 2002. p. 26.

[4] Tortora, Gerard J. & Nicholas P Anagnostakos. **Principles of Anatomy and Physiology. Sixth Edition.** NY: Harper, 1990. p.403

[5] **Catani, Marco**. *Brain Imaging Reveals New Language Circuits*. **Annals of Neurology**. December 13, 2004. http://www.interscience.wiley.com/journal/ana.

[6] Witelson, Sandra. *Einstein and Other Brains*. **Science**, May 1995. (Witelson, a Professor in the Department of Psychiatry at McMaster University in Hamilton, Ontario, Canada, worked directly with Einstein's Brain.)

[7] Giedd, J.N, et. al. *Sexual Dimorphism of the Developing Human Brain*. **Pro-Neuropsychopharmoacol-Biol. Psychiatry Journal**, 1997 (vol. 21:8), pp. 1185-1201.

[8] Witelson, Sandra., 1995

[9] Hannaford, Carla L. *Educational Kinesiology ("Brain Gym") with Learning-Style Discriminated K-12 Students*. Unpublished Ph.D. Dissertation, 1993.

[10] Hannaford, Carla. **The Dominance Factor, How Knowing Your Dominant Eye, Ear, Brain, Hand & Foot Can Improve Your Learning**. Salt Lake City: Great River Books, 1997, pp. 155-158.

[11] Monti, Daniel A., et. al. *Muscle Test Comparisons of Congruent and Incongruent Self-referential Statements*. **Perceptual and Motor Skills**, 1999 (vol. 88), pp. 1019-1028.

[12] Wu, Brother John, (Principal of Salesians of Don Bosco Ng Siu Mui Technical School, Hong Kong) and Amy Choi, educational consultant. Research was done on the Technical School in 1999 and Lam Woo Secondary School in 2002. Communication with researchers.

[13] Mattson, A., et. al. *40 Hertz EEG Activity in Learning Disabled and Normal Children*. Poster presentation, International Neuropsychological Society, Vancouver, B.C. February, 1989

[14] Albert Einstein quoted in Howard Gardner, *Frames Of Mind,* p. 190.

[15] Brewer, Chris & Don Campbell. *Rhythms of Learning, Creative Tools for Developing Lifelong Skills*. Tucson: Zephyr Press, 1991.

[16] Gardner, Howard, *Frames of Mind, TheTheory of Multiple Intelligences*. NY: Basic Books, 1983.

[17] Given, Barbara K. *Learning Styles, A Guide for Teachers and Parents*. CA: Learning Forum Publications, 2000.

[18] The College Board, *1992 Profile of SAT and Achievement Test Takers*, College Entrance Examination Board, p.3

[19] *The Folkeskole*. *Education in Denmark*. Ministry of Education and Research. March, 1991. (Department of Primary and Lower Secondary Education, Frederiksholms Kanal 26, DK-1220 Copenhagen K.)

[20] Eden, G. F., et. al. *Differences In Visuospatial Judgement In Reading Disabled And Normal Children*. *Perceptual and Motor Skills Journal*. February 1996, vol. (82:1), pp. 155-177.

[21] Wheatley, Grayson H. *The Right Hemisphere's Role in Problem Solving*. *Arithmetic Teacher*, 1977 (11), pp. 36-39.

[22] Samples, Bob. *Educating for Both Sides of the Human Mind*. *The Science Teacher*, January 1975, pp. 21-23.

[23] Epstein, Herman T. *Growth Spurts During Brain Development: Implications for Educational Policy and Practice*. IN: J. Chall & A.F. Mirsky (eds.), *Education and the Brain*. Chicago, IL: University of Chicago Press, 1979. pp. 343-370.

[24] Myers, John T. *Hemisphericity Research, An Overview with Some Implications for Problem Solving*. *Journal of Creative Behavior*, 1982 (vol. 16:3), pp. 197-211.

[25] Czikszentmihalyi, Mihalyi. *Creativity, Flow and the Psychology of Discovery and Invention*. N.Y: Harper Collins, 1996, pp. 57-123.

[26] McCarthy, Bernice. *The 4-MAT System*. Barrington, IL: Excel, Inc., 1986.

[27] Kolb, David. *Experiential Learning, Experience As the Source of Learning and Development*. Englewood, NJ: Prentice-Hall, 1984. p. 96.

[28] Given, Barbara, 2000

[29] Gardner, Howard. *Frames Of Mind*. pp. 59-70.

[30] Richardson, Ken and Robert J. Sternberg. *Scientists Search for the Biology of Smarts*. *Science News*, February 8, 2003 (vol. 163), p 93.

[31] Hannaford, Carla. *The Dominance Factor; How Knowing Your Dominant Eye, Ear, Brain, Hand & Foot Can Improve Your Learning*. Salt Lake City: Great River Books. 1997.

[32] *Letter to a Teacher*. *The Native Perspective* (Perth, Western Australia), July-August 1977.

14   DRUGS AND HYPERACTIVITY

[1] Breggin, Peter R. and Ginger Ross Breggins. *The War Against Children*. NY: St. Martin's, 1994. pp. 3, 62, 78.

[2] Chopra, Deepak. *Quantum Healing, Exploring the Frontiers of Mind/Body Medicine*. NY: Bantam Books, 1990. pp. 66-67

[3] Pert, Candace, *Molecules of Emoton, Why You Feel the Way You Feel*. N Y: Simon & Schuster, 1999.

[4] Fischback, Gerald D. *Mind and Brain*. *Scientific American*, September 1992, pp. 54-55.

[5] Mostofsky, Stewart. *ADD and ADHD*. *Neuro News*, April 20, 1999.

[6] Matochik, John A. *Brain Images Delve into Hyperactivity*. *American Journal of Psychiatry*, May 1994.

[7] Winslow, W. and R. Markstein. *The Neurobiology of Dopamine Systems*. *Second Symposium of the Northern Neurobiology Group*, Leeds, U.K., July 1984.

[8] Ellison, Gaylord. *Amphetamine, Cocaine: New Brain Link*. *Brain Research*, *Science News*, January, 1993, vol. 143.

[9] Breggin, Peter R. and Ginger Ross Breggin. *The War Against Children*. p. 85.

[10] The President's Council on Bioethics. *Human Flourishing, Performance Enhancement, and Ritalin*. December 2002. http://bioethics.gov/background/humanflourish.html.

[11] Pert, Candace. *Molecules of Emotion*. Teaching and Learning with the Brain in Mind Conference, Toronto, Ontario, Canada, August 2001.

[12] Johnson, Dorothy Davis. *I Can't Sit Still — Educating and Affirming Inattentive and Hyperactive Children*. Santa Cruz, CA: Education, Training and Research Association, 1992. pp. 153-154.

[13] Hartmann, Thom. *Attention Deficit Disorder: A Different Perception*. Novat, CA: Underwood-Miller, 1993. p. 73.

[14] Whalen, C., and B. Henker. *Hyperactivity Children*. NY: Academic Press, 1980.

[15] Rapaport, Judith L. et. al. *Dextriamphetamine; Cognitive and Behavioral Effects in Normal Prepubescent Boys*. *Science*, 1978 (vol.199), p.560-563.

[16] Ellison, Gaylord. *Amphetamine, Cocaine: New Brain Link*. *Brain Research*, *Science News*, January, 1993, vol. 143.

[17] DeGrandpre, Richard. *Ritalin Nation: Rapid-Fire Culture and the Transformation of Human Consciousness*. NY: W. Norton, 1999.

[18] Blackman, Ann, et. al. *The Age of Ritalin*. *Time Magazine*, November 30, 1998, pp. 84-94

[19] American Psychiatric Association. *Treatments of Psychiatric Disorders, A Task Force Report of the American Psychiatric Association*. Washington, DC: APA, 1989. p. 1221.

[20] Breggin, Peter. *Toxic Psychiatry: Why Therapy, Empathy and Love Must Replace the Drugs, Electroshock and Biochemical Theories of the "New Psychiatry."* NY: St. Martin's, 1991. p. 15.

[21] Swanson, J.M., D. Cantwell, M. Lerner, K. McBurnett, L. Pfiffner, & R. Kotkin. *Treatment of ADHD: Beyond Medication*. *Beyond Behavior*, 1992 (4:1), pp. 13-22.

[22] Ellison, Gaylord. *Amphetamine, Cocaine: New Brain Link*. *Brain Research*, *Science News*, January, 1993, vol. 143,

[23] Mannuzza, Salvatore, et. al. *Adult Outcome of Hyperactive Boys: Educational Achieve-*

ment, Occupational Rank, and Psychiatric Status. **Archives of General Psychiatry**, July 1993 (vol. 50), pp. 565-576.

[24] Nasrallah, H., J. Loney, S. Olson, M. McCalley-Whitters, J. Kramer, & C. Jacoby. *Cortical Atrophy in Young Adults with a History of Hyperactivity in Childhood.* **Psychiatric Research**, 1986 (17), pp. 241-246.

[25] Shaffer, David. *Attentional Deficit Hyperactive Disorder in Adults.* **American Journal of Psychiatry**, May 1994 (vol. 151), pp. 633-638.

[26] Moll. G. H. et. al. *Early Methylphenidate Administration to Young Rats Causes a Persistent Reduction in the Density of Striatal Dopamine Transporters,* **J. Child Adolescent Psychopharmacol**. 2001 (vol. 11), pp. 15-24.

[27] Hartmann, Thom. **Attention Deficit Disorder**. p. 76.

[28] Arby, Ronald and William J. Gole. **Physicians' Desk Reference**, 1995. Montvale, NJ: Medical Economics, 1995. p. 897.

[29] Blackman, Ann, et. al. *The Age of Ritalin.* **Time Magazine**, November 30, 1998, pp. 84-94.

[30] The President's Council on Bioethics: December 2002.

[31] *What Teachers Check For,* **Wisconsin State Journal**; 4G. September 22, 1996.

[32] Parker-Pope, Tara, *Risk of Over-Diagnosing ADHD,* **Wall Street Journal**, *Health Journal*, Jan. 25, 2005.

[33] President's Council on Bioethics. December 2002.

[34] McKearney, J. W. *Asking Questions about Behavior. Perspectives.* **Biology and Medicine**, 1977, p. 116.

[35] Mercogliano, Chris. **Teaching the Restless: One School's Remarkable No-Ritalin Approach to Helping Children Learn and Succeed**. Boston: Beacon Press. 2003

[36] Stein, David B. **Ritalin Is Not The Answer: Action Guide, An Interactive Companion To The Bestselling Drug-Free ADD/ADHD Parenting Program**. San Francisco: Jossey-Bass, 2002.

[37] Berne, Samuel. **Without Ritalin, A Natural Approach To ADD**. Chicago: Keats Pub., 2002.

[38] Mann, Eberhard M. *The Ritalin Controversy.* Paper Presented at the Attention Deficit Hyperactive Disorder Conference in Honolulu, Hawaii, March, 1994.

[39] Panksepp. J. et. al. *Modeling ADHD-Type Arousal With Unilateral Frontal Cortex Damage In Rats And Beneficial Effects Of Play Therapy.* **Brain and Cognition Journal,** June, 2003 (vol. 52:1), pp. 97-105.

[409] Gavin, Kara. *Autistic Kids Make Progress with Play.* University of Michigan Play Project: www.playproject.org/research/index.htm.

[41] Galaburda, Albert. *Ordinary and Extraordinary Brains: Nature, Nurture, and Dyslexia.* Address presented at the Annual Meeting of the Orton Dyslexia Society. Tampa, Florida, Nov. 1988.

[42] Vail, Priscilla. **Smart Kids With School Problems**. NY: Dutton, 1987.

15: LOOKING OUTWARD FOR MODELS

[1] MacLean, Paul. Personal communication.

[2] Interview with Occupational Therapists working with the Sunfield Home School, Verulum, South Africa, March, 1993.

[3] Langburg, Arney. Principal, High School Redirection, Denver Public School System, Denver, Colorado.

[4] Hannaford, Carla. *Awakening the Child Heart, Handbook for Global Parenting*. Captain Cook, HI: Jamilla Nur Pub. 2002. pp. 141-143.

[5] Wald Kindergarten. Patrick Friedrich, Zartenerstr. 7, 79199, Kirchzarten, Germany. Phone: 07661/627272 Personal communication with originator of the school.

[6] Ministry of Education and Research, International Relations Division. *Characteristic Features of Danish Education*. Copenhagen, Denmark, 1992. pp. 1-39.

[7] Henriksen, Spaet, Svend Hesselholdt, Knud Jensen, & Ole B. Larsen. *The Democratization of Education*. Department of Education and Psychology, The Royal Danish School of Educational Studies. 1990.

[8] Nielsen, Jorgen & Thomas Webb. *An Emerging Critical Pedagogy. Rethinking Danish Educational Philosophy in the Light of Changing Concepts of Culture*. Huanistisk Arbog Pub., No. 4, Roskilde Universitetscenter. 1991.

[9] Hahn, Carole L. and Paulette Dilworth. *Preparing Participating Citizens in the European Community*. Presented to the Comparative and International Education Society, San Diego, CA, March 21, 1994.

[10] Kovalik, Susan J. and Karen D. Olsen. *Exceeding Expectations, A Users Guide to Implementing Brain Research in the Classroom, Second Edition*. Covington, WA: Susan Kovalik & Assoc., 2002.

[11] Kolb, David. *Experiential Learning, Experience As the Source of Learning and Development*. Englewood, NJ: Prentice-Hall, 1984. p. 2.

[12] Messier, Paul, Barbara Given and Charlene Engel. *National Learning Foundation Mission Statement*. Presented in February 1994. National Learning Foundation, 11 Dupont Circle, N.W., Suite 900, Washington, DC 20036-1271, www.nationallearningfoundation.org.

Index

~

Carla Hannaford, Ph.D. is a biologist and educator with more than thirty years of teaching experience, including twenty years teaching biology at the university level and four years as a counselor for elementary and intermediate school children with learning difficulties.

She is an internationally recognized educational consultant, having presented more than six hundred lectures and workshops in thirty countries over the past seventeen years. She was selected as a guest educator with the AHP-Soviet Project in 1988, has been recognized by Who's Who in American Education, and has received awards from the University of Hawaii and the American Association for the Advancement of Science for outstanding teaching in science.

Since *Smart Moves* first appeared in 1995 it has sold over one hundred thousand copies in English and been translated into nine languages, with more on the way. Her second book, *The Dominance Factor, How Knowing Your Dominant Eye, Ear, Brain, Hand & Foot Can Improve Your Learning*, (Great River Books, 1997), has also been translated into six languages. She is the author of *Awakening The Child Heart, Handbook for Global Parenting*, (Jamilla Nur Publishing, 2002), the author and co-producer of the video *Education in Motion*, and presenter (with Candace Pert and Susan Kovalik) of the video *Emotions: Gateway to Learning*. She has contributed over one hundred articles to educational and science journals and magazines and been featured in scores of radio and TV interviews in the U.S. and abroad.

She lives with her musician husband Ahti Mohala in Hawaii and Montana.